Hospitality Retail Management
A unit manager's guide

Conrad Lashley

BUTTERWORTH
HEINEMANN

OXFORD AUCKLAND BOSTON JOHANNESBURG MELBOURNE NEW DELHI

Butterworth-Heinemann
Linacre House, Jordan Hill, Oxford OX2 8DP
225 Wildwood Avenue, Woburn, MA 01801-2041
A division of Reed Educational and Professional Publishing Ltd

ℛ A member of the Reed Elsevier plc group

First published 2000

British Library Cataloguing in Publication Data
Lashley, Conrad
    Hospitality retail management: a unit manager's guide
    1. Hospitality industry – Management
    2. Hospitality industry – Personnel management
    I. Title
    647.9'4'068

ISBN 0 7506 4616 0

Composition by Genesis Typesetting, Rochester, Kent
Printed and bound in Great Britain

FOR EVERY TITLE THAT WE PUBLISH, BUTTERWORTH-HEINEMANN
WILL PAY FOR BTCV TO PLANT AND CARE FOR A TREE.

Contents

List of figures

List of tables

Hospitality, Leisure & Tourism Series

Foreword

McDonald's Restaurants Limited operate more than 1,000 restaurants in the United Kingdom. Ensuring uniformity and consistency across all of our restaurants is an important part of our approach to managing the business. The managers and staff who serve and meet the needs of our customers are the key to building a loyal customer base and establishing competitive advantage in the Quick Service Restaurant sector. The company's overall performance is, therefore, dependent on the effectiveness of the managers in each of our restaurants. Management training and development continues to be a number one priority for our company.

It gives me great pleasure, therefore, to write a foreword to this book by Conrad Lashley. I believe that *Hospitality Retail Management* will provide a valuable support to any management development programme.

The book is written in a way that is accessible to busy managers without being too simple or patronizing. It contains valuable practical guidance on how to manage high volume hospitality operations and reveals the underlying management principles involved. At root, the book sets the recruitment, selection, induction, training, leadership, empowerment and retention of staff as core management concerns. In our business, we recognize that effective team leadership, development and motivation provide the basis on which service, quality and marketing objectives are built. These management competencies are, therefore, absolute prerequisites for commercial success.

Andrew Taylor
Chief Executive
McDonald's Restaurants (UK) Limited

Acknowledgements

This book aims to provide a resource for both in-company management development programmes, and for students on taught higher national and degree programmes. It is focused on the needs of unit managers in branded chains of restaurants, bars and hotels. In an attempt to make the material accessible and relevant to the practical training needs of unit management, I have consulted with individuals typical of the target audience and wish to acknowledge my gratitude for the helpful comments and suggestions that I have received from students at Leeds Metropolitan University and a number of industry practitioners.

Specifically I want to thank Zoe Moss, Jean O'Sullivan, Tracey Allport and Mark Sokol, all students on the hospitality management programme, for reading early sample chapters and giving me invaluable guidance about the tone and structure of the chapters. Similarly, Jeannette Roe of McDonald's Restaurants and John Walker of the British Institute of Innkeeping have provided invaluable advice and support about the overall content of the book, and the needs of managers of hospitality retail units. In addition, many managers across the industry have helped me to establish a view about the development needs of managers in hospitality retail businesses. Not the least of whom Chris Ripper, of Scottish and Newcastle Retail, has been extremely generous with his time and provided invaluable insights in developments in the licensed retail sector. Finally I want to single out Hazel Spinlove, a former student within the School of Tourism and Hospitality Management, at Leeds Metropolitan University. Her help in reading the materials and editing the text has been much appreciated and highly valued.

Conrad Lashley
School of Tourism and Hospitality Management
Leeds Metropolitan University

Introduction

For almost three decades, the hospitality industry has experienced rapid and fundamental changes. Although the hotel and catering industry in the twentieth century has seen examples of chains of hospitality business, such as Lyons Tea Shops that offered customers a consistent experience, the last twenty-five years have witnessed the exponential expansion of branded hospitality businesses. These branded operations offer customers a clearly defined array of reliable products and services. Faced with the uncertainties that the traditional hotel and catering business offer to customers, branded operations have captured an increasing share of the total markets in bar, hotel, and restaurant services. Many now operate hundreds, and in some cases thousands, of units.

Fundamentally, however, branded hospitality businesses face a number of dilemmas. Customers want the certainties and consistency that the standardized brand delivers, but they also yearn for the personal touch and humanity implicit in acts of hospitality. Customers want mass-produced service encounters that at the same time treat them as individuals with unique needs. From the operators' point of view standard menus and centralized product and service offers, delivered with the aid of standard procedures manuals, are an attempt to meet customer expectations of uniformity and yet present a logistical nightmare when they have to be delivered through hundreds of outlets. Furthermore, the standardized offer requires the immediate unit management and service delivery team to be able to understand what is needed to meet customer expectations of the brand, but also respond to their individual needs.

In these circumstances, the unit manager and the staff directly involved with customers have a particular significance in delivering customer satisfaction. Satisfied customers are much

Hospitality, Leisure & Tourism Series

more likely to return, and building a strong base of loyal customers is a key source of competitive advantage, leading ultimately to sales and profit growth. Although many hospitality retail organizations express these sentiments in official documents and in public pronouncements, detailed investigation of what they actually do in practice reveals this as a somewhat rhetorical set of claims. Many are guilty of claiming that people are their most important asset yet treating them as a cost to be minimized.

At this stage, many British mangers are still developing their understanding of what is needed to manage hospitality retail brands, but one emerging shared truth is that the unit manager is key to the success of each business unit. The performance of the restaurant, bar or hotel is most fundamentally influenced by the skills, talents, priorities and personality of the immediate unit manager. Studies comparing different levels of profitability, sales, staff turnover, customers' satisfaction and employee satisfaction in different units in the same group show how important the performance of the unit manager is to the success of the unit. Indeed industrial experience in many hospitality retail organizations shows that a change of managers in the same unit can result in dramatic changes in the unit's business performance.

This book aims to provide a resource for both unit management programmes in hospitality retail organizations and for academics preparing students for careers in hospitality retail management. It is deliberately written in a way that addresses a *'how to do agenda'* by offering a practical guide to the skills and knowledge needed by those who will be managing bars, restaurants and hotels in fast-moving hospitality retailing contexts. The book is deliberately presented in a non-academic style without the referencing and quotations typical of academic texts. Within a higher education context, it is assumed that the book will be largely used at Level Two in programmes of study. Traditionally, this stage of hospitality, leisure and tourism management programmes focuses on the practical techniques involved in managing hospitality operations. Similarly, the book is written in a way that goes beyond the simple checklist of many distance learning materials found in in-company management development programmes.

The book assumes that managers running what are substantial businesses in their own right need to be *'reflective practitioners'*. The very nature of the task-driven practical immediacy of their work means that they have to be capable of active management and practical solutions to unit management situations. That said, they also need to be capable of standing back and reflecting on their actions so as to be more effective in future. The problem is that many unit managers in hospitality retail operations are by inclination 'Activist' learners, using Honey and Mumford's (1986) term. That is, they are mostly people who are comfortable when taking action and 'sorting things out', but less comfortable with standing back and thinking about what they are doing and why. I recently came across a pub manager who had recruited 287 people in a six-month period – the normal establishment was fifty employees. He was recruiting over ten new staff every week. Indeed the replacement of staff dominated his work for that period. Instead of spending time developing sales, addressing customer satisfaction and increasing profits, he was almost permanently engaged in recruitment. Had he stood back and reflected on the situation he might have come up with some more useful ways of spending his time. This case is not untypical; many managers feel comfortable by keeping busy and spend little time in active self-critical reflection.

Given the learning needs of both current and would-be managers the text attempts to combine theoretical concepts and practical advice in a way that uses theory as a tool but is not overly theoretical. Where appropriate the text is illustrated by examples from different hospitality retail operations. In the main, these are set within a context that assumes that hospitality retail operations are not all the same. Using a model developed with Steven Taylor (Lashley and Taylor, 1998), I suggest that there are three types of hospitality retail offers to customers – uniformity dependent, choice dependent and relationship dependent. Each of these offers involves a different set of customer expectations, critical success factors, definitions of service quality and requirements from frontline staff performance. Hence this text assumes that there is not one best way of managing hospitality retail units, but there is likely to be a match between the offer to customer and the way service employees are managed.

The content of the book is informed by research and contacts within a number of key hospitality retail operators. It is much closer to a programme of manager training and development in industry than a traditional single-disciplined book. Hence the content asks, what does a manager of one of these units need to know? The content, therefore, contains a number of key themes that are rarely found in one text.

Given that managers of branded hospitality retail organizations have little strategic control over marketing, people or financial matters, the text focuses on providing an understanding of these matters and shows how they shape a manager's immediate tactical role. The manager has to understand that people are the key asset of the business and a large part of the book focuses on understanding and working with people. Understanding what makes them tick, team leadership, successful recruitment and staff training are all essential in controlling the hidden cost of staff turnover. Traditionally, many of these businesses have been happy to live with levels of staff turnover that mean each job is filled twice or three times per year. Apart from the high direct costs to the business, high staff turnover creates barriers to building customers' loyalty and competitive advantage through quality service delivery.

A second key theme in the book explores the nature of service difference, and different offers made to customers together with the implications this has for service quality and service quality management. In addition to the variations in key service offers discussed above, customers use a variety of hospitality retail operations on different occasions. The same customer may have different expectations of the products and services within the same bar or restaurant, depending on the 'occasion' of the visit. Unit managers need to have a thorough understanding of service quality management and the critical success factors that will shape customer assessment of quality of the visit.

Finally, and by no means least, the book explores a number of issues associated with managing the unit as a commercial venture. At an immediate tactical level managers need to understand how to manage their own time effectively and how to ensure that other team members are working towards the various aims and objectives set. The business planning process is therefore a core aspect of effective unit operation. It is through this device that team members' efforts are directed towards global goals to manage costs and ensure that revenue exceeds expenditure and generates profits for the organization. Within the framework the book argues for and demonstrates an alternative approach to managing people compared with traditional management approaches in the field. The approach takes for granted that people are the key asset in delivering improved business performance and shows that an investment in people through improved salaries and training budgets can boost the bottom-line performance of the business.

References

Honey, P. and Mumford, A. (1986). *Manual of Learning Styles*. BBC Books.

Lashley, C. and Taylor, S. (1998). Hospitality retail operations types and styles in the management of human resources. *Journal of Retailing and Consumer Services*, **5** (3), 24–35.

Hospitality services management

Chapter objectives

After working through this chapter you should be able to:

- highlight the key features of hospitality retail service
- identify different types of hospitality service operations
- explain the key drivers of hospitality services types
- contrast and compare service management techniques.

What business are you in?

In the past many people thought that the key to successful hospitality business was 'location, location, location'. In other words, the location of the property was the most important factor in determining its success. There are many successful pubs, restaurants and other hospitality businesses, which are in poor locations yet still manage to build sales and good profits. *It's not so much where your unit is located, but what goes on inside it.*

This chapter aims to show that although hospitality retail services are different, customers expect the quality of product and services to match their expectations. A good unit manager understands what customers want and recognizes that employees – their selection, training, motivation, reward and management – are the key to customer satisfaction.

Hospitality retail services

Hospitality organizations provide food and/or drink and/or accommodation in a service context. Each of these terms needs close consideration if you are to understand the nature of the business you are managing at unit level.

Hospitality retail organizations provide these services in a way that is:

- *Branded*: usually sold under a brand name through a chain of restaurants, bars, cafes, pubs or hotels. The brand will represent a cluster of attributes or benefits to customers who have a pretty good idea of what to expect when entering the premises (see Table 1.1).

- *Customer focused*: a consequence of branding is to shape to particular customer types and needs and experiences the nature of the products and services that make up the brand. Issues to do with age, gender, social class, income, region, consumption patterns and service needs help retailers to consider the nature of the brand and the messages required by customers.

- *Standardized*: though this will vary according to the nature of the brand and business, standardization follows from the requirement of customers for consistency and predictability. Typically, the menu of items, the prices charged, décor and building layout are standardized across all units.

- *Consistent in quality*: management of the hospitality experience has to be concerned with ensuring the customers receive the experience they expect. That is, not only the physical products but also the type of service they get from staff must be consistent and in line with customer expectations. Thus the management of service quality, staff training and performance appraisal become important tools in unit management.

- *Managed via operating systems*: consistency and standardization across hundreds or thousands of units usually require that all operate to a centrally designed system which guides the way that products are purchased, assembled and served. In many cases these systems also lay down how training, recruitment and other staff management issues are to be handled.

- *Sales driven*: using techniques from the retail goods sector, hospitality businesses are concerned to ensure that communication with customers is clear. The nature of the product and services on offer are stated in a way that allows minimal confusion and misunderstanding. Point of sale material and staff training in 'up-selling' techniques, together with an array of other techniques, attempt to maximize the sale to each customer.

- *Mass marketed*: to generate customer identification and to shape clear communications with customers, hospitality retailing organizations frequently use mass advertising through television and newspapers, as well as other promotional techniques to inform customers about the brand and services on offer.

Brand name	Hospitality service	Number of units	Owner corporation
McDonald's Restaurants	Quick service restaurants	894	McDonald's Corporation
Pizza Hut (UK)	Restaurants, kiosks, home delivery	563	Whitbread Restaurant and Leisure Division
TGI Fridays (UK)	American restaurant and cocktail bar	18	Whitbread Restaurant and Leisure Division
Harvester Restaurants	Traditional restaurant and pub	128	Bass Plc
John Barras	Community pub and restaurant	175	Scottish and Newcastle
Kentucky Fried Chicken	Quick service restaurants	259	KFC Corporation
Burger King	Quick service restaurants	356	Grand Metropolitan
Costas Coffee Boutique	Coffee bars	178	Whitbread Restaurant and Leisure Division

Table 1.1 A selection of major hospitality brands

Over the past few decades, branded hospitality retail services have taken an increasing share of restaurant, bar, café and hotel business in the UK and other Western countries. The consistency of service, lower costs through the scale of their operations and appeal of a variety of brands to target markets have ensured wide success. Table 1.1 lists some of the major branded businesses in a number of hospitality market segments.

As a unit managers working in one of these branded businesses you need to understand the nature of the brand in which you are working, that is, what it is that customers are buying into. With this understanding you are able to focus on customer expectations and what has to be done to ensure customer expectations are met.

Most importantly, as a unit manager in branded business you need to understand and work within the disciplines of the brand. Customers who experience different services, prices, quality and service in different establishments in the same brand will become confused about what the brand represents. Their expectations become less clear. A likely consequence is that they will seek out a competitor who is more consistent.

Active learning point

In the 'Comments' column add the details of a hospitality brand known to you.

Brand	Comments
Brand name/owner/number of outlets/geographical location	
Food/drink/accommodation offer Number of products/price	
Service attributes/quality/positioning/ the service experience	
Staffing/types/numbers/contact with customers	
Evidence of product/service consistency	
Marketing and sales drives/pricing and promotional strategies	
Description of typical customers – age, gender, income group, consumption patterns, service needs	

Now the downside!

Whilst these branded hospitality services have been very successful in capturing an increased share of hospitality service business, they face some difficult issues to manage. Many of the features of these operations which have brought about their success also lead to problems, and hence the need for this book.

Management skills

The closely defined brand supported with operating systems, quality management techniques and policies derived at head office can lead organizations to adopt a *command and control style* which allows little scope for individual manager or employee initiative. Managers at unit level are expected to work to the 'one best way'. As we shall see, for some businesses this is consistent with the offer to customers, but sometimes it creates unnecessary difficulties because you may feel stifled and discouraged from being creative in your work. This book shows that there are a number of ways in which your skills as a unit manager can be tapped and developed to the benefit of the brand.

Employee dissatisfaction

Again the operating systems, detailed product specification and 'one best way' job design allow little scope for individual flair and creativity. Employees experience jobs that are tightly controlled, routine and monotonous. On top of this the uneven pace of work in many hospitality services, together with difficulties inherent in serving customers, add additional stress to hospitality service work. Consequently, many hospitality retail operations face high labour turnover. It is not unusual for hospitality retailers to experience average labour turnover over 150 per cent per year across the whole brand, with some jobs and units recording labour turnover over 500 per cent per year. Apart from the direct costs of replacing staff, which can be a considerable added cost in itself, you as the manager will face difficulties through the sheer volume of recruitment, selection and training that you have to undertake.

Service inconsistencies

Problems occur for several reasons. First, the very scale of these organizations means that they are attempting to deliver consistent customer experiences through a very large number of units. Thousands of unit management personnel and tens of thousands of staff must all share an understanding of the brand

and be prepared to work within the rigidities of operating procedures. With so many people involved, there are clearly many opportunities for things to go wrong.

The second problem relates to the labour turnover difficulty. When labour turnover is occurring at high levels, a constant stream of new employees are joining and leaving the organization. In these circumstances it is difficult to communicate and train employees to the desired standards.

The very nature of service contact means that both employees and customers may react inconsistently with each other. Customer perceptions of different employees will shape the way they evaluate the service and employees as people. It may be unrealistic to expect employees to always act with good grace and with a desire to delight the customer. Now and again tiredness, boredom, and frustration with management may cause service problems.

Customer service needs

Whilst customers are attracted to the certainties of the branded service operation, they often dislike being treated as a number. Customer expectations vary in different brands. In some cases the individual wants more consistency and standardization, and in other cases they may want the service to be more personal and shaped to them. The same individual may want different experiences from the same hospitality operation depending on their mood, the time of day and the occasion.

Furthermore, customer service needs are dynamic. As more people experience hospitality services their expectations are moving and shifting (Figure 1.1). Hospitality service organizations have to constantly review and audit customer expectations. They can never sit back and assume they know what customers want.

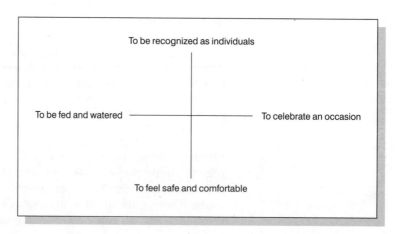

Figure 1.1
Typical pub customer service needs

Local and regional tastes

National branded hospitality services may come across tension between the need to maintain the standardized national brand through which customers learn to know what to expect, and local or regional tastes that cut across the standard brand. That is, customers may expect to be able to order certain drinks or products in the local restaurant or pub, but the brand does not normally stock these items, and instructs managers not provide services 'out of brand'.

The 'big is ugly' syndrome

As we have seen, the scale and coverage of these hospitality retail operations brings advantages through cost reduction and standardization, but large organizations can be unwieldy and slow to change. In fast-moving consumer markets, such as in the hospitality retailing sector, very standardized operating systems and centralized controls can be a disadvantage. The narrow span of control and tall hierarchies that help the organization to manage consistency over a lot of units makes for long lines of communication and slow decision-making processes. It is, therefore, very easy for these organizations to miss changes in consumer taste and be unresponsive to variations in the customer base.

Active learning point

List in below the problems faced by a hospitality brand known to you.

The answer

Many hospitality retail organizations recognize the various problems that they face and are looking for alternative ways of managing their businesses. This book advocates a more *empowered approach to unit management*.

Unit management and staff have the key role in delivering hospitality services, they need to be empowered in its true sense to manage the unit and service encounters in a way which:

1 Gives them the authority to do whatever it takes to deliver the service that customers want. Within the limits of the brand there should be flexibility to meet customer needs.
2 Ensures that all concerned are given the skills to do the job. Adequate training and being allowed to be effective is the basic building block of empowerment.
3 Ensures that managers and staff are recognized and rewarded for their contribution to successful service. Removing barriers to empowerment and developing a sense of personal effectiveness is the defining feature of empowerment. Through this, all concerned share a sense of ownership with customer satisfaction and the success of the venture.
4 Develops organization control systems that need to be both 'tight and loose'. In other words the organization system needs to control those issues which are essential for business success – standardization of the essentials but which also allow for local responsiveness.
5 Manages the organization through a flat structure that minimizes the number of management levels in the organization, thereby enabling short lines of communication and quick decision-making.
6 Encourages initiative and creativity. A learning organization should be prepared for people to make mistakes, provided people are able to think about their errors and learn from the experience.

The following chapters in this book discuss this approach further and provide a course of sessions which will help you as a unit manager to be more effective in managing hospitality retail service operations. Before that, it is important that you understand the nature of hospitality services and variations between different types and levels of service offered.

About services

At the beginning of the chapter we said that hospitality retailing involved *the supply of food and/or drink and/or accommodation in a service context*. The nature of the food, drink and accommodation supplied varies. Hotels, restaurants, bars, cafes, inns and taverns all represent different types of cluster of the three hospitality activities. However, the distinction between establishments is less and less clear as restaurants, for example, encourage diners to come to their establishments and drink, and bars increasingly offer their customers food as well as alcohol.

Whilst the type and quality of products on offer to customers is important, the key feature which as unit managers you need to understand is the precise nature of the service experience which is being supplied, and what customers are expecting of the service encounter. Customer expectations are best understood by building a picture of the key features of service. This shows how different brands offer different bundles of service experiences to customers.

Drivers of service types

Almost all services, including hospitality services, can be said to have four features that make them different from manufactured products. Two of these features – time and face to face – are of lesser importance in shaping service types, but are important in service management. The other two features – the product-service dimension and the predictable-personal dimension – are key factors in building an understanding of the variations in hospitality retail services.

Time ● ● ●

In most cases a service involves an instant interaction between the customer and employee. The service instant is over and gone the moment it has occurred. It cannot be produced in advance, nor can it be taken back and reworked if a problem occurs. The receptionist's smile cannot be re-enacted if it strikes the customer as mechanical and less than genuine.

Clearly, this *perishable* feature of the service encounter means that hospitality retailers have to get it right first time. Service operation systems, communications and staff training are essential in assisting in the delivery of consistent service quality which gets it right every time.

Face to face ● ● ●

In most hospitality retail situations the service received by customers involves face-to-face interactions. Customers and staff can see each other, and customers are evaluating the performance of the employee through a range of conscious and subconscious cues. Thus body language, tone of voice, words used, appearance and personal hygiene help build a picture of the employee which establishes the customer's impression of the organization and its service.

This means that your employees need to be well trained in the various techniques used to develop the appropriate feelings of welcome and the importance of customers as individuals. In addition employee satisfaction and dissatisfaction become crucial. As F. W. Marriott is once said: 'It takes happy worker to make happy customers.

Customer loyalty is likely to be most successfully built on the basis of contacts with staff who make them feel welcome and cared for, and with sentiments that appear to be genuinely felt by the person concerned.

The product-service dimension ● ● ●

All hospitality retail services involve the customer being supplied with a combination of physical products and service based on contacts with customers. In a restaurant the physical elements will obviously involve the food and drink supplied as well as the relationship with service staff.

These *tangible* and *intangible* aspects of the services cover a wide range of issues that can be arranged in a list according to the extent that each is tangible and measurable, and intangible and difficult to measure. The portion size is a tangible and measurable aspect of the customer's meal experience. Operating systems and manuals can specify the consistent size of portion supplied to customers. However, the décor of the restaurant may involve a physical assessment of state of repair and cleanliness, but also involve a psychological dimension in its impact on customer mood and impression which is difficult to measure.

Similarly, the intangible service aspects of the customer's experience involve some factors which are clearly difficult to measure – the impact of the service staff's smile, the tone of voice on the telephone. It is almost impossible to come up with some definition and measure of how this should be delivered. However, role models, best practice and core values can be shared through training. On the other hand, some aspects of the intangible service elements can be measured. The time it takes for a customer to receive their starter after placing the order, or the time it takes to be acknowledged whilst waiting at the reception desk, for example, can be identified and measured against a standard. These aspects contribute to the customer's evaluation of service quality, and can be subject to specific targets and measures in time.

Figure 1.2 provides an example of some of these tangible product and intangible service aspects of the customer's experience for a licensed retail outlet in a bar.

Whilst all hospitality retail services involve combinations of these product and service aspects in the offer to customers, not all are equally weighted. In some cases, the tangible product aspects are more important sources of customer satisfaction. In other cases the intangible service factors become more important. Figure 1.3 shows a continuum of hospitality service businesses that have different bundles of product and service benefits to customers.

In some cases, the same brand may represent a different cluster of benefits, depending on the means by which the customer is

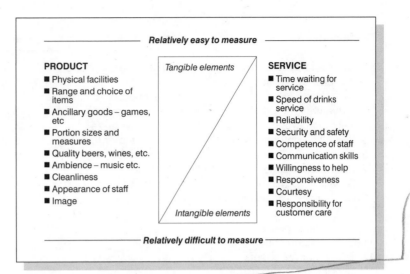

Figure 1.2
Tangible and intangible elements of customer service for a bar

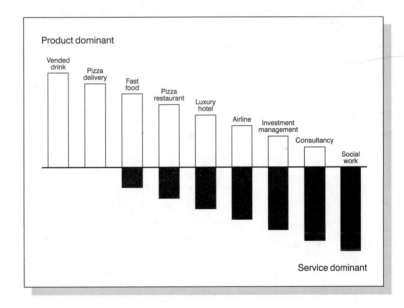

Figure 1.3
Continuum of product and service benefits

supplied with the product and service. Pizza Hut provides a valuable example. Pizza Hut sells pizzas through three types of outlet (Table 1.2). The restaurant operation involves traditional service interactions between customer and staff. The home delivery service requires limited interactions, though issues to do with delivery speed and product temperature will be important. The kiosk sales involve customers buying pieces of pizza and again involve minimum staff interaction.

It can be seen from the above that the range and complexities of hospitality retail services will vary. The source of customer satisfaction will also vary. In some cases, satisfaction largely will

Restaurant	Home delivery	Kiosk
1 Greet and seat customers and give out menus	1 Take order by phone	1 Acknowledge waiting customer
2 Take drinks order	2 Deliver order to customer	2 Accept order
3 Serve drinks	3 Greet customer	3 Fulfil order
4 Take food order	4 Hand over pizza	4 Tell customer the charge
5 Serve first course	5 Tell customer the charge	5 Accept payment
6 Check back – starter OK?	6 Accept payment	6 Salutation
7 Clear starter plates	7 Receipt	
8 Serve main course	8 Salutation	
9 Check back – main course OK?		
10 Clear mains plates		
11 Offer sweet menu		
12 Take order for sweets		
13 Check back – sweets OK?		
14 Offer coffee		
15 Serve coffee		
16 Offer refill		
17 Present bill		
18 Payment		
19 Provide receipt		
20 Salutation		

Table 1.2 Pizza Hut customer contacts in three outlets

be product derived – product taste, variety, size, temperature, etc. In other cases these factors will be important but the range and quality of contact with service will also be important. Following from this, the management of employees will vary according to the complexity and predictability of service needs.

The predictable-personal dimension • • •

Given the personal nature of the service interaction, customers are faced with a difficulty in predicting the quality of the service they will receive. For the reasons outlined in the 'Time' and 'Face to face' sections above, they cannot judge the quality of an experience until they have had it. In part this customer difficulty explains the success of the branded standardized service businesses in hospitality retailing. They attempt to make it clear to each customer what they can expect, and they spend a great deal of time and energy attempting ensure that their expectations are met.

Not all services can be *standardized* in this way; some services have to be *customized* to the needs of the individual. Professional services like dental and medical services provide the most obvious examples. In hospitality retailing there are clearly limits on the degree that services can be totally customized, because the operating systems and standardized offer which attract customers to the brand, also limit the possibilities for giving each customer a totally individual service. It is possible in many ways to personalize the nature of the customer's experiences. It is possible to provide service that either allows a wide choice through which the service is personalized, or through the service interaction it is possible to encourage the customer to feel important as an individual.

It is possible to detect a services continuum which puts different types of service experience in the way they offer the customer a fairly predictable service, and variations in the degree to which different services personalize the customer experience. As with the products-services continuum, most services involve some elements of personalization because of contacts with service personnel, but the degree to which predictability or personalization is important varies between services. Figure 1.4 provides some examples of variations in the mix of predictable and personalized benefits from different hospitality retail services.

These two sets of factors interplay to create a number of ideal service types. Figure 1.5 shows three ideal types of service depending on the nature of the offer on these dimensions. As we have seen, most hospitality retail services supply customers with

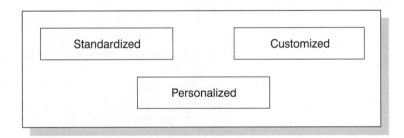

Figure 1.4
Continuum of predictable and personal service benefits

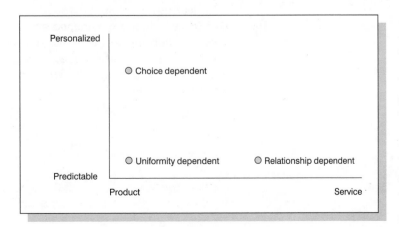

Figure 1.5
Hospitality retail service types

a set of service elements that are at the same time standard and shaped to the customers needs, and they offer service benefits that supply physical products served to them. By bringing these two sets of factors together we can reveal a number of ideal service types, three of which have particular relevance to hospitality retail services.

Uniformity dependent hospitality services

Uniformity dependent hospitality services are based on customer expectations that the goods and services supplied by the brand will be consistent. In many ways they are buying into the certainty that they will be able to predict the experience, the product and even the price they will pay for their hospitality service. Customer satisfaction is more dependent on the food, drink and accommodation that customers receive. It is more dependent on the tangible dimension of service. The intangible service aspects are important, but customers are more concerned with speed and are prepared to accept simpler and shorter contacts with service employees. Many fast-food and self-service restaurant operations are typical of this type of hospitality retail brand. In retail supermarkets, the introduction of self-billing techniques is in part a response to this kind of customer need.

Customers judge the quality of their experience with this kind of brand by the extent that it continues to be consistent and predictable. Quality measurement is based on monitoring consistency and uniformity. Operational standards rigidly define product, such as the size of portion, service presentation etc., and service aspects, such as time, contact, even the words to be used, in very precise ways.

In these types of hospitality retail, operation unit management is chiefly concerned with managing the delivery of the standard product and service. Managers spend a large part of their time monitoring the production of food, drink and accommodation to ensure they meet the standards set. Staff training is concerned with learning the 'one best way' by which goods are produced and served. Staff are managed and monitored to make sure that they are working to the standards set. Staff appraisal, pay and rewards are frequently linked to service consistency. Managers and staff are encouraged to work in the set way and not to use initiative and flair.

Example 1.1

McDonald's Restaurants Limited

McDonald's Restaurants typify an approach to managing service encounters which includes four dimensions in this approach to managing the service process. These dimensions are important sources of customer satisfaction – what people are buying into.

The first dimension is that McDonald's offers *efficiency* in that 'it offers the best way from getting from the state of being hungry to the state of being full'. Work is designed to maximize the use of labour most efficiently through technology and simplified job design. The second dimension is that McDonald's offers services that can be easily quantified and *calculated*. Customers can specify what they are going to get and know the time it will take. Tight job design and productivity levels allow managers to be more certain as to the level of outputs from a given level of labour inputs. Third, customers are able to *predict* products, services and prices. Customers know what they will be offered in different McDonald's Restaurants and even the prices to be charged. From an employment perspective, employee performance and the need for labour hour by hour can be predicted with reasonable accuracy. Finally, customers, through the impact of these other dimensions, can experience a sense of personal *control*. From an employment perspective the design of jobs and management hierarchy aim to ensure maximum control of employee performance.

Standardization and the accompanying psychological benefits are important features of the offer made by the company to its customers, and this shapes much of its management of human resources. Its brand values are tightly drawn and closely managed. Even franchise businesses are bound by the disciplines of the brand. The service dimension is largely shaped by concepts and practices developed in manufacturing industry. The approach draws on principles and techniques such as the division of labour, scientific management and the use of technology to minimize the need for much employee discretion.

McDonald's Restaurants is typical of factory service. Production and service operations are centrally designed and individuals are trained to produce and serve dishes according to the standards laid down. The menu of products on offer, the contents of dishes, their appearance to the customer and the manner of their production, pricing and promotion are substantially planned and executed at national head office in the UK.

Choice dependent services

Choice dependent services have many similar features to uniformity dependent services in that customer satisfaction is largely based on the tangible nature of the food, drink and accommodation supplied. Customers also have a high expectation of consistency in the product and service, but they also want to be able to give their experience a personal touch. In this case the product range is sufficient to allow customers a wide choice of the food and drink that they consume. In some instances the service aspect, too, allows them to be given the kind of service that they want. Staff are trained to give one of a number of service performances, depending on the customer type or occasion.

Customers judge the quality of their experience through a combination of product consistency and feeling that they have been recognized for themselves as individuals. Being able to predict and recognize these service needs becomes important, but through branding and the identification of the customer service types the service is 'customized'. In many ways these organizations supply hospitality services which are similar to customized cars. Mass-production techniques ensure uniformity and lower operating costs, but customers are able to personalize their experience. Operational standards are like those in the uniformity dependent services. Product specifications define the way food and drink is to be prepared and served, with portion sizes and the product range all laid down in the national brand manual. Service methods and service time targets are also defined and measured as an assessment of quality management. However, the importance of making the customer experience more personal and tailored to developing feelings of individuality require the staff to give a range of performance which cannot to be so tightly defined or scripted. Staff performance is vital to ensuring that the customers feel important as individuals.

Management are also concerned with monitoring consistency in production and service. They have to be able to evaluate the quality of customer experiences. This means applying judgements that cannot be so easily systematized. Given the importance of employee performance, managers spend a considerable amount of time and effort recruiting employees who will 'naturally' summon up the feelings and emotions needed to give the customer the service needed. Training and providing staff with role-model examples are key activities. Training in particular has a core significance. All employees are trained to advise the customers about their choice. Knowing the contents and production methods of menu items, for example, is essential in guiding customers. Pay and rewards are typically associated with sales and staff performance.

Example 1.2

TGI Friday Restaurants

There is much about TGI Friday Restaurants which also involves attributes of efficiency, calculability, predictability and control. Customers are encouraged to expect certain service standards, which allow for efficient service. Service standards require that starters are served within seven minutes of receipt of the order and main courses are served within twelve minutes of the order being presented to the kitchen. Information technology is used to ensure that these service targets are met. Like McDonald's Restaurants, menus are fixed and determined centrally, as are prices and production methods. Menus are standardized throughout the country so customers visiting different restaurants know what to expect. The layout of the restaurants, staff uniforms, type of employees, décor, etc. are also standardized. Through the various tangible and supporting intangible standards to the service, customers optimize their control of the meal experience. They can calculate how long the meal will take, the approximate cost and the style of service which they will receive. Standardization enables predictability and control.

Though there are clearly similarities with McDonald's, the nature and degree of standardization is different. For all its standardized approach TGI Friday does allow customers more opportunities to customize their eating and drinking experiences. The food menu, for example, contains over 100 items and the cocktail menu is similarly extensive. This allows customers a wider range of choices over how they construct the experience. Similarly, in the intangibles, employees are encouraged, whilst operating to the service standards, to provide customers with a service experience which is special to them. Thus, if customers wish to linger over their meal or have a special occasion (birthday, etc.), employees alter the service pace or create a celebratory atmosphere accordingly. If the McDonald's offer is best typified as being about mass production, the TGI Friday experience is best typified as being about mass customization.

Relationship dependent services

Relationship dependent hospitality services are those in which the customer is buying into a standardized and predictable offer, but which involves a more elaborate service. The number of contacts between the customer and the service staff are more frequent and customers give priority to the quality of the service as a source of satisfaction. This is not to say that the tangible products – food, drink and accommodation are not important, they are and customers have expectations about these. However, the nature of the service they receive becomes of particular importance. Many hospitality retailers are attempting to compete through the quality of their service offer to customers. Thus there is movement in the way the organization delivers service to its clients.

The nature of the service interactions may require service staff to be flexible. They may need to make some decisions as a response to the customer's service requirement. Typically, employees would be empowered to make some decisions, within prescribed limits, to meet customer service needs or deal with customer complaints.

The service organization is concerned with maintaining the standard products and service targets as well as ensuring that staff take ownership of the service encounter. Empowered employees need to be trained sufficiently to be able to make the decisions needed to give customer satisfaction. Management styles are likely to be more participative because managers are not able to sanction every detail of the service encounter and employees need to be left to make the decisions needed. Employee motivation, training and rewards are particularly important in that they should match the forms of participative management being applied.

Example 1.3

Harvester Restaurants

Harvester Restaurants has some features in common with both McDonald's and TGI Fridays. In many ways brand attributes offer calculability, efficiency and control, but there are additional psychological, intangible elements to the offer which suggest havens of homeliness and tradition in a fast-changing and confusing world.

The core concept is of a family restaurant and pub. Décor conveys a rustic image with menus based on traditional 'English' fare. Pricing strategy pitches the offer in the mid-price range. Although menus offer a reasonable choice of dishes, preparation techniques are based on simple routine tasks and require relatively simple skill levels to complete. Restaurant service style is through waiter/waitress order-taking and plated service of meals. The bar area is designed in pub style and stocked with a typical range of beers, wines and spirits, and offers bar meals.

Service standards reflect the ethos of 'treating customers as though they were guests in your own home'. The style of service is relaxed formality that also reinforces brand values of homeliness, hospitality, tradition and naturalness. Thus the brand can be defined as being standardized in the tangibles. Customers know what to expect and how much it will cost. Whilst the brand also defines core values in customer service, the nature of the business is such that the intangible elements of the brand cannot be standardized in the same way as with tangibles and is thereby reliant on the efforts of frontline staff.

The three examples have shown how the different service offers to customers result in different approaches to managing hospitality retail operations. The idea of 'fit' is important. In other words the nature of the service that customers buy needs to match with marketing strategies, the way employees are managed and the work that managers do in managing the hospitality operation. Figure 1.6 shows how these functional aspects of hospitality service management overlap with each other.

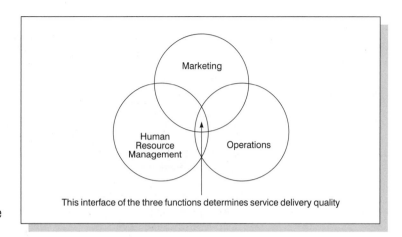

This interface of the three functions determines service delivery quality

Figure 1.6
The functional interdependence
of service management

As a unit manager you need to understand the nature of the service you are supplying to customers so that you are able to manage consistently the operation, the staff and service quality.

Working with customers

As we have seen, hospitality retailing has increasingly used branding as a way of showing customers what to expect. In some cases, the business has been focused at a service offer without being formally branded through common logo, décor, menu, etc., but has been *'blueprinted'* in a way that targets customers and the services that they want to receive. A useful starting point for giving a hospitality business focus is the consideration of *customer occasions*, that is, the reasons why customers use hospitality retail operations. In each case, there are critical success factors that ensure the customer receives the service needed for that occasion. These categories will be discussed more fully in Chapter 12, but Table 1.3 offers some examples.

Clearly, brands and blueprints cluster these customer occasions to attract customers who are using the brand or unit for similar reasons. For example, Scottish and Newcastle's Chef and Brewer brand represent occasions which are 'special meal out' – 'cannot be bothered to cook', 'refuel' and the 'out on the town' customers would not mix with these occasions Whilst children are not discouraged, the offer is essentially aimed at adult occasions. The same company's Homespread brand also offers occasions that cover 'cannot be bothered to cook' and 'refuel', but they are also aimed at 'family outings' and include children's play areas. Again, the 'out on the town' occasions are not compatible.

This consideration of customer occasions recognizes that people use hospitality retail operations in different ways, and the same individuals may be visiting different hospitality retail units for different occasions. This focus allows you, in your capacity as

Customer occasion	Description	Critical success factors
Cannot be bothered to cook	Customers want feeding with minimum effort and formality	Quick service, good value for money, friendly service
Family outing	Visits with children (under 10 years old). May be single parents in the week and two adults at the weekends.	Child-friendly service, value for money – children's menu – female friendly – children's facilities.
Refuel	Shoppers, business people, and tourists having a break – usually lunch time and early evenings	Quick service, easy communication of the menu and drinks, female friendly, smoke-free atmosphere
Special meal out	Couples and groups, spend time over the meal, several courses, high expectations of service and quality, some shared special occasions e.g. Valentine's Day	More paced service, multicourse offer, drinks to support the occasion, table ordering, good quality environment
Out on the town	Typically Friday and Saturday evening, groups and couples, students, having a good time, involves drinks	Lively informal atmosphere, music and atmosphere of something happening, rapid drinks service, fashion drinks

Table 1.3 Examples of customer occasions in hospitality retailing

either the brand manager or the unit manager, to concentrate on the factors which are critical for success, and to consider what other occasions might be explored that are compatible with the brand core occasions. Equally importantly, they also help to identify customer occasions that do not sit well with the core brand occasions – in other words, customer who might upset the core business.

About hospitality

The term 'hospitality' has been used in connection with industrial activities which used to be called 'hotel and catering' for a couple of decades now. The nature of hospitality needs to be carefully considered by organizations that are attempting operate chains of hospitality retail units, because the provision of genuine hospitality can be an important way of building competitive advantage over those who do not understand its true meaning.

To better understand the commercial applications of hospitality it is necessary to explore hospitality in its widest sense. In times past, hospitality and the need to be hospitable were highly valued in the UK. Being genuinely hospitable to travellers and to less fortunate members of the community was considered a good thing and highly valued. In the UK today hospitality and the expectation to be hospitable are not afforded anything like the same status they were in the past, nor as currently given in other societies. That said, there are lessons which commercial operators can learn from a study of hospitality in private domestic settings.

Importantly, being hospitable in a private setting involves the host being responsible for the guest's happiness. There is a special link and the guest is in a mutual pact. The host becomes the guest and the guest becomes the host on another occasion. In private domestic settings hospitality:

- involves mutual giving and obligation
- is generous
- is unselfish
- is open-handed
- is welcoming
- is warm.

Most importantly, hospitality is based on appropriate motives and is more than hosting. A good host may be effective at keeping glasses full, food on the table and the room temperature comfortable, but may be acting for ulterior motives – say to win favour, seduction or vanity. Good hospitality requires the right motives:

- the desire for the guest's company
- the pleasure of entertaining
- the desire to please others
- concerned for the needs of others
- a duty to be hospitable.

Hospitable people are those who posses one or more of these motives for entertaining.

This raises the difficulties faced by many hospitality industry organizations. The commercial rationale in which they operate often distorts the relationship with their guests. The commercial rationale sells hospitality as a commodity. Guests become customers, and both the host and guest develop a reduced sense of mutual obligation. A consequence is that many organizations report difficulties in retaining customers and want to develop more repeat visits by existing customers.

Clearly, individual hospitality organizations cannot change society's sense of hospitality nor run their operations as though they were private domestic hosts, but they might be better able more robustly to build a community of loyal customers if they better understood hospitality in these contexts. For example, genuine hospitality is closely linked to values of generosity, beneficence and mutual obligations. Without wishing to suggest that profit-driven organizations would be willing to give away the product, consideration of how regular customers can be rewarded with extra benefits which celebrate their importance and uniqueness as individuals could be successful. The key here is to making the giving seem like acts of genuine generosity rather than the formulaic 'give-aways' typical of many branded hospitality businesses.

Also, hospitality retailers need to consider the recruitment, selection and training of hosts who are capable of being hospitable, and who display characteristics of hospitableness.

Conclusion

This chapter has attempted to provide you with an overview of some of the key concerns and issues relating to the unit management of hospitality retail services. These were described as multiunit businesses which supplied various combinations of food, drink and accommodation in a branded format where customers were given clear messages as to what to expect of the products and services making up the brand. Hospitality retail service operations have grown in significance and market share over the last twenty years. Hospitality retail organizations have been able to focus the service offer at particular customer segments, and have been able to offer customers standardized service quality through the use of tightly managed operating systems. Customers have increasingly used these brands to predict the service experience.

Whilst there have been substantial benefits to customers and hospitality retail organizations, these organizations are not without difficulties. The highly standardized service offer can be restrictive, inflexible and slow to change in response to change in customer tastes. Furthermore, many hospitality retail organizations experience high labour turnover of employees who find the restricted operation monotonous and boring. High levels of labour turnover create problems for delivering service quality, increase costs and put pressure on managers who have to spend a high proportion of their time recruiting replacement staff.

Although there are some common features to hospitality retail services, not all services are the same. Apart from the obvious differences in the physical food, drink and accommodation offered in different businesses, the nature of the service experience also varies. In particular, the product-services and the standardized-customized dimensions interact to create three service types that apply to hospitality retail services. Customers who buy uniformity dominant services are buying services which are highly standardized and predictable, and more product dependent. Choice dependent services allow customers a wide choice through which to build their own service experience. In this case customers are buying into services which are product dependent but which are capable of being adapted to their personal needs. Relationship dependent services involve services that are standardized but require more significant service interactions. Customer satisfaction is most influenced by the nature of the service experience that they receive.

To varying degrees, each of these service types faces problems of customer loyalty and the need to build a loyal customer base. A common feature is that customers, who may well be called guests, are well aware of the commercial relationship with hospitality supplier/host. Hospitality retailers need to carefully consider the human activity of hospitality and the qualities that make hospitable behaviour.

Reflective practice

Answer these questions to check your understanding of this chapter:

1 List the key features of hospitality retail service.
2 Describe different types of hospitality service operations.
3 Describe the key drivers of hospitality service types.
4 Contrast and compare service management techniques.
5 Highlight the potential management difficulties of each approach.
6 Describe hospitality and the characteristics of being hospitable.

Further reading

Heal, F. (1990). *Hospitality in Early Modern England*. Clarendon Press.

Heskett, S. H., Sasser, W. E. and Hart, C. W. (1990). *Service Breakthroughs: Changing the Rules of the Game*. Free Press.

Lashley, C. (1997). *Empowering Service Excellence: Beyond the Quick Fix*. Cassell.

Lashley, C. and Morrison, A. (2000). *In Search of Hospitality: Theoretical perspectives and debates*. Butterworth-Heinemann.

Lovelock, C. (1981). Why marketing needs to be different for service. In *Marketing of Services* (J. H. Donnelly and W. R. George, eds), American Marketing Association

Schmenner, R. W. (1995). *Service Operations Management*. Prentice Hall.

Telfer, E. (1996). *Food for Thought: Philosophy and Food*. Routledge.

Empowering unit management

After working through this chapter you should be able to:

- identify different forms of empowerment
- explain the benefits and limitations of empowering unit managers
- explain the benefits and limitations of empowering service
- critically discuss the need to feel empowered.

It is more than a name change

One of the problems faced by the branded hospitality businesses is that the standardized and controlled approach, which has been at the heart of their success, restricts employee involvement and commitment. Increasingly these organizations recognize that this can cause customer service problems. Many of these organizations recognize also that true competitive advantage will only come from high-quality service experiences. Customer contacts with service employees and unit managers, therefore, play a crucial role.

Frontline service staff become the key asset on which business success is built. Yet many organizations face major problems in generating employee commitment to customer service goals. Traditional management *command and control* techniques have been seen as the problem and there has been growing interest in alternative approaches to managing employees, and to managers.

Providing it is done properly, employee and manager empowerment can help generate employee commitment, flexibility and authority to make decisions, and meet customer service needs in a controlled manner. This chapter outlines the approach and shows how as unit managers you can both empower your staff and benefit from being empowered yourself. Fundamentally, successful empowerment depends on the supposedly empowered person *feeling empowered*.

Active learning point

Identify some people performance indicators of a hospitality brand known to you.

People performance indicator	Result
Balance of full-time and part-time employees at unit level	
Level of staff turnover – range between units	
Pay and conditions in relation to competition (industry and outside)	
Recruitment and selection procedures	
Staff training – proportion and procedure	
Management training – proportion and procedure	
Staff satisfaction and morale	
Transactions per person hour	
Customer satisfaction – surveys and complaints	

Bearing mind some of the indicators you have identified in the table, consider the nature of the way people are managed in the organization. Could it be described as 'command and control', that is, the dominant style by which managers operate involves *telling* staff what to do, or at best *telling and selling*? Employee involvement is limited to acting on instructions, though in the second instance they are given the reason why the instructions are being issued by managers. This chapter outlines some alternative ways that you can manage staff.

Empowerment: cutting through the jargon

By reading through this chapter you will see that 'empowerment' is one of those words which many people use but which has several meanings. The key claims for empowerment are based on criticisms of traditional organizations of the type that we have called *'branded hospitality services'*, that is, organizations which:

- control one or more major hospitality retailing brands
- operate through many local sites (hundreds of restaurants or bars)
- have a high degree of standardization control
- allow little local discretion to employees or managers
- operate in a command and control culture
- have high levels of staff turnover
- have low levels of employee satisfaction and morale
- experience difficulties in retaining and building customer loyalty.

Many of the problems that these service organizations face are thought to be a by-product of *disempowering* people. That is, the management policies that have extended control have often been at the cost of employee involvement and initiative. Organizations now need to adopt people management strategies to overcome the difficulties which standardization and extended control have created.

So one of the arguments for changing the way organizations are managed is that current practices disempower people and result in many organizations suffering the problems listed in Table 2.1. Low motivation, low morale and high staff turnover, and the other problems listed are therefore a consequence of the way people are managed and the organization needs to explore alternative approaches. *Empowerment* offers such an alternative approach.

Table 2.1
Problems caused by disempowerment in hospitality operations

Problems of disempowerment

Limited authority to meet service needs
Complaints dealt with slowly through senior manager
High level of costs in generating new customers
Low morale and poor motivation
High labour turnover
Low productivity
Low wages but high labour costs
Low quality
Low profits

Advocates of empowerment claim some impressive benefits to hospitality operators who introduce employee empowerment to their organization. Table 2.2 lists some of the benefits to be gained from a more empowered approach. Empowerment of you and your staff can create a more motivated workforce, more satisfied customers, higher productivity and a host of other benefits listed in the table.

Benefits of empowerment

More responsive service
Complaints dealt with quickly
Greater customer satisfaction
More repeat business
More motivated staff
Improved labour stability
Increased productivity
Lower labour costs
High quality
High profits

Table 2.2
Benefits of empowerment in hospitality operations

Some people say that empowerment is democratic and is a move in managerial intentions from *concern for control of employees* to *concern for employee commitment*. Many managers are critical of empowerment because they fear empowerment means a loss of managerial control. Empowerment is concerned with *both* employee control *and* commitment. Contrary to popular management mythology, empowerment is not about industrial democracy or extending workers' control.

Although the empowerment of employees recognizes the importance of employee performance in service delivery and is concerned to ensure greater commitment and involvement in service delivery, employees are generally empowered within defined boundaries. Usually empowerment is restricted to empowerment to the service tasks, or how service tasks are organized.

Empowerment is a management policy that aims to encourage employees to control their own performance to meet business goals. Figure 2.1 shows that control of employee performance can take a variety of forms from *externally* imposed control by the organization and management, through to *internally* self-imposed control. In some circumstances, say where the work is simple and routine, external control may be more effective. In other cases, say where the work is more complex and difficult to predict, the employee will be more effective working within broad guidelines that allow for discretion.

Figure 2.1
Variations in the focus of
control of employee
performance

Traditional	Technological	Social	Self

Organization structure and procedures	Technology	Leadership/ management style	Work groups	Empowerment	Professionalism

External control					Internal control

As we shall see later, three different approaches to controlling employees can be matched against different management and team leadership styles, classically know as:

- *Directive*: also known as command and control. Managers tell, or tell and sell, make decisions and instruct staff (though they may give reasons). Staff receive and act upon instruction.

- *Consultative*: managers tell and test, or seek employees' views about problems or decisions to be made. Staff make suggestions and pass comment before the manager decides.

- *Participative*: managers jointly solve problems and make decisions with staff, or delegate decision-making authority to employees. Employees are either involved with managers in making decisions or make the decisions themselves, within the limits set.

Examples of employee empowerment can involve all these styles, but the most traditional definition is closest to the participative style. One of the key differences with these earlier ideas about the *relationship* between managers and their staff is that empowerment is also a *motivational* concept. That is, empowered employees are supposed to feel more effective and personally committed to the organization and its service objectives to customers.

The examples given so far relate to the empowerment of hospitality service staff. There are examples of empowerment applied to hospitality service managers particularly at unit level. Again, the decision to consider the empowerment of the management structure is a response to the growth in size of hospitality organizations and the increase in levels of management which accompany growth in size in traditional command and control organizations.

Active learning point

In a hospitality brand known to you, identify the number of levels between the customer and board of directors.

Numbers of levels between customers and the board?	
Number of units managed by a multiunit manager?	
Number of multiunit managers in a region?	
Number of managers in each unit?	
How many levels of managers in the unit?	
How many staff to a manager in the unit structure?	

How do you describe the culture:
  – Command and control?
  – Consultative and involving?
  – Participative and empowered?	

As with front line staff, unit managers have been subject to a great deal of centralized control in many licensed retail, fast-food and restaurant chains. Often these controls have been necessary ingredients to establishing the cluster of units as a brand that delivers a consistent experience to customers. Elements include:

- increased control from head/regional office
- national brand marketing
- standard operating procedures
- restricting the role of unit managers to supervisory tasks
- mystery customer reports
- increased use of information technology to monitor performance.

Their role has been to provide team leadership, and local control of the unit. Few managers in these branded restaurants and bars have been encouraged to exercise initiative, creativity or enterprise.

Recently, hospitality service organizations have looked at a number of techniques for *delayering* the organization, that is, reducing the number of levels between the customer and the senior management. The empowerment of unit managers is often a key element in the approach. The unit manager is given more authority to make decisions without reference to more senior managers. The aim is to encourage the unit manager to act more as an entrepreneur, but within the brand context.

Active learning point

List the benefits and limitations of empowering unit managers to act as entrepreneurs within the discipline of the branded hospitality business.

Benefits	Limitations
1	1
2	2
3	3
4	4
5	5
6	6

Empowerment can be said to have four distinct, but overlapping meanings and applications. Table 2.3 lists the different managerial meanings of empowerment, and highlights the forms that empowerment may take. There are examples of applications of each approach. In some cases, an initiative introduced in a firm is

Managerial meaning	Initiatives used
Empowerment through participation	Autonomous work groups Job enrichment ('Whatever it takes training')
Empowerment through involvement	Quality circles Team briefings Suggestion schemes
Empowerment through commitment	Profit sharing and bonus schemes Quality of working life programmes – job rotation, job enlargement
Empowerment through delayering	Job redesign (job enrichment, autonomous work groups)

Table 2.3
Managerial meanings of empowerment

motivated by a mixture of intentions. Empowerment through commitment – empowerment through involvement and empowerment through participation – are initiatives aimed at staff, whilst empowerment through delayering is usually concerned with making the management structure 'flatter', that is, reducing the number of levels of management and empowering the remaining managers.

Empowerment through participation

Where an organization delegates some of the decision-making to employees, which in a traditional organization would be the domain of management, it can be said to be empowering through participation. Employees are making decisions about work organization or scheduling, as in the case of Harvester Restaurants, or are participating in identifying and satisfying customer needs, as in the cases of Marriott Hotels (Examples 2.1 and 2.2).

Autonomous work groups • • •

Autonomous work groups are groups of employees who work together without the immediate direction of a supervisor or manager. The group is given collective authority and is empowered to organize the work, the allocation of tasks within the group, deal with complaints, etc. The group has collective responsibility for the conduct and work done; managers will ask them to account for their actions, but after the event.

The key benefits are:

- increased motivation and commitment to service goals
- flexibility of action and organization as it is needed
- improved problem-solving
- better suggestions for quality improvement
- self-management through internal group dynamics
- reduced management costs as employees manage themselves
- customer complaints dealt with quickly
- improved labour retention and morale.

The approach has been tried frequently in the manufacturing sector, though there have been few examples in hospitality services. Given the history of command and control approaches to hospitality retail brands, it is perhaps not surprising that these approaches have rarely been tried. The following are some of the key weakness or limitations to the use of autonomous work groups in hospitality services:

- requires a high level of labour stability for strong group bonds to develop
- employee training required to provide the skills needed
- potential variations in service
- customer complaints dealt with differently
- potential loss of cost control
- employees cannot be trusted.

Example 2.1

Harvester Restaurants

All staff in Harvester Restaurant units are organized into three autonomous teams which reflect the key operational areas – bars, restaurant and kitchen. Each team has its 'team responsibilities', i.e. those aspects of business performance for which it will be accountable. In the restaurant, for example, the team will be responsible for guest service, guest complaints, sales targets, ordering cutlery and glassware, cashing up after service and team member training. In the more advanced cases, teams take part in the selection and recruitment of new team members.

A Shift Co-ordinator helps co-ordinate the activities of the team. This person is a team member, serving on table, cooking the grills or serving in the bar, but assumes additional responsibilities during the shift. In the restaurant the Shift Co-ordinator would take on the team responsibility for cashing up at the end of service and ensuring table layout was compatible with prior bookings. Several different team members would take on the role of Shift Co-ordinator during the week.

In addition to these roles, one of the staff members operates as the Appointed Person during each shift. This person would again be a member of one of the teams working in the restaurant, bar or kitchen during the shift, but would accept responsibility for securing the building, putting the shift's takings in the safe and handing over keys to the next appointed person. As with the Shift Co-ordinator, Appointed Persons receive no extra responsibility allowances, though in practice they get more pay by being on duty for longer hours. Given that these are often seen as core tasks in a traditional manager's job, it is interesting to note that there were no increases in security problems as a result of this initiative.

Restaurant management consists of just two roles – Team Manager and Coach. In this organization the Team Manager and Team Coach were no longer 'managing' the staff but were responsible for enabling and facilitating staff to be more self-managing and empowered.

The most effective autonomous groups were based on fairly stable groups within the workforce. In some cases, employees had been working in the establishment for five or six years, in some, over ten years. Strong group bonds and stability had been established before the introduction of work groups. Senior executives reported difficulties in establishing groups where there was a stubborn labour turnover problem, or where key members of the work team left and 'pulse turnover' resulted. Some unit managers and coaches also found difficulties in adjusting to the different approach needed.

Senior managers were convinced that the approach had been a success. They reported improved levels of sales, reduced stock holding, reduced labour costs and improved labour retention. Customer complaints were dramatically reduced and some restaurants registered no customer complaints for over several months.

Job enrichment

Job enrichment involves giving people a degree of decision-making authority. In some service organizations the initiative has been called *'Whatever it takes training'*. The key point is that service staff are empowered to make decisions about customer service, and even spend money, to ensure customer satisfaction. As the alternative title suggests, training employees and giving employees role models on which to shape their experience are essential ingredients.

Like autonomous work groups, employees have authority to make decisions about the service they give to customers without reference to a supervisor, but they are required to account for their actions, after the shift. Job enrichment shares many benefits with autonomous work groups, though the initiative is aimed at individuals and not the group. In many cases the more traditional organization structure continues, though supervisors adopt a more 'participatory style' of management. That said, many attempts to empower people in this way have failed because the approach has not been properly thought through, and employees have felt 'empowerment' just meant extra work and responsibility.

The key benefits of job enrichment are:

- increased motivation and commitment to service goals
- flexibility of action and organization as it is needed
- improved problem-solving
- better suggestions for quality improvement
- customer complaints dealt with quickly
- improved labour retention and morale.

Empowerment of individuals in hospitality service operations has a much wider exposure than the autonomous work group model. Given the long tradition of command and control cultures in the UK, it is perhaps not surprising that empowering people to make fairly low-level service decisions is appealing.

The following are some of the key weakness or limitations to the use of job enrichment as a way of empowering people in hospitality services:

- requires a high level of labour stability for employee skills and confidence to develop
- employee training essential to provide the skills needed
- potential variations in service through individual differences
- customer complaints dealt with differently
- potential loss of cost control
- individually based, limited benefits of team self-management
- managers place too many limits on the empowered
- employees cannot be trusted.

Typically, employees have been empowered to make service decisions relating to customer service needs, particularly in response to complaints or unpredictable service requests. This has frequently been linked to cash limits where an employee is able to spend up to a fixed amount to deal with a customer complaint, or service request.

Example 2.2

Marriott Hotels

Marriott Hotels recognized that scope existed to develop a competitive advantage through the quality of service it provided to customers. It was with this objective that Marriott Hotels introduced a *total quality management* (TQM) programme. From the outset, it was recognized that a successful TQM programme would involve a substantial element of employee involvement given the nature of the operation, which equates with a more participative management style and job enrichment. The company labelled this involvement as empowerment which they defined as: 'Employees given authority to create extraordinary service whilst preserving profitability'.

The implementation of this programme of change and its objective of empowering frontline staff and making staff more accountable for guest satisfaction, demanded a substantial investment in both time and money. A number of initiatives were formulated under the umbrella title 'The Quality Guide for Fortune Seekers' which consisted of six separate training modules, designed to communicate senior management's expectations of 'empowered' employees. One such programme was 'Whatever It Takes' (WIT) which involved some forty to sixty hours per employee of training including role-playing exercises. The critical message that management sought to put across was that employees had increased discretion to act in the light of service failures or non-standard scenarios which threatened guest satisfaction. A 'Cost of Non-Quality' (CNQ) programme was introduced which encouraged and authorized employees to take corrective action and then to log the cost of this against the CNQ account. This programme was intended to convey to employees the senior management's commitment to service quality and the trust they placed on employees to exercise their discretion to 'spend money' to ensure quality was maintained.

During the implementation of the TQM programme the company recognized that if changes were to be sustainable it would require the development and maintenance of an appropriate organizational culture. To this end Marriott Hotels have granted individual hotel units a degree of autonomy in the actual content of training programmes, as long as they meet company guidelines, which emphasize the need to look at the service encounter from the employee's perspective and to 'delight the customer' by any means that are legal, safe and profitable. Employee performance is monitored and individuals are given feedback on their performance measured against twelve areas of activity which are seen as critical in achieving the desired outcomes. Thus the TQM programme and the associated empowerment initiatives at Marriott Hotels are calculated to secure the employee control and commitment considered vital in supporting the chosen competitive and marketing strategies.

In managing this process of change at Marriott Hotels, internal marketing has played an important role. To increase employee commitment Marriott Hotels developed a number of 'tools.' This included a scheme aimed at aiding the personal growth of employees through a number of *non-vocational training* schemes. Management believed that helping employees to develop a new, non-job related, skill would help to increase the employee's feelings of self-worth. This, it was hoped, would in turn lead to improved job performance and ultimately increased customer satisfaction. Another element of internal marketing was the *reward and recognition* programme, which consisted of a sophisticated remuneration scheme that was viewed as an essential plank in the company's efforts to introduce and secure its strategy of empowerment. An additional tool was the *employee suggestion scheme* that was already in place but was revitalized for the TQM initiative. Marriott Hotels also utilized a *high profile advertising* campaign to communicate with both its external and internal customers. These advertisements consisted of allegedly true stories of employees demonstrating extraordinary feats to 'delight' customers, and conveyed the company's 'philosophy' to employees as much as it did to the target market.

Empowerment through involvement

Where the managerial concern is to gain from employee's experiences, ideas and suggestions, it may be the intention to empower employees through their involvement in providing feedback, sharing information and making suggestions. Front-line service employees are in a unique position to contribute to problem-solving, and communicate trends in customer service needs and the impact of company policies on service delivery.

The use of quality circles, or suggestion schemes or team briefings are techniques which are attempting to include the ideas and experiences of employees into the managerial decision-making process. Suggestions made may range from the nature of the immediate task, involving both tangibles and intangibles, through to more business strategy and employment policy issues.

Essentially, as a manager you would continue to make the decisions. Employees who choose to participate are directly involved, but participation in these programmes is usually voluntary. The intention is that:

- organizational effectiveness is improved

- there are better communications with front-line employees

- employees feel empowered through being involved in consultation and problem-solving processes

- employees are more committed to organizational objectives and service quality improvement.

Quality circles • • •

Quality circles involve groups of employees who meet regularly to discuss common operational issues. Usually, these meetings are weekly and involve volunteers meeting for about one hour. In the majority of cases the quality circle's activities are co-ordinated by a trained facilitator. Typically, the facilitator is a management appointment, either a supervisor or manager. In some cases the facilitator is a manager from another department. The facilitator acts as the channel of communication with the organization. Quality circles are created usually in a climate of problem resolution relating to either service quality or productivity, but if they are to continue to exist over the initial phase of enthusiasm, quality circles need to be established in an organizational climate which provides an unequivocal long-term role and which demonstrates the support of senior managers.

Typically, quality circles are established to match organizational arrangements. These may be in departments or units. So in a hotel organization, quality circles may be established to cover the kitchen, restaurant, accommodation and leisure operations in each hotel, or they may match just the unit structure, that is, one for each hotel.

Service organizations' motives for introducing quality circles have been identified as:

- a desire to improve communications

- improve staff morale

- improving commitment to service quality

- a good way of learning from employee experiences

- gaining suggestions about changes in customer service needs.

Quality circles can be seen as a means of establishing employee involvement in the service encounter. Quality circles establish employees as important to service quality whilst at the same time minimizing the loss of managerial control, and which also generates genuine improvements to service delivery.

Example 2.3

Accor Hotels

The use of quality circles has been applied in some of the group's hotels to good effect. The first circles were introduced in the company's Paris hotel. Four circles were established to cover the four key aspects of guest service – kitchen, restaurant, accommodation and reception. In each case, the brief requires that the circle focus on an improvement to guest service, and that problem must be capable of being resolved by circle members themselves without major expenditure.

Participants are volunteers, and unpaid for their contributions, though publicity of good ideas in the company's quality circles newsletter, together with the knowledge that quality circles provide formal recognition of the contribution employees can make, helps to generate interest in the programme. Managers report few problems in gaining volunteers for membership of the circles. A manager from another hotel acts as *facilitator*. This is said to assist employees and the facilitator in taking a fresh look at the problem uncluttered by past history and ego-defensive arguments.

Circle members deal with every aspect of the problem – identification, defining criteria for the solutions to the problem, suggested solutions, testing solutions against the criteria, measuring results and then 'rolling out the solution'. Speeding up customer breakfast service and guest checkout times are examples of issues that have been addressed by quality circles. Apart from the immediate benefits arising from the circle improvements, managers report that the most important gains come from improvements in employee morale. Employees are more likely to support changes introduced as a result of quality circles, and they gain an increased sense of worth as managers treat their problems and suggestions seriously. Communications between managers and employees have improved, and there has been a general increase in employee/manager contact.

Team briefings · · ·

Managers and employees meet on a regular basis to discuss operational issues. In some cases, they are used as a means of communicating 'top-down' decisions and organizational issues – shifts in demand, new product lines, successes/failures, etc. In other cases they may be used as vehicles for consultation and suggestion-making from employees. Like quality circles, the key difference with more participative forms is that managers make the decisions, informed to varying degrees, by comments from employees.

The frequency of these briefing meetings varies. When most integrated with operational management, briefings are conducted before or after each shift.

Before the shift team briefings brief the team about the specific requirements of the shift, for example:

- up-coming orders
- stock situations

- likely demand levels

- priority sales targets

- possible sources of operational difficulty

- can be used to enthuse the group.

After the shift team meetings can be useful for learning from operational successes and difficulties, such as:

- to flag up issues to be addressed in subsequent shifts

- correcting individual and group performance

- praising performance

- role modelling

- identifying and sharing best practice.

In both cases they are used to gather suggestions and feedback from team members.

In other cases team briefing sessions may be less frequent, perhaps weekly or monthly. These meetings are often used:

- as a means of communicating progress to employees

- for managers' to target issues for action

- to outline actions and policies being introduced

- to report on unit performance or organizational developments

- to seek suggestions and advice from employees

- for passing on information to employees.

Both quality circles and team briefings involve employees by developing a sense of ownership through communication processes that provide targets and feedback. Through suggestion-making and consultation, managers aim to create a sense of ownership, involvement and commitment to the unit and its success. It is hoped that employees making suggestions, and having their suggestions implemented, will develop pride in their work, feel empowered to detect and correct service faults, constantly improve services and be permanently involved in delighting customers.

Example 2.4

TGI Friday Restaurants

Team briefings occur immediately before the two key shift periods – morning and evening. Usually two teams meet in each unit – the restaurant and bar team meets as one group and the kitchen and back of house team meets as another. These sessions, therefore, involve all employees and are a standard feature of working arrangement. The style of the sessions is informal and managers do not take a formal lead as chair or co-ordinator. They do however, work through a senior member of the team, communicating organizational arrangements, items to be sold up or potential difficulties. Sessions are also used to create a fun atmosphere, with jokes being told by team members. On other occasions they are used to highlight best practice and to share experiences of success and difficulties. Training and shadowing new employees with more experienced employees are all communicated. Team briefing sessions last about twenty to thirty minutes. All employees are paid to attend these sessions, which are regarded by the management as part of 'setting-up' for the shift.

Each session is directed at communication processes and at operational matters, but they are also used to generate a collective enthusiasm amongst the team and to partly limit conflict between individual employees. They bring a collective dimension to the employment relationship. Employees are encouraged to identify primarily with the team with whom they work and with the branch. Both managers and employees repeat the organization's 'canoe theory' which stresses the benefits of members rowing together rather than against each other. During interviews, many employees talked with pride about the position of their unit – its growth, the volume of sales or levels of customer satisfaction. Others are enthusiastic about their relationship with fellow employees as one of the main benefits of working for the organization.

Empowerment through commitment

By empowering employees through greater commitment to the organization's goals it is hoped that:

- employees will take more responsibility for their own performance and its improvement

- employees will be more adaptable to change

- inherent employee skills and talents can be realized

- employees work for the benefit of the organization

- more satisfied customers will be produced

- profits will be improved.

Attempts to achieve greater employee commitment overlap and interrelate with both empowerment through employee participation and employee involvement. However, some initiatives are

Hospitality, Leisure & Tourism Series

quite specifically aimed at greater employee commitment. In these cases, it is hoped that greater commitment will result in the development of attitudes which are positive to the organization, employee performance more closely matched to organizational and customer needs, and more stability amongst the workforce.

Other forms of empowerment intend to gain greater employee commitment through improvements in job satisfaction and feelings of worth to the organization. Thus, changes in job design through increased job rotation, and job enlargement, together with techniques mentioned earlier through both employee participation and employee involvement are intended to change attitudes and reduce feelings of 'Them and Us'.

Basic employment practice ● ● ●

Managers who want employees to be committed have to recognize that employees have some expectations about good employment practice. Loyalty is a two-way street; employers who demand loyal employees have to meet some of these basic expectations.

- *Pay rates* must be fair and compatible with local rates. Employees must also be paid for a reasonable time period. Many organizations lose employee commitment because they forget that fair pay is a key expectation for employees.

- *Selection and recruitment* must be carefully undertaken. Some disciplinary problems are caused because the wrong people have been employed. Recruitment of unsuitable people can have a damaging effect on the morale of other employees.

- *Training and development* of employees is an essential building block of commitment. Employees need to know what is expected of them and they need to have the skills that help them to be effective. Associated with this, as a manager you need to think carefully about operational standards and the skills, knowledge and social skills needed to perform jobs effectively.

- *Performance reviews* need to be undertaken on a regular basis. Training is not enough. You need to ensure that performance is continuing to match the standards and objectives set. Good performance reviews go much further than telling staff what they are doing wrong, if they are to develop employee commitment. There should be opportunities to review expectations, concerns and ambitions as well.

- *Good communications* between management and employers is also an important element in building commitment. Employees need to know how the unit is doing, what the objectives are and what part they play in achieving them.

- *Decent treatment* of staff by managers is also an important feature of winning employee commitment. Employee performance is essential to effective business performance. Employees are people and they expect to be treated with dignity, fairness and respect.

Other employment practices ● ● ●

In business where the service offer is standardized and uniformity dependent, employees are rarely allowed to exercise discretion. Typically, these organizations are managed in a command and control style, which limits employee involvement and participation. Even in the most routine service organization, employee commitment continues to be an important consideration.

Highly standardized job design can make difficulties because job design and tight operating standards can make jobs boring and undemanding. In these circumstances, there are some approaches that can help to overcome the difficulties of working in the 'service factory'.

- *Job enlargement* involves giving staff a wider range of tasks to do. Instead of performing a narrow band of low-skilled and routine jobs, employees are trained to take on a wider number of similar tasks, thereby taking on more of the whole job. The aim is to make the work more interesting by including more of the whole so that employees identify more closely with the final outcome.

- *Job rotation* moves employees round a range of tasks. The aim is to overcome the boredom by moving staff from one job to another. In recent time 'multiskilling' and 'functional flexibility' have involved similar practices but these are more concerned with developing a flexible workforce to undertake more jobs.

Active learning point

Rank in order of importance those factors essential for the success of a hospitality retail business unit.

Factor	Ranking (1 most important)
Good point of sale promotions	
Clean service areas	
Service speed	
Motivated staff	
The personal qualities of the Restaurant Manager	
Trained staff	
A restaurant business plan	
Regular special offers	
Tight operating standards control	
Service quality	

- *Suggestion schemes* that encourage suggestions from staff can, under the right circumstances help to build employee commitment. It is essential that organizations celebrate and reward good suggestions from employees. Schemes are likely to fail if suggestions 'disappear', suggestions take a long time to be evaluated or the rewards from the suggestions are of marginal monetary value.

Barriers to creating employee commitment • • •

- *Staff turnover* makes it difficult to build long-term employment relations and commitment, because employees are typically not there long enough, or staff become demoralized because there is a constant stream of new employees with whom they have to work. Many branded hospitality services register very high levels of staff turnover. High numbers of staff leaving lead to low employee commitment and more leavers, which becomes a self-perpetuating process that can be further compounded if managers see this as an inevitable consequence of the industry.

- *Low discretion job design*, which has been a feature of the growth of branded hospitality services, limits the amount of variety and personal qualities required of employees. Without careful management employees can feel unimportant and that 'a trained monkey could do this job'. Low self-esteem, a sense of disempowerment and low personal effectiveness all create barriers to employee commitment. Again, this can be further compounded if employees are not trained and are put under pressure because the unit is understaffed.

- *Too many part-time or temporary staff* can cause difficulties in creating employee commitment. Whilst many service organizations need some part-time employees to meet fluctuations in demand for services, employees who have limited employment tenure are less likely to make a long-term commitment to the organization and its objectives.

Empowerment through delayering

Over the last two decades many writers have talked about *excellent* companies being 'flatter' and 'close to the customer'. There has been increasing interest in reducing the number of tiers of management in organization structures. Hospitality operators, like their counterparts in manufacturing and other sectors of the economy, have been keen to explore the possibilities of delayering their organizations.

The benefits of delayering an organization include:

- encouraging salaried managers to be entrepreneurial
- cutting overheads by reducing administrative costs
- taking the organization closer to its customers
- quality gains
- greater responsiveness to environmental change.

Typically, empowerment has involved unit managers being given flexibility and authority to run the branded service unit – pub, restaurant or hotel – without the same kind of management from above. Typically, empowered unit managers will:

- develop a unit business plan
- scan the local environment for competitors
- build local alliances with other firms
- identify key customer groups and targets

Hospitality, Leisure & Tourism Series

- undertake local advertising

- reflect local terms and conditions of employment

- have some authority to make capital investment decisions for the unit.

In these cases unit managers work within broad business objectives and do whatever it takes to meet these goals in the way they see fit. Their relationship with multiunit managers becomes closer to that of a franchisee and business consultant. Thus the line manager gives advice and support, and the unit manager is encouraged to make the decisions needed.

Example 2.5

McDonald's Restaurants Limited

As a response to a pilot study, and a report produced on arrangements in the USA, the organization structure focused on unit managers. Using the arrangements for managing the franchised business, the company has produced a structure where a new 'General Manager' role replaced the traditional Restaurant Manager's role. This new role allows each manager more freedom to run the restaurant as an 'independent' business in the same way that it might be run by a franchisee. These managers, therefore, run the restaurant with 'responsible autonomy'. Budgets are largely focused at profit and operational targets. How the individual achieves the targets is, within limits, up to the judgement of the individual. Bonus schemes for the General Managers come into effect only when the business is achieving good grades in the company's customer satisfaction assessment levels, which measure quality, service and cleanliness over a twelve-month period. These service quality measures were said to establish 'green fees' which attracted a bonus, after which further bonuses were calculated on profit growth. Given these bonuses, it is possible for General Managers to earn a further £10 000 over and above the basic salary of £20 000 per annum. Under these arrangements, the General Manager may be responsible for one large unit, or several smaller units.

General Managers, themselves, report to an Operations Consultant, whose role and style is similar to the Field Consultant in the franchisee structure. As the job titles suggest, consultants in both cases act more in a negotiated and supportive role. The General Managers are left to run the business and the Operations Consultant visits them on a less frequent basis than would a Supervisor in the traditional structure. As the General Managers have more delegated authority, the consultant provides advice and guidance as and when required. The agenda of issues to be discussed between the manager and consultant becomes more business rather than operationally focused. Thus, issues related to marketing and profitability are more likely to be discussed under these circumstances than in the traditional relationship between a unit manager and an Area Supervisor.

This form of empowerment allowed managers more freedom to make immediate decisions about the restaurant as a business and encouraged the participants to develop a sense of ownership. This was reinforced by a reward package, which gave managers a considerable material incentive to achieve more business reflected in both quality and profit targets.

Feeling empowered

As we have seen, empowerment is a term with several meanings and which reflects various managerial intentions resulting in different forms of empowerment and changes to what the empowered person can now do. Whatever the nature of the changes to working arrangements – empowerment must result in people 'feeling empowered'. In other words, empowerment produces an emotional state.

Empowerment is motivational and originates in people's internal needs for power and control, and feelings of personal effectiveness. Individuals perceive themselves as having power when they are able to:

- control events or situations

- deal effectively with the situations which they encounter.

Conversely, individuals are likely to feel powerless:

- in situations which they cannot influence

- where they do not have the time, resources or skills to be effective.

The need for power is internal, based on a need for self-determination, and as a manager you should adopt techniques which:

- strengthen employees needs for self-determination and personal effectiveness

- the empowered value and which they have been empowered to do

- employees feel includes actions which are meaningful

- convince employees of their ability to cope in situations

- show employees that their success is valued

- allow employees to exercise a range of judgements and skills.

Figure 2.2 shows Conger and Kanungo's (1988) stages in the process of empowerment. This can be helpful in mapping the processes that unit managers may need to go through to develop the necessary feelings of empowerment in staff members.

- *Stage 1* involves consideration of those aspects of the organization and its operation that lead employees to feel dis-empowered. This might include a range of bureaucratic

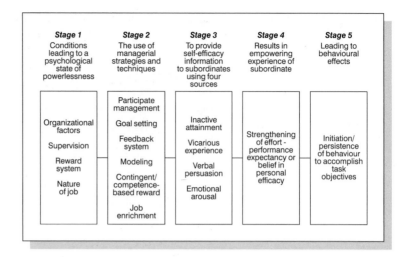

Figure 2.2
Stages in the empowerment process. Source: Conger and Kanungo (1988)

procedures, an overly tall organization structure that limits their ability to take decisions, or a command and control culture that imposes decisions from above. It could be that supervisors operate in an autocratic manner, or treat employees with 'thinly disguised contempt'.

- *Stage 2* includes a range of managerial techniques that assist the employee to enhance their feelings of effectiveness. This might include the introduction of more participatory management techniques. It involves setting goals, training, providing adequate systems of feedback, reward systems which reward competence, management styles that are supportive and designing the jobs to involve diversity, variety and allows the application of discretion.

- *Stage 3* provides self-effectiveness information to subordinates from a variety of sources. Providing information about how the individual is developing is an important feature in developing the individual's perceptions. Information on personal efficacy comes from the personal evaluations of their own development, from watching others, from verbal feedback and through a supportive emotional environment that stresses trust and builds confidence. This leads on to

- *Stage 4* in which empowered employees strengthen their efforts and develop an expectancy of personal efficacy. This in turn leads to

- *Stage 5* which is behavioural change that results in continued efforts to achieve organizational goals.

To be an effective manager, you need to be aware that heightened motivation to complete organizational tasks and aspiration to greater organizational goals, such as increased customer satisfaction, will be achieved through the development of a 'strong sense of personal efficacy'. The development of this strong sense of personal effectiveness becomes the defining feature of empowerment, and thereby, a crucial factor in determining the success or failure of all initiatives which claim to empower individuals.

Conclusion

This chapter has shown that empowerment of managers and staff can improve service delivery. Empowered frontline staff in particular will be committed to customer satisfaction and 'delighting the customer'. Empowered managers are more likely to empower staff within the unit, and have the autonomy to manage the unit in a more flexible and responsive manner. Apart from the direct benefits of empowerment, it is claimed that empowerment helps organizations overcome tendencies to disempower organization members. Large hospitality retail organizations have adopted a range of management and control techniques that have imposed operating standards and working routines which have been successful in establishing uniformity of delivery across different units, but which have also resulted in some major difficulties. Low levels of employee commitment and high levels of staff turnover are two consequences of employees feeling insignificant and powerless.

Exploration of employee empowerment in practice shows that empowerment can take a variety of forms to meet different management intentions. The chapter has shown that empowerment can be both concerned with the relationships between employees and managers, and between managers with the structure. In essence, the empowerment of service staff in hospitality retail operations reflects the nature of different types of service offer to customers. Where the service offer is *uniformity dependent*, forms of empowerment will be mostly concerned with empowerment through commitment because the service offer demands working to tightly defined operational standards. Where the offer is *choice dependent* the forms of empowerment will be more concerned with empowerment through involvement because the employee is acting as a consultant to customers. In the case of relationship *dependent* service it is likely that employees will be empowered in a way which is more participative so that they will provide services required by customers which cannot be predicted or made routine.

In the case of unit management, this chapter argues that organizations can gain much from the empowerment of unit managers. Giving managers more *responsible autonomy* and changing the relationship between unit managers and the next level up (multiunit managers) can have the effect of encouraging the unit manager to act in a more flexible way, which creates a business unit that is more responsive to local customers and

competitors. A major difficulty of giving managers more autonomy stems from the reasons for the growth of hospitality service
brands in the first place – namely the need for standardization
and uniformity. There is a danger that service quality standards
and the nature of the service on offer varies between units as
managers increasingly 'do their own thing'.

Finally, the chapter outlined the central importance of empowerment as an emotional state. To work effectively empowerment
must be more than a name change. It has to result in people
feeling empowered, and developing a sense of personal effectiveness. It must meet their needs to feel that they have the skills to
undertake various tasks and that they are now able to undertake
tasks in which they have some belief and value. From this point
of view empowerment is a motivational concept. In its first phase
it must be concerned with removing the causes of feelings of
disempowerment.

Reflection and practice

Pick a hospitality retail business known to you and answer the
questions below. If needed, use the case study (Chapter 14):

1 Identify the current unit problems.
2 Are any of these linked to employees feeling disempowered?
   Justify your answer.
3 Make a case for empowering staff and managers.
4 What limitations and barriers are there to empowering
   employees in this organization?
5 Devise an outline plan for introducing empowerment.
6 Suggest some performance indicators through which to
   evaluate the success, or failure, of empowerment in this
   situation.

Reference

Conger, J. A. and Kanungo, R. B. (1988). The empowerment
process: integrating theory and practice. *Academy of Management Review*, **13**, 471–482.

Further reading

Barbee, C. and Bott, V. (1991). Customer treatment as a mirror of
employee treatment. *Advanced Management Journal*, **5**, 27.
Conger, J. A. and Kanungo, R. B. (1988). The empowerment
process: integrating theory and practice. *Academy of Manage-
ment Review*, **13**, 471–482.
Foy, N. (1994). *Empowering People at Work*. Gower.
Lashley, C. (1997). *Empowering Service Excellence: Beyond the Quick
Fix*. Cassell.
Stewart, A. M. (1994). *Empowering People*. Pitman.

Team leadership and motivation

After working through this chapter you should be able to:

- identify different styles and approaches to team leadership

- predict the likely impact of management styles on team member performance

- critically discuss the impact of hierarchy on views about team members

- identify stages in team development needs.

'It takes happy workers to make happy customers'

F. W. Marriott's famous quotation provides a reminder of the importance which many firms place on ensuring that the unit team is well motivated under the leadership of enthusiastic managers. Managers need to understand their own approaches to managing the team, and know how to adjust their approach when needed. They must appreciate the benefits that team membership can generate as well as understand the motives and perspectives of team members.

That said, many hospitality retail managers find managing people is their most difficult task. There are many examples of very similar bars and restaurants where the only difference between success and failure, is the local unit manager's ability to motivate and enthuse the team of employees working in the unit. In one establishment, staff are happy, committed to serving customers and clearly enjoy their work, and in the next unit employees are grumpy, unmotivated and clearly desperate to escape. Most frequently the attitudes, assumptions and style with which people are managed by their immediate manager is the only noticeable variable. This chapter suggests some approaches to both analysing management style and understanding the actions of team members.

Active learning point

The table in Exercise 3.1 lists ten sources of job satisfaction. First, rank these in order of importance for yourself but do not think about your current job, just what you think is desirable. Second, rank these in order of importance for a group of employees known to you. In both lists 1 is most important and 10 the least important.

Exercise 3.1

Satisfaction at work

Major sources of satisfaction	Important to you	Important to your subordinates
Steady work and steady wages		
High wages		
Pensions and other old-age security benefits		
Not having to work too hard		
Getting along with the people I work with		
Getting along well with my supervisor		
Good chance to turn out good quality work		
Good chance to do interesting work		
Good chance of promotion		
Good physical working conditions		

At this stage the two lists are important in establishing the similarities and differences between managers and subordinates. We shall return to the findings later, but for now ensure that the list contains two types of factors:

1 Extrinsic sources of job satisfaction are more material rewards:

    (a) High wages.
    (b) Steady work and steady wages.
    (c) Pensions and other old-age security benefits.
    (d) Not having to work too hard.
    (e) Good physical working conditions.

2 Intrinsic sources of job satisfaction make the person feel better:

    (a) Good chance of promotion.
    (b) Getting along with the people I work with.
    (c) Getting along well with my supervisor.
    (d) Good chance to turn out good quality work.
    (e) Good chance to do interesting work.

Hospitality, Leisure & Tourism Series

Looking at your responses to the sources of satisfaction survey:

- Pick out the top three factors which you have identified for yourself. Are they more extrinsic or intrinsic?

- Pick out the top three factors you have identified for your subordinates. Are they more extrinsic or intrinsic?

- Make some notes that explain your answer. Keep these nearby, because we shall return to this exercise.

The relationship between team members and you, the manager, as team leader is important and there are different ways that you can choose to manage your team. As we have seen in Chapter 2, even empowerment has a variety of forms which can be more directive, consultative or participative and involve employees differently – acting on instructions, making suggestions or working without the direct involvement of the manager. These differences are important in team leadership, and we shall return to them later. First we need to show how different managers hold different assumptions about their subordinates and have different priorities about the job and the team.

What kind of leader?

Management at all levels involves a social relationship between manager and the managed. In modern branded hospitality businesses, the relationship between the manager and the team is key to a successful bar, hotel or restaurant. The following four exercises are designed to highlight different elements of the relationship and provide the basis for more discussion later.

Active learning point

Complete the following two exercises as accurately as you can. Use your current job or a recent job as the context for your responses.

Exercise 3.2

How close or distant?

To gauge the sociability of the person (you or your boss), score the individual on each of the dimensions given below. Then add the scores together and divide the answer by 7.

Indicator	1	2	3	4	5	6	7
Use of first names	Never			Boss only uses			Always/ mutual
Sharing break times	Never			Sometimes			Often
Sharing leisure outside work	Never			Sometimes			Often
Exchange pleasantries	Rarely			Usually			Very often
Sharing jokes/humour	Never			Sometimes			Often
Exchanging domestic information	Never			Mostly from subordinates			Often/ mutual
Formality	Very formal			Varies			Very informal

Psychologically and socially distant aloof from subordinates   Remote   Friendly   Psychologically and socially close friendship with subordinates

One aspect of the unit manager's style relates to the way he or she relates socially to team members. As stated earlier, the relationship is personal and involves social relationships. Do you remain psychologically aloof, or try be 'one of the boys/girls'? Many managers find this aspect most difficult to judge, particularly when they first take up a responsible post. An aloof and distant relationship can be perceived as cold and uncaring. The distance between team leader and team can create a barrier that cuts the manager off from the team and thereby prevents effective communication. On the other hand an over-friendly manner can be misunderstood and lead to disciplinary difficulties.

In many ways the sociability style adopted by you as the team leader will be determined by a combination of your own personality, your experience and the context in which the team is working. Some managers are by nature closer or more distant from subordinates. In these cases, it is difficult to suppress your

Psychological distance	Psychological closeness
Benefits	*Benefits*
Disciplinary action easier	Leader has better knowledge of team members
Formality better matched to formal situations	Good communications with team members
Disciplined working methods	Better knowledge of the immediate situation
People 'know their place'	Better able to build strong group bonds
	Better able to tap the creativity of the team
Limitations	*Limitations*
Distance acts as barrier to good communication	Disciplinary difficulties
Remoteness can breed misunderstanding	Team member behaviour is inappropriate in formal settings
Team members fearful and hide the facts	Sloppy working methods
Leads to conflict with the group	Poor follow-through on instructions

Table 3.1 Benefits and limitations of distance and closeness

personality traits and, all things being equal, you will perform to your natural inclination. More experienced managers tend to have the confidence to be relaxed and informal with employees. Many new managers believe that it is easier to be formal first and more relaxed later. Some service situations require a formal approach, particularly in front of house. In other cases, informality is required.

Exercise 3.3

Getting along with others

Read the following reactions by a manager and identify that which is closest to the way you would react. Also identify the reaction which is least like the way you would react.

An employee arrives forty-five minutes late for work. The manager says:

1 'What late again, can't you ever get here on time? You are just too unreliable.'
2 'Oh dear, what happened to you, was the bus late again? Let me help you catch up with your work.'
3 'Please come and see me later. I would like to talk to you about your lateness so that it can be avoided in future. In the meantime do you need any help to make up the lost work?'
4 'I do wish you would get here on time, you know how I rely on you. You have let me down.'
5 'Why does this always happen to me? Whenever I'm on early shift someone comes in late. It really isn't fair.'

These statements are useful in that they each represent different ways that individual managers might feel and act in a given situation. Each makes different assumptions about the position of the manager and the employee, and each represents a different focus for the reaction. The study of *transaction analysis* can assist managers understand the basic modes of behaviour which individuals take up in their relationships with other people. Transaction analysis establishes different kinds of transactions and how to deal with them. You need to understand these as a way of understanding your own behaviour and the behaviour of subordinates, and the psychological games which individuals sometimes play.

Ego states

The above statements each start from different ego states, that is, the assumptions about the communicator (manager) and the relationship with the receiver of the message (the late employee).

Parent ego state

The parent ego state implies a position of power over the receiver. Usually it is learnt from parents, teachers and other authority figures. This may involve an open expression of power 'do this', 'do that', or more implied 'let me help you'.

1 *Critical parent ego state*: openly dominant, critical, controlling, putting others down, minimizing their problems, directing, addressing. **Typical words used:** bad, should, ought, must, always, ridiculous. Tone: critical, condescending, disgusted. **Non-verbal characteristics:** pointing finger, frowns, anger. **Underlying attitudes:** judgemental, moralistic, authoritarian.

   In the example given above, 'What late again, can't you ever get here on time? You are just too unreliable' the manager's reaction is typical of the critical parent ego state. The reaction is blaming and judging without knowing the circumstances of the employee's lateness.

2 *Nurturing parent ego state*: openly supportive, understanding, sympathetic, affectionate, loving, helping behaviour. **Typical words used:** good, nice, I love you, beautiful, splendid, tender. **Tone:** loving, comforting, concerned. **Non-verbal characteristics:** open arms, smiling, accepting. **Underlying attitudes:** understanding, caring, giving.

   In the example above, 'Oh dear, what happened to you, was the bus late again? Let me help you catch up with your work', reaction of the manager is typical of the nurturing parent ego state. The reaction is concerned, accepting and understanding without knowing whether the employee was responsible for the lateness.

Adult ego state • • •

The adult ego state is not related to age. It is concerned with objectively appraising reality and uses information from all sources to make statements and adopt courses of action. It is even handed and avoids being judgemental before all the information is gathered. **Typical words used:** correct, how, what, why, practical, quantity. **Tone:** even. **Non-verbal characteristics:** thoughtful, alert, open. **Underlying attitudes:** straight, even-handed, evaluation of facts.

The third statement, 'Please come and see me later. I would like to talk to you about your lateness so that it can be avoided in future. In the meantime do you need any help to make up the lost work?' is typical of an adult ego state. The manager is registering the fact the employee has arrived late and will want to explore the reasons later, but for now is offering whatever assistance is needed to meet the immediate situation. The manager is communicating an even-handed approach which has avoided making a judgement without more facts.

Child ego state • • •

The child ego state is again not related to age, it is an expression of the feelings and urges which come to a person. These feelings can be expressed directly or indirectly.

1 *Natural child ego state*: involves reactions that are spontaneous expressions of feelings and emotions. It is the ego state which people are in when they are having fun or being affectionate and impulsive. It demonstrates authentic and unfettered emotions that are expressed without concern for the reaction of others. It also includes selfishness, anger and jealousy as well as fun and affection. **Typical words used:** wow, fun, want, won't, ouch, hi. **Tone:** free, loud, energetic. **Non-verbal characteristics:** uninhibited, loose, spontaneous. **Underlying attitudes:** curious, fun loving, changeable.

The fourth response, 'I do wish you would get here on time, you know how I rely on you. You have let me down' is typical of a manager expressing the natural child ego state. The statement expresses the manager's raw emotion and the focus is on the expression of emotions and the self.

2 *Adapted child ego state*: again this is concerned with the self and emotions felt by the individual, though this time these are not directly expressed. The concern is to manipulate others to feel sorry for them, to feel guilty, or to suck up to others. **Typical words used:** can't, wish, try, hope, please, thank you. **Tone:** whining, defiant, placating. **Non-verbal characteristics:** pouting, sad, innocent. **Underlying attitudes:** demanding, compliant, ashamed.

The fifth example, 'Why does this always happen to me? Whenever I'm on early shift someone comes in late. It really isn't fair' is typical of the adapted child ego state. The manager is again expressing emotions and feelings, though in this case is attempting to generate feelings of guilt and sympathy in the late employee. The focus of the communication is not the late employee but the manager's own feelings.

Most people will adopt a mixture of ego states during the normal progress of their working, domestic and social lives, though some individuals may adopt one style more than others, and some situations might encourage individuals to adopt one style more than others. It is important to understand ego states for two reasons:

1 Managers who adopt a dominant style need to understand the potential difficulties it might cause.
2 Managers need to understand the potential reactions to different ego styles.

It is possible to identify the ego state which an individual is engaging from the words used, tone of voice, non-verbal characteristics and underlying attitudes implied in a particular conversation (transaction) between individuals. As stated above, different contexts may mean that individuals use one ego state more than another. Figure 3.1 shows how the same person may use different combinations of ego states at work and at home.

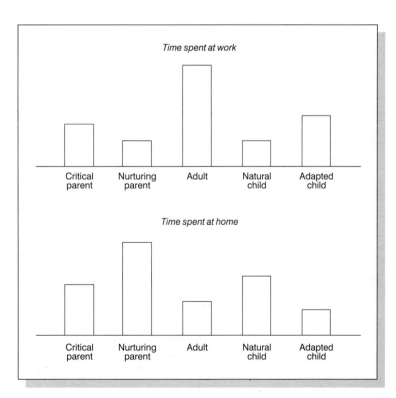

Figure 3.1
Time spent in different ego states at work and at home

It is not unusual for individuals to adopt a favoured ego state at work and the danger is that the individual cannot adapt to the situations which present themselves. It is also possible that if you as the manager have a constant ego state it will create negative reactions amongst your team members.

Constant ego state	Negative employee reaction
Critical parent	Fear Lacking self-confidence Reluctance to use initiative Conflict
Nurturing parent	Lack of discipline Lack of personal responsibility Reluctance to use initiative
Adult	Manager is cold Emotionless boss Unnatural boss Remoteness
Natural child	Lack of respect for manager Matched childishness Sloppy working methods Uncertainty about bosses moods
Adapted child	Manipulated Guilty Lacking confidence Inconsistent decisions

Table 3.2
Disadvantages of constant ego states by managers

In addition to the problems caused by managers adopting a constant ego state, you need to understand the patterns that can be analysed in the way you communicate with team members, but also in the reaction of team members. Analysis of the words used, the tone, non-verbal characteristics and underlying attitudes used by you as team leader and by team members can fit into a number of patterns.

In the examples above, the late employee might respond in a way that matches, or corresponds to, the manager's initial ego state. For example, when the manager says, 'What late again, can't you ever get here on time? You are just too unreliable', the late employee might make one of the following responses:

- 'Don't you speak to me like that, the bus broke down, you are very unfair.' (A paired critical parent reaction.)

- 'It was such a lovely day I decided to walk, it was fun.' (A paired natural child reaction.)

- 'Yes I'm afraid I am late. I'll start work straight away and make up the lost time.' (A cross adult reaction.)

In the first two cases, the employee response matches the initial ego state of the manager, either by dropping into the same ego state or by creating a paired reaction – child to parent. In the other case the employee crosses over from the matched response by reacting in an adult ego state. Obviously, these different patterns of response can work in all directions as adult to child or parent, etc. You need to be able to understand these patterns to communications, because they can provide a useful device for reducing conflict. For example, where a colleague or team member is adopting a parent or child ego state the adult responses can help to reduce the potential conflict.

Active learning point

Complete the following two exercises as accurately as you can, or give it to a colleague to complete on your behalf.

Exercise 3.4

Management priorities

Respond to each item in the questionnaire according to the way you are most likely act as the leader of a work group. Circle the response that most accurately describes the way you would behave: always (A); frequently (F); often (O); seldom (S); or never (N).

1	I would most likely act as spokesman for the group	A F O S N
2	I would encourage overtime	A F O S N
3	I would allow members complete freedom in their work	A F O S N
4	I would encourage the use of uniform procedures	A F O S N
5	I would permit the members to use their own judgement in solving problems	A F O S N
6	I would stress being ahead of competing groups	A F O S N
7	I would speak as representative of the group	A F O S N
8	I would needle members for greater effort	A F O S N
9	I would try out my ideas in the group	A F O S N
10	I would let the members do the work the way they think best	A F O S N
11	I would be working hard for promotion	A F O S N
12	I would tolerate postponement and uncertainty	A F O S N
13	I would speak up for the group when there were visitors present	A F O S N
14	I would keep the work moving at a rapid pace	A F O S N
15	I would turn the members loose on a job and let them go to it	A F O S N
16	I would settle conflicts when they occur in the group	A F O S N
17	I would get swamped by details	A F O S N
18	I would represent the group at outside meetings	A F O S N
19	I would be reluctant to allow the members any freedom of action	A F O S N
20	I would decide what should be done and how it should be done	A F O S N
21	I would push for increased production	A F O S N
22	I would let some members have authority which I would keep under review	A F O S N
23	Things would usually turn out as I had predicted	A F O S N
24	I would allow the group a high degree of initiative	A F O S N
25	I would assign group members to particular tasks	A F O S N
26	I would be willing to make changes	A F O S N
27	I would ask members to work harder	A F O S N
28	I would trust the group members to exercise good judgement	A F O S N
29	I would schedule the work to be done	A F O S N
30	I would refuse to explain my actions	A F O S N
31	I would persuade other members that my ideas are to their advantage	A F O S N
32	I would permit the group to work at its own pace	A F O S N
33	I would urge the group to beat its previous record	A F O S N
34	I would act without consulting the group	A F O S N
35	I would ask the group members to follow standard rules and procedures	A F O S N

T _____ P _____

Scoring the questionnaire:

1 Circle the question numbers for the following questions 8, 12, 17, 18, 19, 30, 34 and 35 – circle the actual number, e.g. ⑫.
2 Write a number 1 in front of the circled item number if you responded S (seldom) or N (never).
3 Also write a number 1 in front of questions not circled if you have answered A (always) or F (frequently).
4 With a different colour pen circle the number 1s you have written in front of the following question numbers 3, 5, 8, 10, 15, 18, 19, 22, 24, 26, 28, 30, 32, 34 and 35.
5 Count the circled number 1s. This is the score for 'concern for people'. Record the score against the P in the space at the end of the questionnaire.
6 Count the uncircled number 1s. This is the score for 'concern for tasks'. Record your score against the T in the space at the end of the questionnaire.
7 Take the smaller number away from the larger number, e.g. T8 – P4 = T4.
8 Record your answer on the scale given in Figure 3.2.

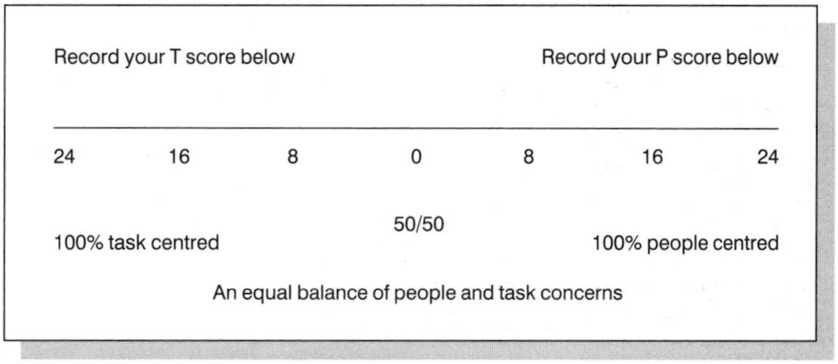

Record your T score below					Record your P score below
24	16	8	0	8	16	24
100% task centred			50/50		100% people centred
		An equal balance of people and task concerns		

Figure 3.2
Management styles: people–things priorities

Exercise 3.5

A question of balance

Using the same context as in Exercise 3.4, rank the following paragraphs as a description of your behaviour as a team leader. Start with the statement which is most typical of your behaviour and rank it 1, and so on until the least typical is ranked 5.

(a) I accept the decisions of others. I go along with opinions, attitudes and ideas of others or avoid taking sides. When conflict arises I try to remain neutral or stay out of it. By remaining neutral I rarely get stirred up. My humour is seen by others as rather pointless. ____

(b) I place high value on maintaining good relations. I prefer to accept the opinions, attitudes and ideas of others rather than push my own. I try to avoid conflict, but when it does occur, I try to soothe feelings and to keep people together. Because of the disturbances a temper flare produces, I strive to keep my emotions under wraps. My humour aims at maintaining friendly relations or, when strains do arise, it shifts attention away from the serious side. ____

(c) I place high value on making decisions that stick. I stand up for my ideas, opinions and attitudes, even though it sometimes results in stepping on toes. When conflict arises, I try to cut it off or win my position. When things are not going right my temper wells up. My humour is hard hitting. ____

(d) I search for workable, even though not perfect, decisions. When ideas, opinions or attitudes differ from my own appear, I initiate middle-ground positions. When conflict arises, I try to be fair but firm and to get an equitable solution. I rarely lose my temper but tend to be impatient when things are not moving. I sell myself or a position. ____

(e) I place high value on getting sound creative decisions that result in understanding and agreement. I listen for and seek out ideas, opinions, and attitudes different from my own. I have clear convictions but respond to sound ideas by changing my mind. When conflict arises, I try to identify the reasons for it and resolve the underlying causes. I rarely lose my temper, even when stirred up. My humour fits the situation and gives perspective; I retain a sense of humour even under pressure. ____

Exercises 3.4 and 3.5 identify management priorities regarding concerns for people and tasks. Whilst some managers will have registered a balanced score between the concerns for people and concerns for task, most managers will be prone to prioritize either people or tasks.

Mainly technical/task priority:

- Priority for task, systems, solutions, planning or action related to systems, operational methods, rules and procedures.
- Priority to monitoring and measuring task and the work of others.
- Priority to things focus – finance, strategy, planning, control, work study.
- Enjoys paper work and systems.
- Can have a problem with understanding people.

Mainly people priority:

- Focusing on the personal needs or problems of others, decisions, solutions, planning or actions related to morale, conflict and motivation problems.
- Priority to people related activities – interviewing, selecting staff, appraisal, counselling.
- Enjoys communicating with individuals and groups.
- Can find figures and systems difficult.

Exercise 3.5 also identifies different management priorities though it is more concerned with balance between degrees of concern for each. The exercise shows five potential positions and these can be mapped on a grid which uses both a high and low degree of concern for people and a high and low degree of concern for task/production (Figure 3.3).

The managerial grid shows how the balance between concern for production and people can vary between managers. These positions are likely to have different impacts upon subordinates and the team's morale.

- *People low, production low* (paragraph a): this registers a fairly neutral position with little concern for either dimension. The team leader is not sociable, tends to abdicate decisions and has minimal communications with the team. Subordinates are likely to react in an equally negative manner – many will move to a corresponding low concern for both people and task – morale will be low and staff turnover will be high.
- *People high, production low* (paragraph b): the team leader would be concerned with maintaining social relationships.

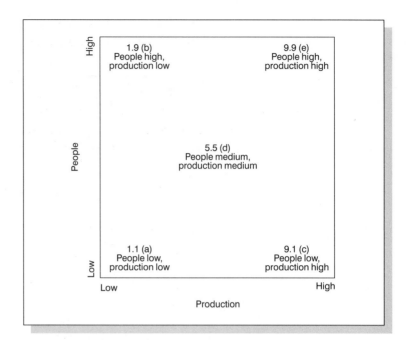

Figure 3.3
The managerial grid

A sociable team leader means less formal working conditions. The team leader is close to the team, though would avoid conflict and places production and tasks as a second priority. Subordinates are likely to be committed to the individual manager. A happy atmosphere to work in, but low output. Conflict within the team is stifled rather than resolved. May stifle creativity. Pulse turnover occurs when the manager or other key team members leave.

- *People low, production high* (paragraph c): the team leader prioritizes production, output levels and tasks. Low sociability and more directive styles of decision-making are typical. The team leader is more comfortable with systems and rules – sets standards for team to work to. Subordinates are likely to react unfavourably to the manager's assumptions that they cannot be trusted. Low commitment is typical. Often team members work steadily when the team leader is there but they slack off when not being directly supervised. Conflict is generated – may be individual or organized in collective forms.

- *Moderate people, moderate production* (paragraph d): priorities are balanced between concerns for people and concerns for production, but not strongly prioritized. The team leader is moderately sociable, and decision-making will tend to be a mix of directive and consultative – tell and sell, tell and test. Subordinates are likely to be more instrumental – not too much effort, enough to satisfy the leader. Not outstanding quality of work or output. Standards not as good as they might be. Conflicts are never fully resolved.

- *People high, production high* (paragraph e): a high priority is placed on both production and the team. The team leader recognizes the significant role team members play in achieving high levels of high-quality output. The leader is sociable and adopts more participative styles of leadership and decision-making. Subordinates are highly motivated, staff turnover levels are lower. Conflict is low and the employees are committed to service and production goals. Quality of work is good and both employee and customer satisfaction are high.

Chapter 2 explored some of the issues to do with the relationships between managers, as team leaders, and team members through the use of empowerment. One of the key points was that different applications of empowerment involve and empower employees in different ways. These variations in employee involvement in empowerment link to variations in the way managers and team members make decisions. In principle there are only three basic approaches (see also Table 3.3):

1 *Directive*: managers make the decisions with little input from employees who merely act on instructions.
2 *Consultative*: managers make the decisions but with suggestions or information provided from employees.
3 *Participative*: managers involve employees in making decisions jointly or delegate decision making to them.

The initiatives discussed in Chapter 2 suggested that there were broadly consistent approaches to empowering employees at an organizational and strategic level. In practice, however, the day-to-day management of a restaurant, bar or hotel may involve managers and employees in using a combination of styles, though one may be more dominant. Exercise 3.6 provides a chance to map these different styles in a work place known to you.

Active learning point

Complete the following exercise as accurately as you can. Use your current job or a recent job as the context for your responses.

Style	Directive		Consultative		Participative		None
	Tell	Tell and sell	Tell and test	Seek	Joint problem-solving	Delegate	Abdicate
Manager involvement	Makes decisions and instructs	Makes decisions and instructs with reasons	Makes decisions but reviews after seeking views	Defines problem and seeks employees view before deciding	Defines problem and makes decision jointly with employees	Defines scope of decision-making authority and monitors decisions	Provides limited direction or support to employees
Employee involvement	Acts on instructions	Acts on instructions and explanation given	Gives views on bosses proposed decision	Discusses alternatives and makes suggestions	Joins in the decision-making process	Makes decisions within boundaries set by boss	Employees decide for themselves and react to events

Table 3.3 Making decisions

Exercise 3.6

Mapping decision-making styles

Using a manager well known to you – your boss or a colleague, identify the proportion of their time making decisions in the various styles which we have identified.

Mode	Directive		Consultative		Participative		None
Style	Tell	Tell and sell	Tell and test	Seek	Joint problem-solving	Delegate	Abdicate
% time							

On the basis of this exercise you will be able to identify a more predominant style, from amongst the range of possibilities. In each case there are limitations to and benefits of an overuse of each style, particularly if the style is at odds with the setting and the people who are being managed.

1 Directive
   (a) Benefit: the directive style works best where there are few options to the tasks to be done – 'one best way', standardized, limited discretion, safety, high risk situations, where a task has to be done now.

   (b) Limitations: the directive style discourages personal initiative, often results in poor morale and poor communications. Can be inflexible and unresponsive to change. Frequently output levels are high under direct supervision, but drop when the manager is not present.

2 Consultative
   (a) Benefit: the consultative style works best where managers want to gain from the knowledge and immediate experiences of the workforce. The manager retains control of decisions. Can be useful for overcoming service quality problems or making suggestions for achieving goals.

   (b) Limitations: the consultative style is limited where managers continue to make decisions with little or no reference to employee suggestions. Manager control of decisions can be demotivating. The processes of consultation can be time-consuming and costly, and the benefits more difficult to cost financially.

Hospitality, Leisure & Tourism Series

3 Participative

(a) Benefit: the participative style works best where managers need to allow employees to make immediate operational decisions, or where employees have better knowledge and experience. Can be useful for gaining employee commitment to service quality, customer and other business goals. Employees have more of a sense of 'ownership' if they make the decisions.

(b) Limitations: the participative style is difficult for many managers because it involves letting employees make decisions and can represent a loss of control. If employees make decisions, they may make decisions which managers do not like. The processes of participation can be time-consuming and costly. The benefits may be difficult to cost financially.

A matter of choice?

We have seen that as a team leader you can behave in a number of ways – your closeness to or distance from the team, the ego states you adopt, your decision-making style and the priorities of concern for the team or concern for production and tasks – and these can all be varied. Your personality, experience and training clearly influence the approach, but are these matters solely a matter of choice?

The first two chapters have suggested that hospitality retail services vary in the offer made to customers. These variations require staff to exercise different amounts of discretion to meet customer service needs. The way you manage the service team needs to correspond to the service offer.

Uniformity dependent

This is where customers are buying into a highly standardized product and service encounter. Managers may have limited scope to involve employees because 'one best way' job design reduces scope for discretion. Management styles will tend to be directive but with some consultation. Some customer service jobs and supervisory jobs might even allow a little participation in the form of delegation and joint decision-making but, for most team members, involvement is limited.

That said, managers in these units can still be sociable and can adopt ego states which treat the employees like adults and with dignity. The team leader and team may be restricted by the operating system but as the team leader you need to give high priority both to the people and production.

Choice dependent

In many cases hospitality retail services that offer a wide choice in a branded context are offering mass customization. That is, the customers are offered standardized products and services, but these are personalized by the customer's choice opportunities or they are offered bundles of products and services that create predictable variations of customization. Employees have to act as consultants and so advise customers. In these cases, some aspects of the process will be directive but the service requires more consultation and participation. Team member involvement may require formal mechanisms for tell and test, seek and joint problem-solving. In some cases, the service encounter needs employees to be delegated to do whatever is needed to create guest satisfaction, and it includes some aspect of participation, though this might be limited to managing the service encounter.

If you are a manager in these units you need to be sociable and adopt ego states which treat the employees like adults and with dignity. The team leader and team needs to adopt generally consultative approaches, and you as the team leader need to give high priority both to the people and production.

Relationship dependent

This type of hospitality retail service may also involve some degree of standardization, but the service encounter involves many more stages and staff contact takes on increased significance as a source of customer satisfaction, or dissatisfaction. Again there may be some elements of standardization required of the national brand, but employees need to be delegated to meet customer service needs – dealing with unusual requests, responses to service failure, acting in way which exceeds customer expectations. Joint decision-making as well as the more consultative approaches may also be advisable in this type of service.

As with the other approaches you need to consider your sociability, and adopt the adult ego state and treat employees with dignity. The team leader and team needs to adopt generally participative approaches, and as the team leader you need to give, as always, high priority both to the people and production.

Active learning point

Complete the following exercise as accurately as you can. The exercise uses the sources of satisfaction survey at the beginning of the chapter. Give this list to one or more subordinates of the post for which you made the assessment.

Exercise 3.7

Measuring employee sources of satisfaction

The following is a list of possible attractions to a job. Please read them all and rank them from 1 to 10 in order of their importance to you. Thus if you consider 'Pensions and other old-age security benefits' are most important to you write '1' by it and so on until all ten factors are numbered. Do not think about your present job, just what you think is desirable.

Major sources of satisfaction	Important to you
Steady work and steady wages	
High wages	
Pensions and other old-age security benefits	
Not having to work too hard	
Getting along with the people I work with	
Getting along well with my supervisor	
Good chance to turn out good quality work	
Good chance to do interesting work	
Good chance of promotion	
Good physical working conditions	

When you have completed the survey of employees, collate the results, and note the differences or similarities with your own assessments of sources of satisfaction.

1 Were your top three responses more intrinsic than extrinsic?
2 Compare these with the top three responses of subordinates in your survey.
3 Compare this with you own assessment of subordinates' sources of satisfaction.
4 Typically, many managers assume that their subordinates are more extrinsically motivated than they are themselves.

In many organizations the hierarchy creates a situation where managers higher up the organization believe that their subordinates are more intrinsically motivated. Yet when the same test is given to lower levels of management the same results are found – the respondents mostly rank the intrinsic factors higher than the extrinsic factors and they, too, rank their subordinates as having more extrinsically driven sources of satisfaction, and so on down the organization.

Misunderstanding as a consequence of organization hierarchy can:

- lead managers to make errors when judging the motives and drives of subordinates

- result in reward packages being aimed at sources of satisfaction which are less important to the employee

- cause employee dissatisfaction

- lead to conflict

- result in poor quality work and customer dissatisfaction.

Working in teams

Even in situations where the work is highly standardized and employees are allowed little discretion to do their work in their own way, you can organize the management group into a team and operate the unit in a way which encourages the employees to see themselves as team members with a significant contribution to make. The major benefits of doing this are:

- improved communications between all managers and employees ensures that the unit's objectives and goals are understood and shared by all team members

- there will be improved commitment through a greater sense of ownership

- better suggestions and ideas

- more creative ideas available

- people learn from each other

- improved morale and motivation because people are included

- communication is improved by being involved in the decision.

Types of teams

Working with the management team will involve each individual team member having specific areas of responsibility. In many hospitality retail units, junior managers will have responsibility for a specific area of the operations – kitchen, bar, restaurant, accommodation, reception. These *functional* departments have to work to common goals and it is up to the unit manager as team leader to ensure that all sections work in co-operative way. A common problem in many hospitality operations is that these divisions based on departments can produce an 'us and them' culture with a lack of co-operation or even conflict occurring between teams. Building a strong management team across the unit is an essential feature of effective management.

Setting up *multifunctional teams* is another way of developing the culture of co-operation and reducing tensions between teams. Often these are based round the identification and resolution of common problems such as service quality improvement, employee satisfaction improvement, reduced wastage and improved operating procedures. Some of these teams are permanent features of the unit's organization; in other cases the teams are set up to deal with specific issues.

In addition, both this chapter and Chapter 2 have discussed different arrangements for consulting with or involving team members in making decisions. In all cases, as the team leader, you need to clearly understand the stages that teams go through in their development, and the factors likely to inhibit team development.

Stages in team development

As the team is established and begins to develop it goes through a number of stages that need to be understood by managers. An experienced team leader aids the team through each stage, and recognizes the danger of inaction and cynicism which can occur if team members feel their efforts are not valued.

1 *Searching stage*: often team members in new teams feel a thrill of enthusiasm as the team is first created. Particularly where team members are unused to being consulted, the team may experience a high level of commitment to the team and its goals. As the team leader you need to recognize the benefits of this enthusiasm, but ensure that team members do not develop an overoptimistic expectation of outcomes.

Team members are also searching for a shared definition of the objectives during this stage. A good team leader will either provide the team with clear objectives or facilitate the team in developing the shared objectives necessary for effective performance. Most effective team leaders avoid 'telling' team members what they must do; 'asking' is much more effective. The tendency to underestimate the degree of disagreement cannot be overstressed. The enthusiasm felt by members often leads members to assume they all share the same objectives, but do not want to argue them out.

Hospitality, Leisure & Tourism Series

2 *Exploring stage*: once the team members have agreed the broad objectives, they have to spend some time raising questions, making suggestions, evaluating alternatives and deciding on the appropriate course(s) of action. This stage will involve conflict as different team members suggest different courses of action. Disagreements will occur and team members may form into subgroups as they come together round different suggested courses of action.

Team leaders need to be aware that this is a necessary stage through which the group must travel. You need to help the team to establish mutual understanding and a healthy respect for the creative tension the group needs in order to be most effective. Negative conflict can be harmful because it can prevent innovation and the working out of agreed paths. However, too much conformity or conflict avoidance can be equally damaging, because disagreements are never resolved and the team never formulates a consensus of action plans and priorities.

3 *Alliance stage*: the team eventually reaches a point where the members share both an understanding of the objectives and what needs to be done. Each member understands not only their role, but also the role of other group members. There is also a shared understanding of the strengths and weaknesses of all team members. The team has a uniformity of purpose, they are committed to the outcomes but respect the diversity within the group, recognizing that different views and interests are essential for the team to work effectively.

The team leader needs to help and enable the team to keep working towards the goals and outcomes identified, and to encourage the team to constantly review objectives and action plans. There is a great danger of the team developing 'frozen thinking' at this stage. That is, the team, having decided on a course of action, continues to support the action, even when circumstances change and the action is no longer relevant.

Any disruption to the dynamics of the team – the loss of a member, a new team leader, new members or changes in the focus of the problem or purpose of the team – may cause the team to slip out of the alliance phase into an earlier stage. In these cases, the team will drop back and work through *searching* and *exploring* again.

Threats to team development

Effective teams develop as the product of group bonds set up between specific individuals. In these circumstances, individual behaviour is influenced by a combination of individual and group motivations. The following are some of the key causes of team failure:

- high levels of instability due to staff turnover or movement around the organization

- limited opportunities for the team to meet and work through the stages needed

- limited support from more senior organization members

- restrictions placed on the team's ability to resolve the problem

- poor morale or intergroup conflict.

Benefits of working in teams

Clearly the reasons why teams have been set up differ and the benefits which teamworking can generate will also vary, but there are some general benefits to be gained by the individuals involved, the management and the unit.

Benefits of teams to individual members

- Increased job satisfaction.

- Personal development and growth.

- Career planning.

- Reduced fear of risk-taking.

- More involvement in decision-making.

- Increased recognition for their contribution.

Benefits to unit management

- Decisions are made by people most closely involved.

- Managers share the workload with others.

- All are focused on the same objectives.

- Improved commitment and support for decisions.

- More flexibility amongst team members.

Benefits to the hospitality retail unit

- Improved quality of products and services.

- Creates a culture of continuous improvement.

- Improved trust and openness.

- Better communication reduces misunderstandings.

- Reduced duplication.

- Improved working relationships.

- Improved customer satisfaction.

- Increased opportunities to achieve or beat performance targets.

- Improved employee satisfaction.

- Reduced staff turnover.

- Improved sales and profit performance.

Different types of teams will deliver different clusters of benefits. Thus team briefing sessions prior to the shift, or occasional briefings to the staff, will deliver different benefits to team structures based on autonomous work teams. In each of these examples the relationship between you, as the team leader, and team members is different. The amount of discretion allowed to the team is different and the extent to which they can make decisions is also different. In some cases team members merely receive information, whilst in others they are actively managing their own work situation. Clearly, the impact that these different arrangements have on your team members is also influenced by the nature of the team members themselves. The following chapter explores more fully some of these differences between individuals.

Conclusion

This chapter began by reproducing F. W. Marriott's well-known comments drawing the link between the management of employees and customer satisfaction. These views are widely shared in many hospitality retail organizations that pay increasing attention to employee attitudes and 'internal customer satisfaction'. Though influences outside the immediate unit cannot be dismissed, the key to employee satisfaction is the immediate unit management in its role of team leader. There is very clear evidence that the relationships created by you as the unit manager can either enthuse and inspire team members or confuse and demotivate them.

The ideas that the manager holds about employees, as team members, is often crucial to shaping the approach to team leadership. In some cases, managers adopt a *critical parent ego state* and are *psychologically distant* from team members. In addition these managers give key priority to managing output through their *high concern for production and low concern for people*. Compound this with a *directive* decision-making style and assumptions that employees are all 'just here for the money' (*extrinsically motivated*), and many employees will react negatively to working in the unit. Poor moral, absenteeism, low job satisfaction, high staff turnover and dissatisfied customers are likely consequences.

Effective team leaders are more likely to be *psychologically close* to team members and adopt an appropriate array of *ego states* with a high proportion of the *adult* ego state. They will have priorities that give equally *high concern for people and high concern for production*. They adopt an approach to managing employees through *team membership* – even in situations where highly standardized production and service systems limit employee discretion. Even in these circumstances their personal decision-making style is prone to be *consultative* and *participative*, wherever possible. In addition, effective managers understand that employees have an array of needs and priorities from work and that employee satisfaction will depend on rewards which both *make the person feel better* as well as *provide material benefits*. Associated with this approach, effective team leaders understand the many benefits that teamworking can bring, and have a thorough grasp of team effectiveness that can be enhanced and developed.

Reflection and practice

Answer these questions to check your understanding of this chapter:

1 Using the case study at the back of the book identify the management styles of the key management roles.
2 What action would you take to change the remaining manager's approach?
3 Show how the style of management has impacted on employee behaviour and business performance.
4 Make a case for working with teams in this case. How would you organize these? Devise an action plan showing how you would introduce team working. What are the potential difficulties and benefits?
5 What measure might you use to check team effectiveness?

Further reading

Argyle, M. (1989). *The Social Psychology of Work*. Penguin.
Biddle, D. and Evenden, R. (1993). *Human Aspects of Management*. Institute of Personnel Management.
Boella, M. (1996). *Human Resource Management in the Hospitality Industry*. Stanley Thornes.

Goss-Turner, S. (1989). *Managing People in the Hotel and Catering Industry.* Croner.

Maghurn, J. P. (1989). *A Manual of Staff Management in the Hotel and Catering Industry.* Heinemann.

Mullins, L. J. (1995). *Hospitality Management: A Human Resource Approach.* Pitman.

Roberts, J. (1995) *Human Resource Practices in the Hospitality Industry.* Hodder and Stoughton.

Rothwell, S. (1980). *Labour Turnover: Its Costs, Causes and Control.* Gower.

CHAPTER 4

Working with people

After working through this chapter you should be able to:

- identify ways of analysing differences between individuals

- critically evaluate the management of groups and behaviour of individuals as group members

- apply principles of assertion and deal with conflict

- devise plans for motivating team members.

It is people, people, people

The hospitality industry is often described as a 'people industry'. As we have seen in earlier chapters, frontline employees are the means by which an organization delivers its service to customers, and the management of employees needs to tap employees' commitment and enthusiasm to 'delight customers'. The service interaction in most hospitality retail organizations is 'inseparable' in that the customer is present when the service is 'delivered'. Customer reactions and involvement in the service are also important features of the service. Customer expectations and moods will form a basis for judging the success or failure of the service encounter.

Chapters 2 and 3 showed the contribution that employee empowerment and effective team leadership can make to creating the best circumstances for quality service delivery. This chapter aims to further develop your understanding, as a unit manager, of people as employees and as customers. The chapter first explores some features of how individuals differ and may react in their own ways to similar circumstances. Second, the chapter considers the behaviour of individuals as group members. Chapter 3 dealt with benefits of managing individuals in formal work teams; this chapter considers some of the influences of group memberships that arise out of the work relationships. Third, the chapter will consider techniques to assist unit managers in their relations with customers both in assertiveness and in dealing with resolution of conflict. Finally, the chapter explores some of the actions you can take to develop the motivation of your employees and their satisfaction at work.

Individual differences

There are many different ways of explaining people's behaviour and motives. The following section provides a basic introduction to some ideas about people that might help you as a manager to better understand customer and employee behaviour. At the very least they lay down a model for analysing different people.

Personality

There are a number of explanations as to why people do what they do, the *trait theory of personality* suggests that people's actions and personalities can be understood through an analysis of their personality traits. These traits are reasonably consistent characteristics, which are probably developed through a combination of inheritance and social and physical environment. The 'nature versus nurture' debate amongst various psychologists puts different influences on the relative importance of each. For our purposes, it is probably true to say there is most probably a combination of both.

One simple technique for understanding individual differences involves mapping people against two axes – extraversion/ introversion and stable/unstable. An extravert person is most interested in the outside world of people and things, whereas the introvert is more interested in their own thoughts and feelings. A stable person tends be calm and even-tempered, whereas the unstable personality is changeable and touchy. Figure 4.1 shows how positions on the two continua can reveal how personality types can be located in one of four quadrants.

The scales in Figures 4.2, included against each dimension of extraversion/introversion, build a model of personality traits in which the extreme extravert is active, sociable, risk-taking, impulsive, expressive, practical and irresponsible. The classically introverted personality on the other hand is inactive, unsociable, careful, controlled, inhibited, reflective and responsible. In reality, few people are purely extravert or purely introvert, or purely stable or purely unstable. Personality testing shows that people usually possess a combination of traits that are more or less extrovert, and more or less stable (Figure 4.3).

Figure 4.1 shows how these variations might result in different personality types depending on their location on the four quadrants produced by comparing introversion/extraversion and stability/instability.

- *The stable extravert* tends to be warm-hearted and outgoing, demonstrates a temperament which is sociable, outgoing, talk-ative, responsive, easygoing, lively, carefree and with leadership qualities.

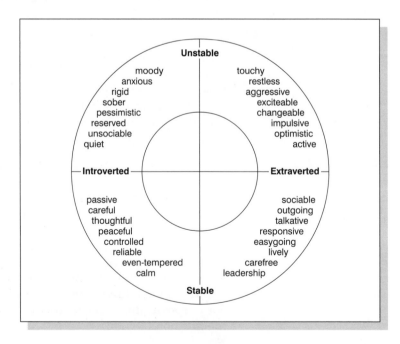

Figure 4.1
Personality profiles

Average		
Extravert		**Introvert**
Active		Inactive
30 29 28 27 26 25 24 23 22 21 20 19 18 17 16		15 14 13 12 11 10 9 8 7 6 5 4 3 2 1
Sociability		Unsociability
30 29 28 27 26 25 24 23 22 21 20 19 18 17 16		15 14 13 12 11 10 9 8 7 6 5 4 3 2 1
Risk-taking		Carefulness
30 29 28 27 26 25 24 23 22 21 20 19 18 17 16		15 14 13 12 11 10 9 8 7 6 5 4 3 2 1
Impulsiveness		Control
30 29 28 27 26 25 24 23 22 21 20 19 18 17 16		15 14 13 12 11 10 9 8 7 6 5 4 3 2 1
Expressiveness		Inhibition
30 29 28 27 26 25 24 23 22 21 20 19 18 17 16		15 14 13 12 11 10 9 8 7 6 5 4 3 2 1
Practicability		Reflectiveness
30 29 28 27 26 25 24 23 22 21 20 19 18 17 16		15 14 13 12 11 10 9 8 7 6 5 4 3 2 1
Irresponsibility		Responsibility
30 29 28 27 26 25 24 23 22 21 20 19 18 17 16		15 14 13 12 11 10 9 8 7 6 5 4 3 2 1

Figure 4.2
Dimensions of extraversion/introversion

Average		
Emotional instability		**Emotional stability**
Inferiority feelings		Self-esteem
30 29 28 27 26 25 24 23 22 21 20 19 18 17 16		15 14 13 12 11 10 9 8 7 6 5 4 3 2 1
Depressiveness		Hapiness
30 29 28 27 26 25 24 23 22 21 20 19 18 17 16		15 14 13 12 11 10 9 8 7 6 5 4 3 2 1
Anxiety		Calm
30 29 28 27 26 25 24 23 22 21 20 19 18 17 16		15 14 13 12 11 10 9 8 7 6 5 4 3 2 1
Obsessiveness		Casualness
30 29 28 27 26 25 24 23 22 21 20 19 18 17 16		15 14 13 12 11 10 9 8 7 6 5 4 3 2 1
Dependence		Autonomy
30 29 28 27 26 25 24 23 22 21 20 19 18 17 16		15 14 13 12 11 10 9 8 7 6 5 4 3 2 1
Hypondraisis		Sense of health
30 29 28 27 26 25 24 23 22 21 20 19 18 17 16		15 14 13 12 11 10 9 8 7 6 5 4 3 2 1
Guilt		Freedom from guilt
30 29 28 27 26 25 24 23 22 21 20 19 18 17 16		15 14 13 12 11 10 9 8 7 6 5 4 3 2 1

Figure 4.3
Dimensions of stability/instability

- *The stable introvert* tends to be listless and slow, demonstrates a temperament which is calm, even-tempered, reliable, controlled, peaceful, thoughtful, careful and passive.

- *The unstable introvert* tends to be more depressed and sad, and demonstrates a temperament that is quiet, unsociable, reserved, pessimistic, sober, rigid, anxious and moody.

- *The unstable extravert* tends to be easily angered and quick to react, demonstrates a temperament which is touchy, restless, aggressive, excitable, changeable, impulsive, optimistic and active.

Whilst this trait theory approach is attractive because it is easy to understand and seems to reflect 'common sense' – the ancient Greeks identified four similar types of personality – there are several problems with these personality 'types':

- They tend to assume too much about the person and that people will always react in the predicted way.

- They tend to assume these types are unchanging over time.

- They take little account of cultural or other environmental influences on temperament.

That said, the traits identified can be useful in building a more detailed picture of individual behaviour or the type of person needed for a particular role or job.

Active learning point

Complete Exercise 4.1.

Exercise 4.1

Selecting traits for hospitality jobs

Using the seven dimensions of extraversion/introversion and the seven dimensions of stability/instability given in Figures 4.2 and 4.3, map the ideal personality traits of one front of house job (bar person or waiting staff) and one back of house job (cook or room attendant)

People drawn to work in the hospitality industry tend to have more extravert personalities. Yet it would be a mistake for you to employ staff who are extremely extraverted, that is, registering a high extravert score on all seven dimensions. For all the obvious benefits to hospitality businesses of people who are active, sociable, expressive and practical, individuals who are risk-taking, impulsive and irresponsible may create problems as employees.

Research on hospitality managers and managers training for the hospitality business show that the overwhelming majority has *learning style preferences* that are *activist*. That is, they enjoy learning best through a combination of experience and learning by doing. They like to learn from concrete situations and do not find that reflection and theorizing come easily. This type of manager:

- puts a lot of energy into doing things, tries out new ideas, likes to get things completed, enjoys activity, likes the present and expresses feelings readily

- often acts without thinking, makes mistakes because of a lack of planning, may repeat mistakes, can operate unpredictably and spread confusion.

It is essential that effective hospitality managers are *reflective practitioners*, and management development programmes in both industry and at university or college need to understand that the learning style preferences of hospitality managers are based on their personality profiles. People with extravert personalities who do things because they 'feel right' are attracted to management careers in the hospitality industry. Management development must work from these preferences by developing skills in reflection and theorizing.

Beliefs

Beliefs are a reflection of what people 'know' about the world. Knowledge in this sense is not just a reflection of factual knowledge, although factual knowledge is a belief system. Beliefs may include:

- factual knowledge – water is made up of two atoms of hydrogen and one atom of oxygen

- what a person desires to be true – my favourite football team will win the cup

- how a person identifies themselves in relation to others – political and religious beliefs play this role

- knowledge which individuals cannot prove but they accept as a matter of faith.

Beliefs and perceptions often interact. Perceptions are in part shaped by beliefs – people perceive things in line with their beliefs. Beliefs are also reinforced perceptions – individuals perceive things that they notice because of their beliefs.

An understanding that individuals, managers, employees and customers may have different beliefs is important to you as the unit manager.

- The manager must be aware that differences in beliefs can be a source of tension and conflict.

- Differences in beliefs about dress, language and conduct etc. can cause offence.

- Managers must be sensitive to the beliefs of others and that humour or ill-considered remarks can be offensive.

- The manager must aim to establish a shared belief in the success of the unit, standards needed and that effective performance will be recognized.

Values

These are what people want to be true, what individuals value in the long run and from themselves. There are two types of values:

- End values: how things should be in the long run – a comfortable life, a sense of accomplishment, a world at peace, equality, wisdom, self-respect, etc.

- Instrumental values: how a person should conduct themselves – broadminded, cheerful, helpful, obedient, polite, self-controlled.

Tests show that different individuals will rank these differently. Values tend to be bundled. A person is frequently expressing a view of what they consider to be important through their values. Some people give priority to the 'state of the world' whilst others give priority to values about their relationships with others or about how they themselves should be. In some aspects, values reflect tendencies towards extraversion and introversion.

In addition, to these general values which individuals hold, there are several different sets of assumptions which people make about the values and priorities of others.

Active learning point

The following exercise will help you evaluate how you think about the values that people apply at work.

Exercise 4.2

Values at work

From each of the pairs of statements listed below select the *one* statement which you most support.

1.1 People are mainly interested in money at work.
1.2 The most important thing at work is money.

2.1 People work best if there is a good team spirit.
2.2 The best motivation is self-motivation.

3.1 People like to be left alone to get on with the job.
3.2 Feelings get in the way of doing a good job.

4.1 People will value their self-interest above all else at work.
4.2 People need a boss who is easy to get on with.

5.1 The most important thing at work is your colleagues.
5.2 What people most want from work is a chance to use their skills and abilities.

6.1 The best motivation is self-motivation.
6.2 People have to be controlled if they are to work well.

7.1 Feelings get in the way of doing a good job.
7.2 People are more influenced by their colleagues than their boss.

8.1 People need a boss who is easy to get on with.
8.2 An interesting job is the best guarantee of good work.

9.1 What people most want from work is a chance to use their skills and abilities.
9.2 People are mainly interested in money at work.

10.1 People have to be controlled if they are to work well.
10.2 People work best if there is a good team spirit.

11.1 People are more influenced by their colleagues than their boss.
11.2 People like to be left alone to get on with their job.

12.1 An interesting job is the best guarantee of good work.
12.2 People calculate their self-interest above all else at work.

Exercise 4.2 consists of statements reflecting common stereotypes about people at work:

- rational economic stereotype
- social stereotype
- self-fulfilment stereotype.

Each statement is paired with a statement from one of the other stereotypes. The key given later shows how to work out the score.

Hospitality, Leisure & Tourism Series

As a manager you may have developed fixed ways of thinking about people and the things they value at work. These stereotypes can cause difficulties when dealing with employees, because you see what you expect to see rather than what is actually there. Chapter 3 identified a widespread tendency for those in higher positions to consider the motives of people in lower positions to be more concerned with materials than they were themselves. Using this model, they tend to apply the *rational economic stereotype* when thinking about the values and priorities of subordinates. The stereotype favoured by an individual manager reflects much about the manager's own values, and less about the values of employees. To understand people at work it is necessary to:

- accept that people are different to ourselves

- treat people as individuals and expect the unexpected

- use frameworks and theories as a guide, not as rigid rules.

Rational economic stereotype

This stereotype views people as chiefly motivated by economic incentives and material rewards. The assumption is that people's values prioritize material and personal benefits. Dominant values prioritize *ambition, achieving a comfortable life* and *obedience* for example. Managers holding this view believe that people will act to maximize material rewards in preference to any other benefits from work. Frequently this set of manager values prioritizes output efficiency, monetary incentives, competition between individuals and the close supervision of employees together with a directive style of management.

Social stereotype

Social stereotypes view people as being motivated by social needs and being part of a group. It is assumed that values that focus on the relationships with and obligations to others are most important to individuals at work. It is assumed that group membership gives individuals a sense of identity and support. Dominant values will prioritize *true friendship, social recognition* and *helpfulness*. Managers holding this view place emphasis on the human relationships at work and provide opportunities for individuals to identify with group needs through team membership, department and organization identity.

Self-fulfilment stereotype

This views people as being motivated to a sense of accomplishment, and the need to develop abilities and skills. It is assumed that dominant values give priority to the quality of working life and opportunities for personal growth and development. Dominant values will prioritize *a sense of accomplishment*, *self-respect* and *self-control*. Managers holding this view place emphasis on job design, employee satisfaction, and autonomy. The focus is on delegation and participative management, training and employee development.

The scoring key for Exercise 4.2 • • •

The twelve sets of paired questions match a statement of one stereotype with another. By working through your preferences it is possible to detect your ways of generalizing about people. Using the grid below put a circle round each statement you have selected for each of the twelve pairs – each will fall under one of the three columns which identify the stereotype. For example, if you have indicate a preference for statement 2 to the first pair put a circle round 2 opposite 'statement pair' 1 in the 'social' column.

Statement pair	Rational economic	Social	Self-fulfilment
1	1	2	
2		1	2
3	2		1
4	1	2	
5		1	2
6	2		1
7	1	2	
8		1	2
9	2		1
10	1	2	
11		1	2
12	2		1
Totals			

There are twelve pairs of statements reflecting three stereotypes, so the maximum score for any one is eight. When you have indicated all the preferred statements, add up the scores in each column. A score of more than four indicates that you use this stereotype as a way of generalizing about people.

If your scores are fairly even on all three stereotypes, it may mean that you do not hold any of these stereotypes. If you score six or more on one stereotype and two or less on the others, you may have a stereotype in the way you think about people.

The problem with stereotypes ● ● ●

The main problem is that stereotypes are restrictive and assume 'people are all the same'. Managers who can hold a stereotype believe them and act as though they are true, but they may not apply to some people and only partially apply to others. To be an effective manager you should recognize that:

● people are complex

● people are highly variable and change as a result of experiences

● it is a mistake not to oversimplify people's actions and motives.

Attitudes

Attitudes are expressions of what a person feels about things they believe exist. These are usually expressed as statements of *like* or *dislike* and *agreement* or *disagreement*. Attitudes are frequently expressions of inner emotional states of fear or envy as well as expressions of values and beliefs. Though people do not always act in line with their attitudes, many organizations use surveys to gauge both employee and customer satisfaction.

The example given in Exercise 4.3 is an employee satisfaction survey which explores employee attitudes on a number of dimensions including the employment terms, relations with management, the nature of the job and relations with co-workers.

Active learning point

The following exercise will help you evaluate employee satisfaction. Either complete the tasks yourself or give it to a colleague, or reproduce it and give it to your subordinates.

Exercise 4.3

Employee attitudes

Employee survey
The following questions aim to measure employee satisfaction.
Please answer the following questions as frankly as possible.

You may give *one* of seven answers to each question:

- Ex Dis – I'm extremely dissatisfied
- V Dis   – I'm very dissatisfied
- Mod Dis – I'm moderately dissatisfied
- Not Sure – I'm not sure
- Mod Sat – I'm moderately satisfied
- V Sat   – I'm very satisfied
- Ex Sat – I'm extremely satisfied.

Please tick

	Ex Dis	V Dis	Mod Dis	Not Sure	Mod Sat	V Sat	Ex Sat
1 The physical working conditions	Ex Dis	V Dis	Mod Dis	Not Sure	Mod Sat	V Sat	Ex Sat
2 The freedom to choose your own working method	Ex Dis	V Dis	Mod Dis	Not Sure	Mod Sat	V Sat	Ex Sat
3 Your fellow workers	Ex Dis	V Dis	Mod Dis	Not Sure	Mod Sat	V Sat	Ex Sat
4 The recognition you get for good work	Ex Dis	V Dis	Mod Dis	Not Sure	Mod Sat	V Sat	Ex Sat
5 Your immediate boss	Ex Dis	V Dis	Mod Dis	Not Sure	Mod Sat	V Sat	Ex Sat
6 The amount of responsibility you are given	Ex Dis	V Dis	Mod Dis	Not Sure	Mod Sat	V Sat	Ex Sat
7 Your rate of pay	Ex Dis	V Dis	Mod Dis	Not Sure	Mod Sat	V Sat	Ex Sat
8 Your chances to use your abilities	Ex Dis	V Dis	Mod Dis	Not Sure	Mod Sat	V Sat	Ex Sat
9 Industrial relations between management and workers	Ex Dis	V Dis	Mod Dis	Not Sure	Mod Sat	V Sat	Ex Sat
10 Your chance for promotion	Ex Dis	V Dis	Mod Dis	Not Sure	Mod Sat	V Sat	Ex Sat
11 The way the unit is managed	Ex Dis	V Dis	Mod Dis	Not Sure	Mod Sat	V Sat	Ex Sat
12 The attention paid to suggestions you make	Ex Dis	V Dis	Mod Dis	Not Sure	Mod Sat	V Sat	Ex Sat
13 Your hours of work	Ex Dis	V Dis	Mod Dis	Not Sure	Mod Sat	V Sat	Ex Sat
14 The amount of variety in your job	Ex Dis	V Dis	Mod Dis	Not Sure	Mod Sat	V Sat	Ex Sat
15 Your job security	Ex Dis	V Dis	Mod Dis	Not Sure	Mod Sat	V Sat	Ex Sat

Full-time employee   Part-time employee   Casual employee

Male   Female

Job title _____

As stated earlier, the link between attitudes and behaviour is not absolute, but in the above exercise there is an attempt to identify what employees feel about work so that sources of dissatisfaction can be understood, and acted upon. In addition there is assumed to be a link between employee satisfaction and

- customer satisfaction

- service quality

- productivity and up-selling

- staff turnover and retention.

In Exercise 4.3 what, if any, were the common causes of satisfaction and dissatisfaction? What actions might you as the manager responsible take to overcome dissatisfaction?

Active learning point

Look at the picture in Exercise 4.4 and write down in the space provided what you see. Then go on and complete the exercises that follow.

Exercise 4.4

Interpreting information

Look at the picture in Figure 4.4. What do you see? Try it with a colleague or group of colleagues

Figure 4.4
Interpreting information

Can you see the partial face of the bearded man? If not, look at the upper edge of the picture and imagine the picture of a bearded man with long hair where the picture cuts off the top of the head above the eyebrows. If you still cannot see it, ask a colleague who can see it to explain it to you.

Exercise 4.5

Differing perceptions

Look at the picture in Figure 4.5 with a colleague or group of colleagues, and say what you see. Do you all see the same thing?

Figure 4.5
Differing perceptions

Do you see the picture of an old woman? Do you see the picture of the young woman? Do you see both? Keep looking at the picture until you can see both a young woman and an old woman. If you have difficulty, pair up with a colleague who can see the image that you cannot see.

Exercise 4.6

Seeing things in context

Look at the picture of three men in Figure 4.6. Which man is the largest?

Figure 4.6
Seeing things in context

Is it the man on the right, or is it the man on the left or in the centre? They are, in fact, all the same size. Take a ruler and measure them. The narrowing lines make it look as though the man on the right is larger than the man on the left. The context in which the image is set influences how people see the image.

Exercise 4.7

Say what you see

Look at the three triangles in Figure 4.7 for ten seconds. Cover the book with a piece of paper and write down what you can remember.

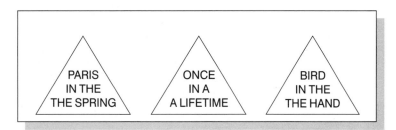

Figure 4.7
Triangles

Did you write down PARIS IN THE SPRING, ONCE IN A LIFETIME and BIRD IN THE HAND? If so, look again. What you should have written is PARIS IN THE THE SPRING, ONCE IN A A LIFETIME and BIRD IN THE THE HAND. Most people look at these three triangles and see what they expect to see. They do not see the extra 'THE' or 'A'.

Perceptions • • •

Consideration of Exercises 4.5, 4.6 and 4.7 establishes some useful points about human perception:

- People interpret information and give it meaning.

- Different people may perceive the same things differently.

- The context influences the way people perceive things.

- Prior knowledge and experience influence perceptions.

- In some cases perception is distorted by expectation.

Although the examples used are all based on visual perception, these general observations can be applied to the way people perceive through all the senses. In fact, a high proportion of human perception is shaped via the visual sense.

As a unit manager, you need to understand these influences of perception because customers, staff and even managers are all subject to these influences, and conflicts of perception are at the heart of many business problems.

Hospitality, Leisure & Tourism Series

Customers have different perceptions of service quality than do managers and staff. Similarly, employees may perceive their relationship with managers differently and there may even be differences amongst the employees.

As we have already seen, stereotyping is a common problem in human interactions. People expect other people to act in a predetermined manner and interpretation of their actions more often than not distorts perceptions to confirm the prejudgement. Managers need to understand their own predispositions as these might end up causing self-fulfilling outcomes. For example, exercises in this and earlier chapters show that some managers have a view that employees cannot be trusted. Managers often set up control systems that overcontrol their staff and produce situations that fulfil the prediction.

Active learning point

In the table in Exercise 4.8 write down fifteen words you might use to describe yourself to someone you have just met.

Exercise 4.8

The social individual

| Descriptor | Type | |
	Group	Other
1		
2		
3		
4		
5		
6		
7		
8		
9		
10		
11		
12		
13		
14		
15		

Typically, most people cannot describe themselves without making reference to some social groupings which give them a sense of identity: nationality, regional origin, religion, political party, social class, occupation, family relationships, football club supporter, etc. How many of these words have you used to describe yourself?

Individuals in groups

Group membership, even when people cannot know all the other members, help individuals define who they are and also, importantly, who they are not. These labels shape behaviour and expectations, helping to establish codes of expected actions and beliefs.

Individuals belong to two types of groups. *Secondary groups* are groups to which people belong, or to which people affiliate, where the members are mostly unknown to each other. In other words, a person may declare him or herself to belong to a national group, say English, without knowing all the other people who make up the nation – the English. Yet membership of this group can result in all sorts of positive and negative behaviour – supporting the football team, conflict with supporters of other teams, etc.

Individuals also belong to *primary groups*. These are small groups, usually not much larger than ten people, where all the members are known to each other. Typically, individuals belong to families and work groups that are in the form of primary groups. In a formal way, the use of teamworking and autonomous work groups recognizes these social dynamics but, even in situations where teams and group membership are not part of the management structure, group membership will influence behaviour at work. Group influences on individual behaviour:

- provide a sense of identity

- develop a structure including roles such as leader

- establish norms and expectations about how members behave

- pressure individuals to conform to the norms

- provide individuals with a sense of security

- will defend individuals from threats outside the group

- can improve collective output through mutual support

- can result in conflict with other groups

- are able to act in a unified manner

- provide a means of communication and developing shared knowledge.

Hospitality, Leisure & Tourism Series

The potential benefits of group membership in providing a self-disciplining, mutually supporting framework for guiding individual performance are at the root of the use of work teams, and autonomous and semi-autonomous work groups. Yet the social psychology of group influences means that all the positive and negative influences on behaviour are to be found in the workplace, and as a manager you must be aware of their influence.

Individual employees are members of the formal group structure that the organization sets up:

- departments within the unit

- occupational and job role differences

- different unit membership

- units in different brands within the group

- units in other companies, etc.

Managers can use these group memberships arising from the formal structure to develop a sense of common purpose and shared expectations. Thus, creating a sense of 'us and them' can assist you to give unit staff a sense of common purpose to see the unit succeed in comparison to other units in the group or against competitors. At the same time the formal structure can create a climate in which people in different departments are in conflict with each other and form as a barrier to effective operation. The traditional conflicts between kitchen and restaurant are a good example of the negative effects excessive conflict can produce.

At the same time, individuals belong to informal groupings that are a natural consequence of people working together. These, too, can have both positive and negative effects. Informal group membership can provide mechanisms for mutual support and shared purpose, which lead to high morale and commitment. At the same time, informal groups can result in norms of behaviour which restrict production and have a conflictual stance with management. Informal leaders can perform an important role in challenging you, the unit manager, as the formal leader.

To effectively manage the unit you have to recognize the influences of informal group membership on individual behaviour and attempt to work with informal leaders. As was stated in the earlier chapters, teamworking and autonomous work group membership provide techniques. At the very least you can:

- work with group members to reduce staff turnover

- use groups to assist in problem-solving

- encourage a sense of common purpose and shared objectives

- recognize and incorporate unofficial leaders from their groups

- aim incentives at group performance

- provide opportunities for effective group working to be established.

Influencing others

Effective unit managers need to be able to exercise a range of skills, attitudes, energies and behaviours to persuade others to act in a desired way. This book has shown that well-motivated and committed employees are essential to high-quality hospitality business performance. Traditional techniques of command and control and authoritarian management styles are not compatible with the development of employee motivation and commitment. Managing more involved and participating employees requires persuasion rather than instruction.

You need to exercise *personal power* that goes beyond structural power and, even, expertise. Personal power is used to influence people and actions. It is used to work through other people. As was shown in Chapter 2, the positive use of power aims to empower others and work through and with them without diminishing their personal power. By empowering others, more committed employees deliver better quality decisions in an environment of mutual trust. It produces a win-win situation in which all benefit.

Having personal power, therefore, involves the exercise of skills in influencing others. Exercising personal power is not about bullying or threatening others through displays of aggression and conflict. Influencing others is the process of modifying, effecting or changing another person's thoughts, attitudes or behaviour. There are a number of ways this can be achieved, though this section deals with being *assertive*. Assertiveness training is about empowering people and making them more self-confident.

Assertiveness

Assertiveness involves standing up for yourself without damaging other people's rights. It is about being aware of the rights and dignity of others without giving up one's own rights and dignity. The approach requires individuals to develop an appreciation of each other's views and feelings without being aggressive or non-assertive, in other words, without standing up for your rights at the expense of others or allowing other people's rights to be expressed at your expense.

Suppose a work colleague keeps giving you some of their work to do. You decide that you do not wish to do it any more. The person has just asked to you to take on some more. You say:

1 'No Joe I'm not going to do any more of your work. I've decided that it's not right for either of us for me to do both my work and yours'.   *Assertive*

2 'Forget it, it's about time that you did it. You treat me like your slave. You're an inconsiderate . . .   ' *Aggressive*

3 'I'm rather busy. But if you can't get it done I think I can help you'.   *Non-assertive*

Active learning point

Complete the questionnaire in Exercise 4.9. Each question has three answers reflecting assertive, aggressive and non-assertive response. Can you identify which is which?

Exercise 4.9

Recognizing assertive, aggressive and non-assertive behaviour

Identify the assertive, aggressive and non-assertive response in each case.

1 You are working the unit's weekly returns and your unit manager colleague telephones to talk to you about next week's unit managers meeting. You would prefer to finish what you are doing.

(a) 'I'm happy to talk about the meeting, but I'm busy right now. I'll ring you back this afternoon.'
(b) 'Look I'm busy. It's always the same, as soon as I get the figures out I can't get on because of pointless interruptions.'
(c) 'Well I'm busy, but I guess I can find time if you want to speak to me right now.'

2 Your Area Manager has criticized one of your staff. You feel the criticism is unjustified.

(a) 'I feel your criticism is unfair. He/she is not like that at all'.
(b) 'I'm the manager and know this person best. You should allow me to deal with my own people in my own way.'
(c) 'I hadn't thought about it but I suppose you are right.'

3 A customer arrives late for a table booking. You are concerned that customers booked in later may be delayed.

(a) 'We have been holding the table for you. I would have appreciated it if you had telephoned.'
(b) 'Shall I show you straight to the table?'
(c) 'There are other customers waiting. This is very inconsiderate.'

4 A colleague compliments you for your report to the unit managers meetings

(a) 'Thank you.'
(b) 'It's nothing really.'
(c) 'What do you expect from me, I only do excellent work.'

5 One of your staff deserves a low appraisal rating because of continued poor timekeeping – a matter which has been raised before.

(a) 'Look the company expects you to be here on time. It's very difficult for me. What problems have you got that cause you to be late?'
(b) 'I'm disappointed that your timekeeping has not improved since the last appraisal. Let's try to get things sorted out once and for all this time, so you can do well.'
(c) 'You never learn do you. It's time to get yourself sorted out. You are for the high jump this time.'

Key to Exercise 4.9

1 (a) Assertive   (b) Aggressive   (c) Non-assertive

2 (a) Assertive   (b) Aggressive   (c) Non-assertive

3 (a) Non-assertive   (b) Assertive   (c) Aggressive

4 (a) Assertive   (b) Non-assertive   (c) Aggressive

5 (a) Non-assertive   (b) Assertive   (c) Aggressive

The assertion approach provides a very powerful way of developing influencing skills and avoiding other overaggressive behaviour or being treated as a 'doormat'.

A common manager error is to wrongly assume that the only way to get the best of staff is to treat them in an aggressive way. The assumption is based on the misguided notion that discipline can only be imposed. Adopting an assertive approach is assumed to be a sign of weakness. Yet nothing could be further from the truth. Assertive behaviour helps to share understanding, develop mutual respect and build self-discipline.

Similarly, some individuals feel that non-assertive behaviour creates harmony, because displaying disagreement results in conflict and disharmony. Again this is a mistake, because avoiding conflict does not remove the differences in perceptions or interests. Conflict is frequently based on different perceptions and misunderstanding. Conflicts often reflect irreconcilable differences of interest, in which case recognizing and managing the differences in an atmosphere of mutual respect is essential.

Dealing with conflict

Conflict occurs when the concerns of two or more people are incompatible. Conflict is an inevitable feature of hospitality service organization life. Fundamentally, the relationship between organization and employees; between employees and customers; and between customers and the organization are all bound to result in different parties having needs which conflict with others. Even though customers, employees and the organization's management may work together in harmony for much of the time, deep-seated conflicts of interest are always under the surface, for example, in the:

- employee/organization dimension wages for employees are costs for the organization;

- employee/customer dimension the customer's service need represents work and effort for employees

- customer/organization dimension customer service satisfaction is sales revenue for the organization.

Figure 4.8 shows the conflicts of control between the three key parties to the service encounter. On another level personal conflicts also occur between employees, between managers and between customers. These conflicts, though not a fundamental part of the relationship, are bound to be a natural part of hospitality retail organizations as a consequence of differences in personalities, beliefs, values attitudes and perceptions amongst the people in involved.

Much hospitality organizational rhetoric can be unhelpful because it suggests a harmony of interests where none exists. Employees are not internal customers, they are employees who work for wages; and the organization will only want to delight external customers as long as there is a profit to be turned.

If conflict is a natural and consequential part of organization life, it is not always a bad thing. Conflict can produce creative tensions that add to the vigour of decision-making and problem-solving. By recognizing the natural tensions and conflicts which stem from the very nature of organization life, as a manager you

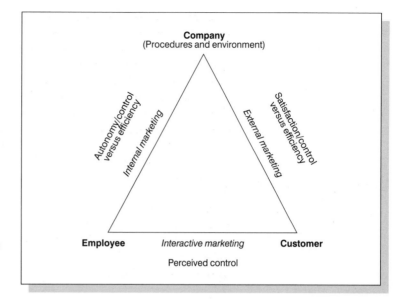

Figure 4.8
Control conflicts in the service encounter
Source: Adapted from Bateson (1985).

CO-OPERATIVE

Accommodating	**Collaborating**
Neglecting own position to satisfy those of other parties, e.g.:	Working with the other party to find some solution which satisfies the concerns of both parties, e.g.:
■ *selfless generosity or charity;* ■ *accepting an instruction when one would prefer not to;* ■ *yielding to another's point of view*	■ *exploring disagreements in order to learn from each other;* ■ *agreeing to share scarce resource;* ■ *confronting and finding a solution to a problem*

Compromising

Finding a convenient mutually acceptable solution, partially satisfying both parties, e.g.:

UNASSERTIVE ——— ■ *splitting the difference* ——— **ASSERTIVE**
■ *exchanging concessions*

Avoiding	**Competing**
Not pursuing own interests nor the interests of the other party, i.e., not addressing the conflict, e.g.:	Pursuing one's own concerns at the expense of the other party, using ability to argue, power and status, e.g.:
■ *diplomatically side-stepping an issue;* ■ *postponing the issue until a later date;* ■ *withdrawal from a threatening situation*	■ *'standing up for your rights';* ■ *defending a position which you believe is correct* ■ *concern to win at all costs.*

UNCOOPERATIVE

Figure 4.9
Strategies for handling conflict

can use these conflicts to aid improved performance. At the very least, recognition of the potential harmful effects and an understanding of how conflict can be handled are essential (Figure 4.9). The following sections deal with conflict and how it can be managed.

The means of managing the conflict can be mapped against two sets of issues. The extent that the manager is being assertive or non-assertive, and the extent that the manager is attempting to be co-operative or unco-operative. The interplay of these two factors suggests that there are five potential approaches to dealing with conflict situations. Without consideration and thought the approach will be largely driven by the manager's personality, values, beliefs, attitudes and perceptions. In each case, there may be situations where the approach is appropriate and, in all cases, managers must be aware of the consequences of their approach. That is, in conflict situations each party will react to the actions of the other party.

Collaborating

Collaborating is based on being assertive and co-operative. It recognizes the conflicts of interests and considers an approach which is mutually acceptable to both parties:

- Both sets of concerns are too important to be compromised.
- The objective is to learn by sharing the views of others.
- Bring together the diverse interests of different parties.
- Gain commitment to the decision reached.
- Deal with difficulties in interpersonal relationships.

Several techniques for managing employees in more a participative style are examples where this approach can be used to great effect. Managers who recognize the conflictual basis to the employment relationship recognize that this approach will not necessarily resolve the conflict but it will ensure mutual respect and commitment to common goals. You should explore the possibilities of a win-win outcome. On the other hand, decisions may well take a long time to make.

Collaboration can be applied in dealings with employees, suppliers and customers.

Competing

Competing is based on being assertive and unco-operative. The approach is essentially pursuing one party's interests at the expense of the other party. Managers recognize the conflict of interests with employees, suppliers or customers and are determined to get the upper hand. The approach involves a win-lose outcome. One party wins at the expense of the other. It is often applied when:

- a quick decision is vital

- one party is convinced they are right

- the other party is attempting to take advantage of the situation.

Many hospitality retail managers operate this way in relation to employees. In situations where employees have little opportunity to stand up to managerial power, even with the collective power of trade union membership, employee resistance to this managerial approach takes an individual form – absenteeism, poor quality working and high levels of staff turnover are a consequence.

Avoiding

Avoiding is based on a non-assertive and unco-operative approach. Generally this approach has negative consequences because it avoids conflict and the problem remains unresolved. It is a lose-lose position. However, there may be times when this is appropriate when dealing with customers who are making complaints that are, in your judgement, unjustified. In other cases it might be appropriate:

- when other issues are more urgent

- where there is a limited chance of a satisfactory outcome

- where the damage of conflict outweighs the benefits of its resolution

- to resolve an immediate tense situation

- when the conflict can be resolved later

- where the issue is a symptom of a bigger problem.

Giving customers the benefit of the doubt and avoiding conflict has the advantage of building customer satisfaction, but there is the risk the some customers may use the knowledge to make unjustified complaints as a way of obtaining discounts, etc. Similarly, avoiding conflicts with employees can have negative impacts when the problem remains unresolved, or where the employee gets the impression that 'anything goes'.

Accommodating

Accommodating is based on an approach that is unassertive and co-operative. It recognizes that the other party has a justifiable point and that the individual should concede to it. It is a lose-win position. Dealing with justified customer complaints and over-compensating for the problem caused is an example. This approach has particular relevance in the following circumstances:

- when a party realizes they are wrong

- when the issue is more important to the other party than to you

- when continued conflict would damage your cause

- to avoid disruption

- to develop subordinates by allowing them to learn from mistakes.

This approach may also apply when dealing with employees, particularly where the manager recognizes the justice of the employee's cause. The approach can, however, cause negative effects if you concede just to keep the operation running and the problem remains unresolved, or employees and customers gain the impression that the concession is an ongoing right.

Compromising

Compromising involves moderate elements of assertion and co-operation. This approach accepts that the two parties have mutually powerful but different points of view, or that continued conflict is not worth the effort. It is a half-win-half-win position. It may involve negotiations with employees in industrial relations matters or with suppliers in disputes over supplies and payment. It is likely to be applied:

- when the cost of the potential disruption is greater than the point to be won

- when there are two mutually powerful parties committed to mutually exclusive goals

- to achieve temporary settlements of complex issues

- when time pressures require an expedient solution to the problem

- as a fall back position when collaboration or competition fail.

Again the main danger is that conflicts may remain unresolved as the parties reach a settlement which they 'can both live with'. At heart, however, both feel they have conceded more than they wanted and this resentment is stored up for the future.

The model in Figure 4.9 gives a useful insight into conflict and how it can be handled. However, there are only a limited number of outcomes from conflict. These five positions highlight each possible outcome and the relationship of the parties. Key to resolving conflicts are the skills of effective influencing through assertiveness and active listening. Being able to recognize the other person's point of view and ensuring that they understand your position is essential.

Motivating people at work

Unit managers in hospitality retail businesses depend on employees for delivering the defined service standards that represent the brand. Working to set procedures, not cutting corners and working 'one best way' are common requirements of work in branded hospitality services. In addition, effective service is more than behaving like a preprogrammed robot. Customers expect to be treated like individuals, they want to feel the person serving them is genuinely concerned about their needs. It is often said that employees have to supply *emotional labour* – to feel for the customer. Furthermore, hospitality retail employees are frequently expected to 'up-sell' and persuade the customer to buy more than they intended. Thus employees are expected to:

- work to a routine

- delight customers by treating them as individual

- feel committed to the customer

- accept the commercial objectives of the organization

- manage all these conflicting pressures.

Employee motivation and commitment are essential for the success of the hospitality brand. Yet employee motivation is often left to a haphazard process. The following sections suggest some ways you can build your employees' motivation and commitment.

Understanding individuals

As we have seen, individuals differ in their personalities, beliefs, values, attitudes and perceptions at work. They are also different in their orientations to work. For some people work is a major aspect of their lives, which provides social benefits and a sense of identity. In other cases, work is a means to an end – they work because they have to and gain social benefits and a sense of identity through other aspects of their lives. Many hospitality organizations structure their motivation strategies on the stereo- types introduced earlier:

- rational-economic

- social

- self-actualizing.

The more appropriate model is *complex* people. Thus the same individual may well prioritize different rewards from work at different times, and may well want to satisfy all sets of needs at one time. The acceptance of the complex person model is important because it:

- prevents the manager from making wrong assumptions about people and their motives

- allows managers to be more responsive to employee needs

- recognizes that people may change over time.

To understand people at work it is, therefore, necessary to consider the individual and the total situation at work. Herz- berg's dual factor theory is a useful model for understanding people and the factors likely to shape their motivations.

Satisfiers and dissatisfiers

People experience an array of emotions at work. Some things make them feel happy and motivated, and others make them disgruntled and demotivated. There are expectations about work which employees take for granted as returns for their labour:

- physical working conditions

- company policy and administration

- security

- relations with supervisor

- salary and material rewards.

If these provisions are not appropriate, employees become dissatisfied. They may well constitute 'push factors' (Chapter 5) that cause employees to leave the firm. However, unexpectedly good provision will not generate motivation. Thus an increase in pay may lead to increased effort, but this will only last for a short period.

It is possible for employees to experience an absence of dissatisfaction without being motivated.

Motivators are aspects of work that make the individual feel better – the intrinsic factors discussed in Chapter 3. They arise from the way the job is designed and, most importantly, how they are treated as employees:

- developing a sense of achievement
- recognition for work done
- the nature of the work itself
- developing a sense of responsibility
- potential for advancement.

Employees who experience these outcomes from work are more likely to be motivated by their work experience. They make the extra effort and actively engage with the job and the objectives set. Chapter 2 touches on these motivations as an outcome of empowerment.

Motivators create good feelings and increase the will to work well.

Money as motivator

Using the rational-economic stereotype, many firms consider financial incentives are a powerful inducement to work well. Tips from customers or commission on sales are used to stimulate workers in hospitality retail organizations. In some cases the reward package is made up of a low basic wage, commission on sales and tips from customers. Clearly these reward schemes are intended to generate sales and customer satisfaction. In many ways they can be effective because:

- financial rewards are linked to achievements
- they focus the employee on the desired objective
- they create an interest in the success of the business
- they encourage an entrepreneurial approach in staff
- they are a fairer reward for effort.

The problem is that they can generate negative effects as people focus more on doing whatever will maximize the financial reward – at the expense of other objectives. Tips, for example, put the employee in the position of having to work for two bosses – organization and customer. Sometimes the employee does things against company policy in order to maximize the tip. Commission based on sales also can have negative consequences if employees are overly pushy and offend customers. In both cases, competition for the highest tipping customers or the busiest stations in the restaurant can create harmful competition between employees.

Conclusion

This chapter has provided some tools for thinking about the people who are the employees and customers of hospitality retail businesses. It is important in your role as manager that you recognize employees and customers as complex beings, that the models in this chapter are useful starting points and that people are rarely consistently one thing or another.

Individuals differ in their personalities in degrees of extraversion/introversion and stability/instability. Even using these measures, individuals may be more prone to be on one dimension than others but are rarely extreme extraverts or extreme introverts. Employee recruitment needs to take account of these factors. On another level, people are different in their beliefs, values and attitudes, as well as having different perceptions of similar things. Differences in employee, manager and customer perceptions can cause difficulties when expectations clash.

In addition to understanding employees as individuals, they also form informal groups in the workplace. The groups to which individuals belong influence individual behaviour. Earlier chapters have highlighted the use of group membership as a management device for influencing individual performance, however, informal group memberships are also important because of the impact on employee morale and behaviour.

As the unit manager you have to be able to exercise personal power and influence others. Understanding assertiveness, aggression and non-assertiveness provides you with some valuable tools for reducing disagreement and for winning support. In particular, the impact on conflict resolution is valuable. Unit managers have to deal with conflicts on a number of levels and dimensions. Many of the relationships between customers, the organization and the employees are based on fundamental conflicts of interest. Identifying and using approaches that minimize the negative effects of conflict are essential.

Finally, you need to motivate employees to work well. Understanding the motives and drives of the employees, and individual differences, is an important starting point. In addition, recognize that employees have expectations about how they are to be treated, which if not met will create dissatisfaction and, more importantly, employees have an array of needs that you can satisfy and which will lead to feelings of harmony and well-being.

Reflection and practice

Answer these questions to check your understanding of this chapter:

1 Using the case study (Chapter 14), devise a personality profile of a manager capable of resolving the situation.
2 How does an understanding of individual differences assist the hospitality retail manager in dealings with employees and customers?
3 Show how an understanding of the influences of group membership on individual behaviour enables a unit manager to be more effective.
4 Using the case study (Chapter 14), critically discuss the main strategies for influencing people that are being used by some of the main actors.
5 Show how you would resolve some of the conflicts that exist in the case study.

Reference

Bateson (1985). Perceived control and the service encounter. In *The Service Encounter* (J. A. Czepiel, M. R. Solomon and M. R. Superenant (eds). Boston MA: Lexington.

Further reading

Biddle, D. and Evenden, R. (1993). *Human Aspects of Management*. Institute of Personnel and Development.
Mullins, L. J. (1995). *Hospitality Management: A Human Resource Approach*. Pitman.

CHAPTER 5

Staff retention and turnover

After working through this chapter you should be able to:

- identify the causes of staff turnover

- calculate staff turnover and retention using a range of techniques

- estimate the costs of staff turnover

- suggest ways of reducing labour turnover in given situations.

Hidden problem, hidden costs

Staff turnover continues to be a contentious issue in the hospitality industry. Many managers see the process of staff leaving and being replaced as a natural and inevitable feature of industry employment. Providing they can continue to recruit people when needed, this is 'just the way things are'. It is not unusual, for example for many organizations to keep no record of the numbers of staff who leave and are replaced, and it is rarer still for firms to cost staff turnover or value the benefits of staff retention.

Some managers even consider staff turnover to be a good thing because it allows managers to manipulate the size of their workforce without resistance from employees and the need to make compulsory redundancies when trading conditions worsen. Increasingly, however, managers in large hospitality retail organizations recognize labour turnover as both *costly* and *creating operational* difficulties, particularly when trained or frontline staff leave. Consequently many now have detailed records of the levels of labour turnover, though few account for it when measuring unit performance. This chapter argues that staff turnover can represent a considerable additional cost to the business. Unit managers can reduce the numbers of people who leave the organization, but fundamentally the organization needs to understand:

- the levels of staff turnover
- the causes of staff turnover
- the costs of staff turnover
- the value of staff retention.

Causes and types of staff turnover

Staff turnover is best understood as the movement of labour out of and into a working organization. As indicated earlier, some practitioners and academics see positive benefits to *controlled staff turnover*:

- if poor performers are the ones to leave the organization
- if new employees bring new skills and ideas
- if the organization is refreshed by change brought in by new staff.

However, all too often it is the better staff who leave and staff turnover is *uncontrolled*. In these circumstance staff turnover can:

- wreck planning
- have a disastrous effect on staff morale
- represent a considerable extra cost to the business
- reduce service quality
- cause customer dissatisfaction.

Active learning point

Using an organization known to you or the case study in the final chapter, list the benefits and problems caused by staff turnover.

Benefits of staff leaving	Problems caused by staff leaving
1	1
2	2
3	3
4	4
5	5
6	6
7	7
8	8
9	9
10	10

Frequently, a vicious cycle is established where high staff turnover results in hurried recruitment and selection, poor induction, limited training, supervisory and management pressure, and low morale leading to further instability and labour turnover. Figure 5.1 shows this vicious cycle, and represents the experiences of many branded hospitality organizations.

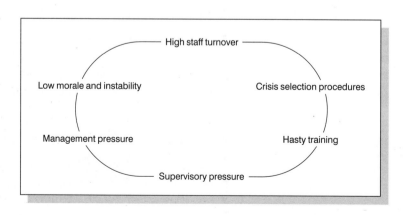

Figure 5.1
The vicious cycle of staff turnover

Some departures from the organization, through retirement, illness, pregnancy, etc., are unavoidable – an inevitable aspect of organizational life. Table 5.1 lists some of the causes of unavoidable staff departures.

Table 5.1
Some common reasons for unavoidable staff turnover

Unavoidable staff turnover
Retirement
Illness
Death
Marriage
Pregnancy
Leaving the area
Students returning to college or home

However, where labour turnover is high, it is usually due to avoidable reasons which, as a unit manager, you can manage (Table 5.2). Thus employee dissatisfaction with training and personal development, wage levels, management styles and policies, colleagues and overall job satisfaction are issues which you can attempt to match with employee expectations.

Table 5.2
Some reasons for avoidable staff turnover

Avoidable staff turnover
Dissatisfaction with wages
Relationship with management
Lack of training
Work pace and stress
Relationships with other staff
Hours of work
Transport difficulties

Frequently, no single factor causes people to voluntarily leave an organization and often their decision is shaped by both *push* and *pull* factors. Push factors are those issues that cause dissatisfaction with the current organization, and pull factors are perceived benefits being offered by competing employers (Table 5.3).

In these circumstances, it is important that managers understand the local labour market and pay attention to the employment terms and conditions being offered by other firms. Levels of

Push factors	Pull factors
Discontent with leaders	More money
Poor image of the organization	Better hours
Poor terms and conditions	Permanent employment
Uneven work patterns	Alternative employment
Poor pay	Improved career prospects
Unsuitable hours of work	Improved training and
Lack of autonomy	development
	Empowerment

Table 5.3

Some push and pull factors in staff turnover

employment and unemployment have an effect on levels of staff turnover in hospitality retail organizations. Staff turnover is likely to be higher when there are many employers looking for the same type of staff. In these circumstances, you must ensure that terms and conditions of employment are as good as, or better than, the local competitors and that *push factors* are minimized. In other words, ensure that staff satisfaction is high and the staff have few reasons to leave. Remember most branded hospitality retail organizations:

* employ people to do routine unskilled tasks
* use a large number of part-time staff
* compete for staff with other hospitality organizations
* compete with supermarkets and other retailers
* often employ people during unsociable hours
* recruit people from the local community.

Active learning point

Using a hospitality retail unit known to you, identify the terms and conditions of employment which operate within the local labour market.

Terms and conditions	Unit	Local labour market Minimum	Maximum
Hourly pay rates			
Average hours worked:			
F/time and P/time			
Other benefits:			
Money and non-money			
Training given			
% part-time workers			
Interesting/boring work			
Management/staff relations			
Employee satisfaction			
Levels of staff turnover			
Image of organization			
Travel arrangements			

Similarly, it is important to consider *involuntary* withdrawal from the firm as well as the *voluntary* cause suggested earlier (Table 5.4). Involuntary labour turnover occurs against the wishes of the individual employee. In some cases, where a fixed term contract ends or there is a downturn in the business cycle, the turnover is perhaps understandable, but where misconduct, absenteeism or poor performance are concerned you cannot absolve yourself of responsibility. Hurried and sloppy recruitment or poor training are frequently important contributors to the cause of unacceptable employee behaviour.

As indicated earlier, many managers are unaware of the problem of staff turnover and adopt a fatalistic acceptance of people leaving the organization as a fact of hospitality sector life.

Voluntary	Involuntary
Another job	Conclusion of temporary
Return to college/school	employment
Marriage	Reduction in work force
Medical reasons	Poor performance
Relocation	Loss of licence
Dissatisfaction with wages	Incapacity to do the job
Dissatisfaction with work	Misconduct: absenteeism,
Dissatisfaction with conditions	lateness
Resignation without notice	Gross misconduct:
Career advancement	dishonesty, disobedience,
Personal development	drinking, violence and
	swearing

Table 5.4
Some voluntary and involuntary forms of staff turnover

Providing it is possible to find enough people to fill vacant posts, managers frequently do not see high levels of labour turnover as a problem. In many cases, they have no knowledge of whether the levels of turnover in their organization are high, low or average for the industry. In some cases, managers do not even keep records of how many staff leave and are replaced in any one trading year. These managers have no means of monitoring trends nor, most importantly, of assessing the costs of staff turnover.

Counting the cost

Staff turnover represents both direct and indirect costs to the business. In the case of direct costs it is possible to calculate direct expenditure related to filling each vacancy. Advertising for replacements, recruitment agency fees, additional overtime payments, or payments to agency staff brought in to cover gaps, etc., are all examples of additional costs incurred when a job vacancy has to be filled. In addition, indirect costs can be identified which, whilst difficult to physically calculate, represent genuine costs to the business none the less. Management time spent in all the stages of recruitment, selection, interviewing and induction could be spent in other ways. Similarly, lost training investment and the time taken for new recruits to match the job performance of the former employee, as well as lost business due to customer dissatisfaction, all involve additional costs (Table 5.5). In the hospitality business in particular, regular customers like to be recognized and acknowledged by staff when they visit the establishment. This is difficult to deliver if there is a permanently high level of staff turnover.

Direct costs	Hidden costs
Advertising for replacements	Management time spent recruiting, interviewing,
Recruitment agency fees	selecting, inducting, training
Travel expenses for interviews	Lost investment in training
Postage and stationery	Lost staff expertise
Induction and orientation	Reduced service quality
Training	Reduced productivity
Overtime cover	Increased wastage and costs
Agency staff cover	Customer dissatisfaction
Processing new recruit's documents	Negative impact on remaining staff
Processing ex-employee's documents	Opportunity cost of lost management time
Uniforms	

Table 5.5 Some direct and hidden costs of staff turnover

The costs of staff departures can have very negative impacts on the business. However, there are different costs associated with replacement of different levels of staff. Figure 5.2 reproduces a graduated scale of different replacement costs through unskilled, craft and management positions. According to their calculations the Institute of Personnel and Development (1997) estimated that at the time of the study average replacement costs ranged from £735 per unskilled employee to £5008 for managerial and administrative posts.

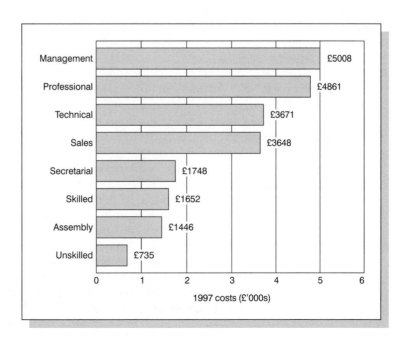

Figure 5.2
National estimates of staff turnover costs (£)
Source: Institute of Personnel and Development (1997).

Example 5.1

The Wise Owl Hotel: costs

The Wise Owl Hotel is located in a popular attraction in northern Britain. At the time of the study the hotel had been operated by Mr and Mrs Straw for six years. The hotel contains nine double bedrooms, a meeting room for twenty delegates, a large bar and a function room capable of seating 150 people. The hotel's most profitable business comes from hosting conferences and weddings.

The management of the hotel is headed by the owners who act as General Manager (Mr Straw) and Chief Administrator (Mrs Straw). A Hotel Manager and Deputy Manager together with Restaurant Manager, Bar Manager and Head Chef make up the remainder of the management team. Like many other hotel businesses, the Wise Owl Hotel used numerical and functional flexibility in staff employment. With the exception of chefs, most staff were expected to work in different departments as business demand determined. The full-time staff, including the management team below the owners, was twenty and normally about forty part-time staff were registered as being regularly employed by the hotel. In some cases part-time staff worked as many as thirty-five hours per week. Only the staff employed to cook food were expected to be qualified in appropriate craft qualifications. All other staff received fairly basic levels of training and most gained skills and job competence by actually doing the job.

Audited accounts for the period being studied show the total sales revenue for the hotel was just under £1 million per annum, and the profit and loss account registered a net profit of £295 000 (29.9 per cent). Salaries and wages accounted for £195 000 (20 per cent of sales revenue). On the face of it the company was making a healthy operating profit, and Mr and Mrs Straw felt their management of the business was successful because they had 'turned the business round'.

Fifty-seven people left the employment of the hotel during the twelve-month period of the study. Compared to a nominal role of sixty employees, this represented a total labour turnover of 95 per cent. However, the rate for full-time employee was 130 per cent (twenty-six leavers) and 77.5 per cent for part-time employees. Whilst a small minority of the leavers were voluntary, just under half of the terminations in employment were involuntary due to dismissal.

Typical for an organization experiencing high labour turnover, a large number leaving employment at the Wise Owl Hotel had only been with the organization for a short period. Twenty-eight of the leavers left the organization within the first three months of their employment, and over 68 per cent of the employees leaving the hotel did so within their first six months of employment. This pattern of labour turnover reveals a strong 'induction crisis' suggesting a problem in the recruitment, selection and induction of new recruits.

The overall estimate of the costs of replacement tends to underestimate rather than overestimate the costs. The total cost of replacement of employees in the year of the study is £60 857 and this represents an additional 31 per cent when compared to the total wages bill of £195 000. When compared with net profit on the profit and loss account, £60 857 would add another 20 per cent to net profit if these costs could be avoided. In addition these figures take no account of the costs to the business of lost custom when ill-trained staff, or ever-changing staff cause customer dissatisfaction. Nor do they account for extra wastage or theft when inappropriate recruitment takes place. Neither do these figures include the opportunity cost to manager's time, that is, what could managers be achieving if they were not spending so much time recruiting new staff?

These amounts may appear to be high for hospitality retail organizations, but recent research for the Hospitality Training Foundation showed that staff turnover in a major hospitality retailer costs directly £450 per head, and this did not take into account some of the impacts on customer satisfaction, service quality or employee satisfaction. Just taking these figures into account, staff turnover was costing the company in the region of £16 million per year.

Whilst some costs will be incurred in replacing staff who have left the organization for unavoidable reasons, many of the costs of avoidable labour turnover represent, for most organizations, a hidden but real additional cost.

Measuring staff turnover

The measurement of staff turnover is an essential first step in both recognizing the nature of the problem and identifying the actions needed to reduce it. As with all other management information, the more detailed the information, the more you are able to understand the nature of the problem. There are a number of different measures that can be applied. The following will provide a brief overview of some of those more widely used.

Staff turnover rate

This is the most commonly used statistic and merely compares the number of leavers with the normal complement of staff. The rate is calculated as a percentage, so it is possible to express the rate using uneven bases. For example, it is possible to calculate the rate for:

- the national economy
- the industry
- different firms
- individual units in the brand
- departments
- different jobs
- full- and part-time staff.

The measure can be taken annually, quarterly or monthly. The staff turnover rate can be calculated to suit your need, but it is commonly calculated as a 'rolling twelve months average'. The key to its attraction and wide use is that it is simple to calculate and it gives a broad indicator from which to compare time periods, jobs, departments, etc.

The formula is:

$$\frac{\text{Number of leavers}}{\text{Average number employed}} \times 100 \qquad (5.1)$$

If forty staff have left and been replaced during the year and the unit normally employs twenty-five staff, the calculation is:

$$\frac{40}{25} \times 100 = 160\% \qquad (5.2)$$

As shown above, it is possible to build a more detailed picture by making the calculations for each job, for different departments, or different units in the firm. These calculations help pinpoint some of the problems, but this calculation can produce a false impression. For example, the bald figure:

- suggests that all staff have left and been replaced
- suggests that all jobs are equally affected
- gives no information about the time staff have stayed with the unit.

The staff retention rate

The staff retention rate allows you to calculate the number of jobs not affected by staff turnover. Thus it helps to feature the general extent or limited nature of the turnover taking place. The calculation is again concerned with a comparison with the normal establishment, but this time it takes account of the number of jobholders who can be described as *long-term employees*, typically having been with the firm for over one year.

To calculate the staff retention rate the formula is:

$$\frac{\text{Number of long-term employees}}{\text{Average number employed}} \times 100 \qquad (5.3)$$

In the above example forty staff have been replaced during the year, but fifteen of the twenty-five staff have been with the unit for over one year. The calculation is then:

$$\frac{15}{25} \times 100 = 60\% \qquad (5.4)$$

In other words, although there is a general level of staff turnover in the unit of 160 per cent, the majority of staff are long-term employees. Sixty per cent have been with the organization for over twelve months. The pattern appears to show that just ten jobs have accounted for forty staff leavings in the year. If this is evenly spread, the ten jobs each have four new members of staff who have joined and left over the year.

Clearly the staff retention rate can be calculated against any base. Usually, a long-term employee is defined as having been with the firm for over one year. However, this could be a two-year period, and it is possible to calculate *length of service charts* that then plot the employment histories of staff who have been with the firm for two, three, four years and beyond. For most units this type of information is interesting but not essential.

The survival curve

The survival curve helps to develop a picture of new entrants and the organization's ability to retain new employees. As the name suggests it concerns itself with the staff leaving the organization and then plots them against their length of service. The key statistics are gathered according to how long each leaver has been with the organization, and are then compared with the total number of leavers. The formula is:

$$\frac{\text{Number of leavers after 3 months}}{\text{Total leavers this year}} \times 100 \qquad (5.5)$$

$$\frac{\text{Number of leavers after 6 months}}{\text{Total leavers this year}} \times 100 \qquad (5.6)$$

$$\frac{\text{Number of leavers after 9 months}}{\text{Total leavers this year}} \times 100 \qquad (5.7)$$

$$\frac{\text{Number of leavers after 12 months}}{\text{Total leavers this year}} \times 100 \qquad (5.8)$$

$$\frac{\text{Number of leavers with over 18 months service}}{\text{Total leavers this year}} \times 100 \qquad (5.9)$$

The calculations can be extended to meet the specific needs of the organization. Typically most turnover occurs within a short period of staff joining the organization, and in some cases the calculations for the first quarter need to be further broken down into monthly figures. The survival curve is valuable for identifying an *induction crisis*, that is, a problem that occurs when the new recruit first enters the organization. The induction crisis may be caused by:

- poor recruitment and selection
- limited use of job description and person specification
- a lack of a formal induction
- limited training
- poor staff morale amongst other staff
- team membership problems
- poor communication with the new recruit
- excessive job stress.

In the example used above, forty staff have left in a twelve-month period. Records reveal that the leavers had been with the organization for the periods shown in Table 5.6:

Leavers left after	3 months	6 months	9 months	12 months	15 months	18 months
Numbers	30	5	3	1	1	0
% of all leavers	75.0	12.5	7.5	2.5	2.5	0

Table 5.6 Example of staff leavers during a twelve-month period

In this example the majority of staff who left the unit did so within three months of joining (Figure 5.3). This pattern is one that is typical for a business which is experiencing high labour turnover. Given the information from the staff retention rate, there is an induction crisis, which may be a problem restricted to a particular type of job or may be a problem facing all new recruits and be caused by one of the reasons suggested above.

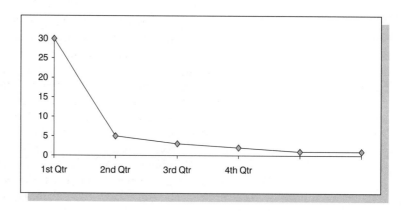

Figure 5.3
Example of a survival curve

Seasonal and temporary staff

Many hospitality retail organizations use temporary or seasonal staff to meet the demand for staff in predictably busy periods. In many cases, Christmas or summer trading represents a disproportionate additional sales volume and the unit manager needs to recruit extra staff to meet the peak in demand. Recruiting these individuals and releasing them after the period finishes does represent staff turnover, but it is planned and predicted. Calculations can, however, be distorted if no special account is taken of these employees.

In some cases, a student works in a unit during holiday periods, and then goes away to college or university where he or she might work part time for the same organization, only to return to the original unit in the vacation. It is possible to predict a student joining and rejoining units in the same organization six times in a year. The staff turnover could appear to be a problem if no special account is taken of this type of person. Many organizations now have a code for employees who are students so that they can be extracted from the calculation of staff turnover.

Active learning point

Using the information given to you in the case study (Chapter 14), prepare an analysis of the staff turnover. This should include using all the techniques outlined above, and an estimate of the costs of staff turnover to the organization. Use the IPD's estimates of the cost of staff replacement.

Whilst many hospitality retail organizations are now calculating the rate of staff turnover, very few account for the total cost of staff turnover for the business. In part, this can be explained because of the difficulties in accurately measuring the true impact of losing staff, who may have worked in the unit for varying times, and knowing the true cost of the impact of lost staff on customer satisfaction and service quality. Taking into account these points, all units should attempt to both calculate the level and cost of turnover as part of the assessment of unit performance.

If a restaurant has sixty employees on the books at any one time, experiences staff turnover of 140 per cent and has estimated the direct cost of turnover as £450, the calculation will be as follows:

$$60 \times 140\% = 84 \text{ staff replaced each year} \tag{5.10}$$

$$84 \times £450 = £37\,800 \text{ spent on the direct cost of staff replacement}$$

Using the Institute of Personnel and Development's estimate of the wider costs through lost customers, etc. this could be costing the unit over £65 000 per year.

Keeping your staff is not rocket science – everyone can do it

As yet, few organizations attempt to value the cost of staff turnover, though increasing numbers of the larger branded hospitality retailers are now concerned with the impact of staff leavers on service quality and customer satisfaction. And the link between employee satisfaction and customer satisfaction is well established. Increasingly managers are being asked to come up with strategies for reducing staff turnover and for managing *internal customer satisfaction*.

The following sections suggest some steps that you can take to keep staff and reduce the amount of unwanted and unplanned staff turnover.

Keeping records and costing staff turnover

To be able to manage staff turnover you must keep accurate records of staff leaving and joining the unit. There are a few suggestions to consider when you create a system within the unit.

1 When setting up the file think carefully about the aims you have for the information. Resist the temptation to store too much information as this will increase your workload.

2 Usually you will be interested in a few key issues:

(a) the total volume of staff turnover
(b) departmental or job title variations
(c) evidence of staff retention and stability
(d) the percentage of staff leaving within a short period of joining the unit
(e) potential variations by employee characteristics
(f) differences between full-time, part-time and casual staff.

3 Whether to include all employees. You may need to make allowance for certain categories of staff leavers who are not a 'problem':

(a) seasonal or temporary staff
(b) students returning to college or home
(c) staff leaving for 'unavoidable' reason – retirement, death, etc.

4 Try to create as accurate a picture as you can of the reasons for staff departures. Are the reasons:

(a) due to push or pull factors
(d) due to avoidable or unavoidable reasons
(c) voluntary or involuntary?

5 Attempt to cost out staff turnover. Many organizations have some estimate of the costs involved in replacing members of staff. If not, the national survey figures given in Figure 5.2 can be used. Failing that, try to work out the direct costs of losing staff yourself. Table 5.5 suggests some of the factors which you might want to include.

Exit interviews

Many unit managers attempt to build up a picture of the reason for staff departures through the use of exit interviews. These are conducted after a person has given notice of their intention to quit, but prior to departure. At the least they give the manager some opportunities to explore the experiences and motives of those who have decide to leave. The problem is these interviews are notoriously inaccurate as sources of information. Employees, particularly dissatisfied employees, often find it difficult to express their views openly. A situation made more difficult if the unit management team is the key source of the employee's dissatisfaction. Here are some tips that will should help make the interview more effective:

1 The rules of good interviewing apply, so a quiet room without interruptions, and the appropriate preparation are essential.
2 The interview is intended to discover the reason for the departure, not to persuade the person to stay on. The quality of information gathered will be a reflection of the trust and relationships between the manager and staff member. An open trusting relationship will usually result in a more honest exchange of views.
3 Open-ended questions that allow the person to explain in their own words, means their views are more likely to be helpful.
4 The style and tone of the interview needs to be friendly and open, rather than aggressive and argumentative.
5 Above all, recognize the difficulty which the employee faces and attempt to make the event as comfortable as possible so that you achieve an accurate view.

Monitor the local labour market

If you are to avoid some of the problems caused by competition in the local labour market, you need to be aware of current trends and reward packages being offered by competitors. Pay rates and working hours are issues of particular concern to most employees. Many managers forget that whilst labour is a significant manageable cost to the business, that 'cost' is a wage on which to live for the employee. Competitor firms offering regular hours and better rates of pay appear very attractive to employees who experience low wages and short working hours.

Conduct a regular audit of local competitor pay rates, term and conditions, and the other factors suggested above. These are particularly important when trade is booming and there is competition for staff.

Employee satisfaction

When an employee makes a decision to leave the organization for a voluntary reason the employee is, in one way or another, expressing dissatisfaction with the current employer. Employees in hospitality retail organizations, in particular, have few courses of action open to them if they are unhappy with things. Few hospitality retail organizations, in the UK, have any sizeable trade union membership, and few organizations recognize and negotiate with trade unions. Grievances can be taken up, but these often put the individual in a difficult position with little power to change things they do not like. For many members of staff, therefore, the only way of dealing with a situation they do not like is to either put up with it or withdraw from it.

It takes happy workers to make happy customers.

(J. W. Marriott)

Bearing in mind J. W. Marriott's famous statement, the level of employee satisfaction is an important issue for you as unit manager. Apart from the linkages with staff turnover, service quality and the concern to 'delight customers' requires service staff to actively deliver service that goes beyond predictable customer needs. Dissatisfied employees are unlikely to respond appropriately to customers.

Most branded hospitality retail organizations have instruments (questionnaires) for measuring employee satisfaction, however, these can be both infrequent and long-winded. In some cases the questionnaires are too complex to fill out and response rates from staff can be low.

An example of a questionnaire that is simple to use and analyse is given in Chapter 3. This provides a seven-point scale against which the employee responds to fifteen questions that have been selected to test the employee's attitudes to various employment factors.

Employees have a number of concerns that influence their motivation to work and, ultimately, their levels of satisfaction and commitment to the organization. There are many theories about motivation, but you need to think carefully about the nature of your relationship with your employees and the *different* views they have of work, their reasons for working and the rewards from working.

Like customers, your employees have expectations about work and to successfully manage them you need to keep in touch with these expectations regarding:

- pay and rewards
- shifts and working time
- relationships with managers
- relationships with fellow workers
- the levels of interest in the job
- what is a fair amount of effort
- the amount of commitment to the job.

Some organizations go so far as to call employees *internal customers*. The intention is to make the Marriott-type link, but this should not be overplayed. Employees are not customers. Their relationship with the organization is not that of a customer. They come to work to earn money to live, and for a cluster of other material, social and psychological benefits.

There is a natural conflict of interests between employees and employers, which has particular impact in service industries because:

1 Wages make a significant part of total service costs.
2 The labour element is often the most easy cost element to cut.
3 Operating profits can be expanded at the expense of employee incomes.

If you expect employees to be loyal, that loyalty has to be earned and it has to be seen as a two-sided arrangement. You need to be loyal to your employees and respect their needs.

Good communications

Developing a strong mutual understanding helps both you as a unit manager to understand employees and their needs, and employees to understand what they are doing and why. Clearly, the employee surveys identified above help in this process, but they tend to be a one-way form of communication which can be limited by response rates and by their ability to reflect the issues which really concern employees. The following are some suggestions for improving communications.

1 *Team meetings*, as outlined in Chapter 2, can be before or after service, or on a regular basis, preferably weekly. The more frequent the meetings the better the levels of communication. At their most effective they include everyone, and employees are paid to attend.

2 *Quality circles* or some form of representative group through which the staff can make suggestions is another way of getting staff involved in the business and overcoming problems. Again Chapter 2 has a more detailed outline of these arrangements. Whilst they do not involve all employees, they can help communicate issues to the staff as a whole through their representatives.

3 *Appraisal interviews* with individual members of staff need to be a regular feature of unit management. These can give you a chance to share understandings with staff members.

The key point about these and other processes for improving communication is that a shared mutual understanding is one of the foundations for the development of trust and loyalty. You must understand the need to keep employees informed and to build these mutually trusting relationships.

Pay and rewards

Research with employees shows that this is one of the most important causes of employee dissatisfaction and is a reason why people leave an organization. Clearly pay and money is not the only reward that employees get from work, but it is an important one which has to reflect their expectation if employees are to stay with an organization. It is one of the *tangible elements* of employment, a bit like comfortable beds or clean tables for customers, and pay is a basic requirement on which other aspects of employee satisfaction has to be built.

1 *Hourly rates* have to be in line with the local labour market. Employees soon know if pay rates can be bettered in another restaurant, or supermarket.

2 *Take-home pay* is made up of the hourly rate times the number of hours less any other stoppages or costs of employment that the employee has to make. The number of hours worked can be a particular problem for part-time or casual employees. If you cut back on the number of hours a part-time employee works, this will reduce their take-home pay and may cause dissatisfaction.

Whilst part-time employees allow you flexibility in employment, part-time staff who have constantly changing schedules have difficulties planning their income and personal lives. Irregular hours are one of the most common reasons given by part-time staff who leave hospitality firms.

3 *Incentive pay* is a feature of many hospitality retail firms. The intention is that employees work harder to achieve better sales or profits if they have a financial benefit from the achievement.

In some cases the extra benefits are linked to training and performance to standards. Whatever the objective the incentive will be most effective when it is achievable and valuable to the employee.

4 *Tips* can be a source of considerable extra income for employees, though they can also create tension and conflict amongst the team. Some organizations now actively discourage tipping, because it confuses customers and creates an impression that employees only give good service for money. If you allow tipping you need to consider the system by which tips are gained and shared amongst staff.

In addition to these monetary aspects to rewards, it is possible to reward staff with goods in kind, say letting them act as 'mystery customers' in other units in the brand. A free meal, drinks allowance or free weekend in another unit can be a mutually beneficial way of rewarding staff. Apart from the immediate benefit to the individual, by acting as customers they develop a better understanding of the service that they deliver.

Finally, praise and recognition of good work can be used to reward people for their effort. 'Thank you' costs nothing but can be very welcome to the individual employee.

Recruitment and selection

Recruiting the right employees with a clear view of what the job entails is the key to reducing staff turnover. As we have seen, high labour turnover is often fuelled by an induction crisis that, in part, is caused by sloppy recruitment and selection. Chapter 6 provides a more detailed outline of the approach, but the key elements for the reduction of staff turnover are:

1 *Forward planning* of recruitment is more likely to result in better recruitment of people who are likely to stay longer. Hurried recruitment is a major cause of subsequent staff turnover.

2 *Job description and person specification* should clearly define what the job entails and the sort of person needed to succeed in the job.

3 *Attracting the right sort of applicants* through advertising, agencies or 'word of mouth' from existing employees. There is no point in attracting applications from people who are unsuitable. Employee stability often can be built through 'word of mouth' from existing employees, thereby building a team of employees who know each other.

4 *Selection interviews* need to be carefully undertaken. Involving more than one manager or undertaking several interviews can help ensure that the right person is selected.

5 *Following up references* helps to ensure that the unit is recruiting people who will behave in a reasonable manner. The failure to follow up references is a frequent cause of staff problems, particularly where someone has a previous record of absenteeism or even theft.

Induction and orientation

Systematic recruitment and selection of new staff needs to be followed by a formal induction and orientation programme. As we have seen, the induction crisis is a common cause of staff turnover. Joining any new organization can be stressful enough. Staff who are 'thrown in at the deep end' and given minimal training or introduction to the organization or the work involved, face additional pressure and many people avoid the pressure by running away from it – by leaving. Chapter 7 deals with these issues in more detail, but if staff turnover is to be minimized you need to consider the following points:

- Plan the start day or time to avoid a busy service period
- Consider pretraining before the first work period.
- Use a 'buddy system' to help ease the new employee into the team.
- Carefully plan the first shifts to avoid undue pressure.
- Check with the individual about his or her experiences and problems.
- Encourage other team members to welcoming and helpful.

Training and development

Training individuals to be effective in their job has an immediate benefit in that it removes the pressure that incompetence or inexperience can add to the individual. Pretraining, in particular can give the individual skills that help them to deliver better customer service and productivity from the start. Research shows that people who are trained prior to their first shift are more productive more quickly than those who receive no formal training. For the individual, training represents an investment in them as an individual, and is likely to encourage staff to stay with the organization, particularly if a formal programme of training can be shown to link to promotion and career development.

Supervision and management style

Chapter 2 has outlined a case for careful consideration of employee empowerment. By building up employees' sense of personal worth and self-effectiveness, they will add value and quality to the service provided to customers. Recognizing the benefit that employees can contribute will have the added impact of encouraging staff to stay in an environment where they feel valued, thereby reducing levels of staff turnover. Similarly, if you treat employees as though they are worthless and adopt an overly autocratic style of management it is likely to add to the pressure to leave. Effective unit supervision and management attempts to reduce the effects of push and pull factors.

Example 5.2

The Wise Owl Hotel: causes

Interviews with new recruits and management confirmed that there was little by way of a formal induction programme. Staff were frequently set to work alongside whoever was the most experienced person on duty at the time. Consequently, the degree of coaching and assistance given by individuals to new employees varied considerably. Many individuals felt anxious about the pressure and responsibility, and were too frightened to ask questions. Interviews with former employees stated that these levels of anxiety pushed them to leave the hotel during this initial period.

The number of dismissals from the organization also suggests a problem with recruitment and selection of staff. Twenty-five employees were dismissed from the hotel. In two cases the individuals were managers brought in to manage the hotel during the owner's absence who were not properly briefed about the limits of their authority, and were subsequently dismissed for making unauthorized changes to the business. In the other twenty-three cases dismissal was due to a cluster of factors. In most cases, problems were associated with behaviour and orientation to work. In one case an employee was dismissed for theft, and it subsequently emerged that he had been dismissed from his former employer for a similar reason. This case was typical. Not one reference was requested for a new recruit during the whole period of the study.

The hotel had neither job descriptions nor person specifications available to help in the recruitment process. Those undertaking the selection process had no formal record from which to check potential recruits' skills and orientations to work. The lack of a formal definition of the duties and responsibilities for job and skills required by those undertaking the role had a number of consequences related to labour turnover at the hotel. Apart from the problem associated with managerial judgements in selecting people with the appropriate qualities to do the job, new recruits themselves were not given enough information to understand what the job entailed. Several former employees confirmed that the job was not what they expected it to be. Flowing from this, the lack of job descriptions and job specifications also meant that management had no instrument to appraise individual employee performance, or devise an appropriate training plan where performance was found to be deficient.

Of the fifty-seven leavers during the period of the study, thirty-two employees left voluntarily. Not surprisingly, career advancement was the most common reason given. Research shows that many employees use this explanation as a screen for the real reason(s) for leaving. Interviews with former employees confirmed that pay and hours of work, together with a lack of training opportunities represented the largest number of reasons for voluntary labour turnover.

A review of competing establishments revealed that full-time rates in the Wise Owl Hotel were as much as £20 per week below local rates of pay in other hotels. Part-time rates were not so far behind, but were at the low end of local rates. Many part-timers resented having to clock off during break times. The pay and hours issue revealed different experiences for full- and part-time employees. For full-timers, 'it's as though they are trying to squeeze every last drop of energy from you'. On average full-time waiting staff worked fifty to fifty-five hours per week. The part-timers were sent home often even when there was work still to complete. Some complained of being sent home after just one hour of a shift period, because the management felt they were 'no longer needed'. The tendency to reduce staffing levels was a general source of dissatisfaction for many employees. Perhaps not surprisingly in these circumstances, many employees sought alternative employment that would give them better pay and conditions of employment.

Interviews with both former and current employees registered concerns about training and promotion prospects at the hotel. The last two senior appointments had been made from outside the organization and several staff registered a sense that they were unlikely to be promoted in the organization. The only formal training being offered at the hotel was for trainee chefs who were enrolled on part-time courses at the local college. For the remaining staff, no opportunities were offered for qualifications such as National Vocational Qualifications, nor were there any other opportunities to develop themselves within the organization. If these employees reflect findings that hotel employees have strong positive ambitions, then the only opportunities for development appear to be outside the Wise Owl Hotel.

Interviews with management revealed a failure to draw the obvious conclusions from their own experience and difficulties. The longest serving employee had been employed at the hotel for four years and he had been sent on the chef's training course at the local college. The hotel management's investment in the individual's development had contributed to his loyalty to the hotel. Similarly, interviews with managers revealed concern about the general lack of skilled personnel in the hospitality industry. Recent appointments to the post of Head Chef and Restaurant Manager had been as a result of 'poaching' staff from competitor organizations, and consequent high salaries being paid to the individuals. When pressed, senior managers did not recognize a responsibility to train their own employees. They felt that other employers would in turn poach their trained staff. There was no recognition that training and the offer of career opportunities to employees would contribute to a reduction in labour turnover.

Conclusion

In many ways the Wise Owl Hotel represents an employment relationship typical of many firms in the hospitality industry. Employers working in environments where demand is subject to rapid fluctuation and labour represents a significant proportion of total cost, manage the workforce in a way that maximizes direct managerial control. Labour costs in such business do represent an element that is the most manipulatable for managers. So the policy of reducing part-time hours and extracting as much effort from full-timers as possible appears to be rational.

However, this takes little account of some fundamental industrial relations issues. As individuals, these employees have limited opportunities to formally challenge the power of the employer. That said, employees are not totally without opportunities to resist their employer, though these take a more individualized form. Absenteeism, lateness, poor performance, theft and, ultimately, withdrawal are all options which are typical of this kind of relationship. Thus the policy to maximize the exploitation of labour is short sighted and costly. The resulting employee frustration and subsequent labour turnover represent a considerable extra cost to the business. Managers are largely unaware of these extra costs because they have no system of recording or monitoring trends in labour turnover or the costs it incurs.

Whilst there are inevitable tensions in the employment relationship – an income for one is a cost to the other – most progressive employers understand that loyalty is a 'two-way street'. Employers expecting loyal employee behaviour must in turn be loyal and fair to their employees. Providing people with fair incomes and with some justice in the way they are treated is not a major challenge to profits and taking a longer view might even enhance them.

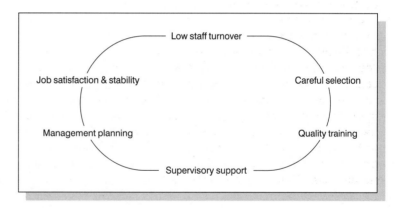

Figure 5.4
The virtuous cycle of staff turnover

At the most basic level, as unit manager you must keep records, monitor performance and account for the costs of turnover in different sections of the business. You need to move to a virtuous cycle, as shown in Figure 5.4 – careful recruitment, selection and induction leading to good quality training, and increased supervisor support, improved management communication, increased job satisfaction and stability; and low labour turnover.

Reflection and practice

Answer these questions to check your understanding of this chapter:

1 Using the case study (Chapter 14) identify the causes of staff turnover in this situation.
2 What steps would you take to reduce it?
3 What priorities would you make for action over the next three months?
4 Make a case for costing the value of employees into an assessment of unit performance.
5 What measure might you use?
6 Some managers argue that high staff turnover is a price worth paying for low labour costs and increased profits: (a) prepare arguments in support of this view; (b) prepare arguments opposing this view.

Reference

Institute of Personnel and Development (1997). *IPD Labour Turnover – 1997 Survey Results*. Institute of Personnel and Development.

Further reading

Argyle, M. (1989). *The Social Psychology of Work*. Penguin.

Boella, M. (1996). *Human Resource Management in the Hospitality Industry*. Stanley Thornes.

Goss-Turner, S. (1989). *Managing People in the Hotel and Catering Industry*. Croner.

Johnson, K. (1986). Labour turnover in hotels: an update. *Service Industries Journal*, **6** (3), 362–380.

Maghurn, J. P. (1989). *A Manual of Staff Management in the Hotel and Catering Industry*. Heinemann.

Mullins, L. J. (1995) *Hospitality Management: A Human Resource Approach*. Pitman.

Roberts, J. (1995). *Human Resource Practices in the Hospitality Industry*. Hodder and Stoughton.

Rothwell, S. (1980). *Labout Turnover its Costs Causes and Control*. Gower.

CHAPTER 6

Staff recruitment and selection

After working through this chapter you should be able to:

- identify the main sources of recruits
- plan and organize staff recruitment
- plan and organize staff selection
- conduct a selection interview.

You cannot train nice

Staff recruitment and selection is important in hospitality service organizations. The ability to attract and recruit people who have a 'natural' affinity with customers is particularly important for frontline staff, and whilst staff performance can be improved by customer care programmes, the essential qualities are related to the individual's personality and commitment to providing good service.

Careful recruitment and selection is also important to reduce staff turnover and disciplinary problems and to improve employee satisfaction. You need to take the time to select the right person to match the needs of the job and who will fit in with the rest of your team. Staff recruitment and selection can occupy a large part of a unit manager's time, particularly where there are high levels of staff turnover. Under time pressures, it is tempting to reduce the effort put into recruitment and selection, but this is often a false economy because it creates problems.

Before starting the recruitment and selection process it is necessary to think about the job the new employee will do and the person needed to do it. Many managers in hospitality retail operations make problems for themselves because they fail, when recruiting employees, to understand the importance of careful planning and the needs of the new recruits. The first step involves thinking about the duties and responsibilities of the job and skills needed to be successful in it. The second considers new recruits, their motives for becoming an employee and their needs in both the early stages of employment and beyond.

Flexible employees

The demand for hospitality services varies through time. In some cases, these variations can be predicted – different days of the week have different sales levels, for example Monday is quiet and Saturday is busy; January has a low level of sales, but December is busy. It is not unusual for these variations to be dramatically different so 50 per cent of the weekly sales occur on Friday and Saturday, or 50 per cent of annual sales occur in November and December. In other cases, the variations are difficult to predict – changes in weather conditions result in higher or lower than normal sales.

In all cases, you need to be able to call on sufficient staff to meet the demand. That means:

- being able to get more staff in busy times
- having fewer staff when sales are lower.

Planning future needs is discussed further in Chapter 8. However, recruiting for the future and deciding how flexible labour needs will be managed is essential. Traditionally, hospitality managers have managed this problem by having a 'numerical flexibility' – lots of staff available to be brought in when needed. Typically, full-time staff numbers have been kept to a minimum and restricted to the more 'skilled' employees, supported by extra employees as needed:

1 *Regular part-time staff*: working regularly for the pub or restaurant on varied number of hours each week depending on the needs of the business.

2 *Temporary/short-term staff*: usually working on a full-time basis for a fixed term – to meet the demands of a busy period or planned staff absence.

3 *Casual staff*: infrequent employees who work during the busiest periods. In some cases they are used for specific types of demand – banquets or parties.

4 *Agency staff*: these people work for an agency or contractor who supplies staff to meet planned or unplanned shortages.

These varied sources have allowed managers to meet staffing needs whilst limiting the financial commitment to employing staff when demand for the unit's services were low. However there are some difficulties caused by this approach:

- Employee commitment to the service, customers and organization may be lower.

- Employee incomes may vary and create dissatisfaction.

- It can lead to higher labour turnover.

- Skill levels may be low because of limited investment in training.

- Service quality may suffer.

- It may lead to reduced productivity and sales per hour.

- Customer repeats are reduced because of increased customer dissatisfaction.

One way round some of these problems is to recruit more full-time employees, but create a more flexible workforce through wide skills training. 'Functional flexibility' results in a more flexible workforce through being able to employ staff in a variety of roles as the demand for the business varies. This will be discussed more fully in Chapter 7.

The main point here is that whatever the form of the employment relationship – full time, part time, temporary or casual – the selection and recruitment process needs to be planned and the steps laid out in this chapter carefully followed. *Ultimately your customers will judge the quality of service on the basis of their experience; they are not interested in the employee's terms of employment.*

The local market for labour

Irrespective of the manner of the employment relationship – full time, part time and so on – recruitment does not take place in a vacuum. Hospitality retail employers are usually competing with other service sector employers for labour and any one business may be recruiting similar people to those recruited by:

- supermarkets
- shops and stores
- other hospitality employers
- offices
- call centres etc.

As we saw in Chapter 5, hospitality retailers who do not at least match the terms and conditions of their competitors for labour may contribute to push factors which lead to employee dissatisfaction with your employment. Similarly, if you are aware of local competitor conditions it is possible to draw up a reward package that creates 'pull' factors for you to attract staff.

Active learning point

Choose a hospitality retail unit known to you and in the table below list the other local organizations competing for the same potential employees

Competitor organization	Approximate annual recruitment	Training and development provided	Pay and benefits provided
1			
2			
3			
4			
5			
6			
7			
8			
9			
10			

Hospitality, Leisure & Tourism Series

The supply of employees

As with all markets, the market for labour in any local area will be a by-product of supply and demand. Thus your ability to attract enough staff of the right quality and characteristics depends on the competition from other firms *and* a cluster of factors which influence the total supply of labour in that market.

1 *Levels of unemployment and employment* represent a major factor in hospitality services labour markets. In areas where unemployment is low, recruitment into hospitality retail organizations can be difficult.

2 *The industry profile* in the area may result in fewer or more potential recruits being available even within any given level of unemployment. It has been difficult to recruit people into hospitality retail operations where local employment has been based on 'heavy' industry. Understanding the potential difficulties can help you to be more focused in your efforts to recruit people in these circumstances.

3 *Participation rates* of people in the labour market varies between areas and regions of the country. Where more women and young people participate in employment as well as men, the potential supply of labour will be greater. The participation rate also varies over the year, as some people want to take on a second job to earn extra money for Christmas or summer holidays. Recognizing the ebb and flow of interest in second jobs can help you to attract people for fixed terms to meet particular difficulties.

4 *Where people* live in relation to the unit and the associated ease of transport to the site will be a factor. Late night working in a remote part of town may restrict potential recruits to those with personal transport. Mapping the major housing estates and transport systems can help build a picture.

5 *Educational establishments* such as secondary schools, further education colleges and universities can all provide useful sources of part-time, temporary and casual labour. Making contacts with significant staff members in schools and colleges can help to improve communications between you and potential employees.

The importance of planning ahead

The more planned and carefully undertaken the recruitment and selection process, the more likely you are to be successful in selecting employees who stay with you and who make a contribution to the unit. Hurried recruitment invariably leads to difficulties later.

As the unit manager you need to think forward over the next few weeks to consider your recruitment needs. Planning ahead means that you will have the employees in place, trained with the right skills when they are needed. Here are some of the points to build into the plan:

1 *Future peaks in demand*: the Christmas build-up, or some other period when sales are above the norm and extra staff are needed.

2 *Holiday arrangements*: when staff take planned annual holidays there is a need for staff to cover absent employees.

3 *Staff turnover*: creates an ongoing demand for replacement staff. Often it is more cost-effective to recruit replacement staff in batches to match the predicted loss, though as Chapter 5 shows, staff turnover is costly and wasteful.

4 *Planned retirements and departures on maternity leave, etc.*: will create some vacancies that have to be filled. They are predictable, and need to be planned into the recruitment process.

It is important to consider the process of recruiting new employees and the time taken to develop an effective performer. Issues such as the time taken to recruit, the number of applicants needed on average, the number of interviews needed, the induction period and training programme all need to be considered. The more time these steps take, the more time you have to plan into the process of planning for the future.

Successful recruitment is unhurried and systematic. The following sections take you through the key steps: considering the job, type of person needed, how to attract applicants, and selection and induction.

Describing the job to be done

Even in the smallest units it is necessary to consider the work to be done by the recruits. By thinking carefully about the job and what has to be undertaken, you will be in a much stronger position to recruit a person who will be able make an effective contribution.

The job description

Start with the job, not the jobholder or the terms and conditions under which they will be employed. The job description should include the following broad headings:

- Job title, department and location: gives the job a name and position.
- Job function: what the job is about.

Hospitality, Leisure & Tourism Series

- Job superior: to whom will the jobholder answer?

- Job subordinates: which jobs will the holder supervise?

- Relationships with others: non-hierarchical relationships.

- Main duties: what is done.

- Occasional duties: what is done now and then.

- Limits to authority: what the jobholder can/cannot decide.

In the following example the duties and other details are written in a way that describe the job and the relationship between it and other jobs. When preparing these documents it is important to consider the job and what you want the jobholder to do. The main duties are described using active verbs. It is a good idea to show the job description to a current jobholder to check whether the job description correctly describes the job as it is being done now – organizations are dynamic and jobs change. See the example in Figure 6.1.

Finally, in all cases you should consider *empowerment*. Could the jobholder be more empowered? In the example in Figure 6.1, could the employee be empowered to sign for goods and consult with the Head Chef over damaged goods and deficiencies?

Job title, department and location	Kitchen Assistant, kitchens in the Dog and Duck
Job function	Simple food preparation in the kitchen
Job superior	The Head Chef
Job subordinates	None
Relationships with others	Delivery staff (food and dry goods) Food service staff
Main duties	1. Assist daily in the initial preparation of the kitchen. 2. Prepare cold food as required by the chef. 3. Assist with preparation of meals. 4. Pass to wash-up or return to stores equipment used in food preparation. 5. Clean and tidy food stores. 6. Assist with unloading kitchen supplies.
Occasional duties	1. Check the quantity and quality of goods received. 2. Assist chef with stock-taking 3. Assist with service as required
Limits to authority	The jobholder is not authorized to sign for goods. Deficiencies or damaged goods must be reported to the Head Chef.

Figure 6.1

Example of a job description for a kitchen assistant

Describing the ideal recruit

Many managers make mistakes in the recruitment of staff because they do not carefully consider the ideal person to be able to undertake the job as outlined in the job description. A well thought out job description helps you to think about the person needed – his or her background and prior experience, education and training, and personality and characteristics.

Drawing up a *staff specification* helps to prepare for the recruitment process. This should be written down, but needs to be done carefully because you need to make sure you are not applying prejudices to the processes – that is, making assumptions which are unfounded. In some cases you may not be able to recruit the ideal person but will need to build the necessary profile through training and further development. The following are some of the categories to be considered:

- Physical make-up: age, appearance, build, health, speech, eyesight. (*Note*: it may be possible to justify a specific sex, e.g. for lavatory attendant, but be careful.)

- Education and training: school qualifications and grades, further or higher education, recognized skills programme (e.g. NVQs), other qualifications or training.

- Work experience: experience in industry, specific industry or sector, similar type of work, work in related sector with transferable skills, responsibilities for people or money.

- Personality: sociability and extraversion, empathy, honesty, stability, leadership, etc.

- Personal circumstances: requirement to work, requirement to work shifts, requirement to live in/out.

Whilst compiling this list of factors it is important to remember the requirement in law and in practice to offer *equal opportunities*. Openly discriminating on the grounds of gender, ethnicity or religion is illegal. However, a good unit manager works beyond the legislation to ensure that all employees and potential employees are treated equally and fairly. Thus, when selecting criteria for inclusion in the staff specification, you must be sure the criteria are genuine requirements of the job to be done, because it is possible to be guilty of *indirect discrimination*, that is, selecting job requirements which by definition exclude people who are capable of effective performance.

Not all the desirable qualities are of equal importance and it is useful to list them under headings that show how desirable or essential they are. It is possible to build up knowledge and skills through training and development. Again, careful consideration

	Essential	Desirable
Physical make-up		
Age	Over 18	20–45
Appearance	Clean	Smart and well groomed, hair and hands important
Health	No record of *notifiable diseases*	Lively and energetic
Speech	Speaks with clarity	
Education and training		
School	Able to read and write and do simple calculations	Able to check invoices and delivery notes
Skills training		NVQ I and II in food preparation and cookery or equivalent
Work experience		
In hospitality industry	Worked in food preparation, over 2 years' experience.	Worked in food preparation in licensed retailing operation
Personality		
Stability	Polite, not easily flustered	Cheerful disposition
Honesty	Evidence of high standards of honesty from past employers	
Personal circumstances		
	Able to work to full range of shift duties through the year	

Figure 6.2
Staff specification for a kitchen assistant

of the essential requirements helps you to be focused in the selection process. See the example of a staff specification in Figure 6.2.

The main point in drawing up the staff specification is to think carefully about those requirements that really are essential for the job. You want to end up with a list which helps you to define the sort of person who can do the job, but which also does not exclude people who in reality could be effective.

Thinking about the sort of person needed also leads to thoughts about:

• how you will check the person's qualities and abilities

• the selection process

• the best sources of this type of applicant.

Active learning point

Using what you know about the operations featured in this book, make a list of the source of employees and the recruitment processes most likely to recruit frontline employees in McDonald's Restaurants Limited, TGI Friday Restaurants, and Harvester Restaurants.

Hospitality retailer	Source of recruits and the recruitment process
McDonald's Restaurants Limited	
TGI Friday Restaurants	
Harvester Restaurants	

Attracting candidates

Once you have decided on the duties of the job to be filled and the sort of person required, you need to consider the best source of likely candidates before considering the best processes required to select them. The aim of attracting applicants is to attract a sufficient number to make the appointment of the ideal candidate(s) likely.

- Too many applicants is as problematic as too few.
- The aim must be to attract suitable applicants.

Sources of applicants

Candidates will be attracted from the local labour market and the following lists represent some common means of communicating with potential applicants to inform them of job vacancies. As with all advertising, the more targeted and accurate the message, the more it will appeal to the most suitable applicants. Vague, misleading and dishonest descriptions of the job or person needed are always counterproductive.

Hospitality, Leisure & Tourism Series

Internal sources of applicants come from within your unit and might include:

- Internal promotions – help to build staff morale and show that employees can progress if they stay with you.

- Present staff who are on temporary, casual or part-time contracts who wish to become full-time employees. As above, this has a motivational benefit, but also you will have a better knowledge of the person than of an external applicant.

- Current staff recommend an individual known to them (family/friends). Again this might lead to a better knowledge of the new recruit. It is cheaper because advertising costs are reduced. However, there is usually an introduction fee to the staff member and a danger of setting up cliques in the workforce.

- Notices and posters on your premises – customers or customer contacts may be a source of potential employees. Relatively inexpensive, though there may be issues about the impression created by ongoing staff turnover. Also some units discourage customers to be employees, others see it as a benefit.

- Records of previous applicants – it is not unusual for the recruitment process to attract more suitable candidates than there are vacancies. It is a good idea to keep the details of these applicants on record so that you can contact them when another vacancy comes up. Consistent interest in working in the unit might be an indicator of future stability.

External sources of applicants come from outside your unit and might include:

- *Newspaper advertising* is in local newspapers, though some management and skilled craft jobs may recruit from a national labour market. The main benefit is that the advertisement will be seen by a large number of people who might be interested in the job. These can take the form of box advertisements, or classified ads. The former are more expensive and best reserved for a major recruitment campaign.

- *Local radio* gives a good coverage and could be used for a major recruitment campaign – say, opening a new unit – but is likely to be too expensive for ongoing recruitment for one unit.

- *Job Centres* and other state employment agencies can provide a permanent, generally low-cost source of applicants. Commercial recruitment agencies are used in some cases, but are usually regarded as too expensive for most frontline staff.

- *Posters and notices* in shop windows or local clubs are usually low cost and visible to people who live in the immediate area.

- *Direct mail shots* to local housing estates. These are again local to the unit and relatively cheap. Often used for openings and relaunches.

- *Universities and colleges* in your locality are a good source of employees. Students on hospitality, leisure or tourism programmes are worth prioritizing, but most students provide a valuable source of potential recruits. It is worth contacting course leaders or careers officers, and the Student Union.

- *Schools careers teachers* are also a good source of recruits both for young people finishing their schooling and looking for permanent employment and for continuing students requiring part-time, casual and temporary employment. Work experience sessions can also be a good source of recruits – many courses have two- or three-week periods to gain work familiarization. Hospitality retail managers can use these sessions to promote careers in their organization.

Time spent cultivating contacts with significant people in these local organizations will prove to be a valuable investment for the future. This is a particular need in hospitality retail organizations experiencing rapid staff turnover. As we have seen, high staff turnover is expensive but a fact of life in some units, and ensuring that you have a strong supply of potential labour is important.

Advertising

Many of the sources of external recruitment available to you as unit manager will be from outside the unit. In some cases, material will be supplied from head office, and you will not be able to spend much money on advertising – perhaps only a display advertisement in the local newspaper. However, whatever the medium, you will be advised to consider some general pointers to successful job advertising.

- *Attract* the attention of the potential applicant. Usually this would boldly show the job title (Kitchen Assistant), or person type you are looking for (Bright young person). Make sure that this key factor is prominent and cannot be missed.

- *Interest* the person once you have attracted their attention. Tell them the who, what, where of the job and the name of the company. Briefly describe the purpose of the job and where it is located, and provide a brief outline of the person needed, the salary, and the opportunities for advancement. You want to both attract suitable applicants and discourage those who are unsuitable.

- *Desire*. You are trying to make the advertisement stimulate a desire in the reader to do something about following up the advertisement. It is here that many go wrong. In some cases the advertisements are just plain boring, in others there is a strong temptation to oversell the job and provide inaccurate information.

- *Action*. Provide instructions as to how the advertisement needs to be followed up – a telephone number or an address so they can apply for an application form. An obvious point, but this is a common error in many advertisements.

Figures 6.3–6.5 show examples of advertisements for hospitality staff.

TRENDY CAFE BARS
invite applications for

TRAINEE MANAGERS

This fast growing bar and restaurant group is looking to develop young people as future managers for planned new cafe bars.

The company is looking for graduates, preferably with a licensed retail or hospitality management qualification. Applicants are invited from candidates who are at least 20 years old and have some work experience in the hospitality retailing business.

The company provides a structured and tailored training programme designed to develop your skills and talents. Typically the training programme covers all aspects of the operation but is flexible to meet the needs of each individual. All management trainees undertake the Professional Diploma in Hospitality Retail Management awarded by Leeds Metropolitan University as part of the training programme. Trainee Managers receive a staring salary of £15,000 per annum as well as company health insurance. Trainee managers work a guaranteed 40 hour week and are entitled to a minimum of 25 days paid holiday in addition to statutory holidays.

Contact the following person for an application form and further details:

Adrian Smith, Management Development Manager, Trendy Cafe Bars, The Retail Park, Luton LU3 9HG. Tel. 0196 121212.

Display advertisement

Figure 6.3
Example of advertisement for hospitality staff

Figure 6.4
Example of advertisement for
hospitality staff

> **Bar Staff Required** at the Trendy Cafe Bar, High Street, Nottingham. Full and part-time staff wanted. No experience needed. All staff are trained leading to the National Bartenders Certificate. Good pay (above national minimum rate) and bonuses available. Good chances of promotion and development. For more information speak to John Brown - the Manager on 0115 980 2264.

Classified advertisement

Figure 6.5
Example of advertisement for
hospitality staff

HEAD CHEF
required

For busy cafe bar restaurant. Restaurant seats over 100 covering substantial lunch and dinner periods. Menu based on modern English cuisine and includes a substantial pub food operation.

Applications welcomed from experienced and qualified candidates who are at least 24 years of age. Good pay plus performance and loyalty bonuses.

Kitchen team includes four full-time staff and six part-time employees. The successful candidate must be able to lead and motivate the team and have a proven record in training and developing a team. Ability to control food costs and to work within agreed budgets.

Apply in writing to

**John Brown Manager
Trendy Cafe Bar
High Street Nottingham**

Semi-display advertisement

Gathering information about applicants

The advertising process will invite interested people to formally apply for the position. In most cases the information about candidates is gathered through an application form, because this enables you to get information about each candidate that will assist in filtering those candidates who appear to meet the staff specification requirements.

The application form needs to be structured in a way that is simple to fill in and allows candidates to communicate the information that you require to decide on their suitability:

- name
- address
- gender
- age
- education and training
- past work experience
- other interests
- personal circumstances
- names and addresses of references.

The application form must be laid out so that the information needed for the decision to progress with the application is easily seen, and most importantly, has been provided by the applicant. A clear layout which asks the candidate unambiguous questions is essential. A common mistake is that application forms do not allow sufficient space for applicants to fill in all their details, and it contains vague questions.

The application only provides part of the information and in most cases, the final selection is based on an interview and other selection techniques that help you to understand the applicants sufficiently well to make a selection.

Making a short list

The applications received need to be considered so that you can decide on those applicants who match, or nearly match, the staff specification. The applications can be sorted in a systematic way by comparing each application with the staff specification criteria using a matrix. This allows you to see how each candidate compares with the requirements outlined in the staff specification, and also allows comparison between candidates. Table 6.1 provides an example of such a matrix for applications received for a post. The example here suggests a code system with + indicating whether the candidate meets the 'essential requirements' and ++ the 'desirable requirements'.

Candidates	Age, etc.	Education and training	Work experience	Personal circumstances
Brown	+	++	++	+
Green	++	++	+	
White	+	+		+
Black	+		++	+
Pink	++	++	++	+
Grey	++	++	++	+
Olive	+	+	+	+
Purple	+	+	++	

Table 6.1 Example of a short listing matrix for a kitchen assistant

In the above example, Pink and Grey are clearly worth interviewing as they are both qualified, have the work experience, are of the preferred age group and are able to work shifts. Brown also might be worth interviewing because the candidate matches all but the desired age criteria. The candidate might be a little younger than desired but may have other strengths. Similarly, Black is underqualified but meets other criteria. This candidate might be worthy of further consideration, perhaps holding on the reserve list?

Making the selection

The aim of the selection process is to continue the process of finding out about the candidates so that the judgement whether to recruit or not is based on as sound information as possible. Usually, the selection of staff to work in hospitality retail units occurs after a simple interview with the manager, but there are alternatives that might be worth considering.

One-to-one interviews

The unit manager, or a deputy, interviews the candidates one by one on his or her own. The process uses less in management time, but the weakness is that just one person's judgement is involved. It is possible for the interviewer to miss an important aspect of the interviewee's qualities or to apply personal prejudices.

Two or more interviewers

The interview is conducted with one or more interviewers – unit manager plus deputy. Here the purpose is to bring in a wide range of perceptions and skills on which to base the selection. In some cases, one person is asking questions whilst the other person observes and makes notes. This method is more costly of management time but results in some safeguards against individual prejudices. Managers involved in the selection process are more likely to support the selection made. Interviewees can find this type of interview more intimidating, particularly if there are more than three interviewers. This form of interview may be subject to collective prejudice, particularly where one of the interviewers is forceful.

More than one interview

In some cases, where there are many suitable candidates, managers may conduct a first round of interviews from which a short list of candidates is selected for a second round of interviews – frequently on another day. This form of selection is costly of management and candidates time. Usually this approach is applied in the selection of skilled staff or management personnel. The benefit is that more applicants are seen, and the selection is ultimately made on the basis of candidate's performance on two occasions. In other cases more than one interview might be arranged on the same day, with a different purpose to each interview or a different person interviewing candidates in each interview. Again the benefits are increased exposure to the candidates, and more managers' opinions are involved in the selection process.

Role plays

Here the intention is to invite the candidate to deal with a situation, or give a performance, which helps to reveal more about the person in non-interview situations. Popular examples involve asking the person to deal with a customer complaint in which the manager acts as the disgruntled customer. In other cases candidates are invited to sing a song or tell a joke. The organization of role plays and the evaluation of performance usually involve more than one manager. This approach is more costly, because candidates go through an interview process as well as the role plays. The key benefit is in providing a wider set of behaviours and information about the candidate.

Personality/aptitude test

Personality tests and aptitude tests both aim to supply further information about the candidates upon which the decision to recruit can be made. Personality tests vary but some of the issues explored in Chapter 4 can be measured with these tests. For example, it is possible to measure the various dimensions of *extraversion and introversion* and the dimensions of *stability and instability* through personality tests. Similarly, aptitude tests are designed to measure a person's general abilities and suitability for certain types of work. The problem with both these sets of measures is that, whilst they both appear to be 'scientific', these tests are not foolproof predictors of future work performance. It is possible for performance to be affected by other factors external to the individual, and it is also possible for a person who is familiar with the tests to give answers which are not true reflections of their personality or abilities. However, used in support of other selection techniques they can be a valuable aid to decision-making.

References

References supplied by previous employers or character witnesses are an important part of the selection process. Example 5.2 in Chapter 5 reveals a frequently made error, that is, not following up the references of selected candidates prior to employment. In the case quoted several people were recruited who had poor records with previous employers. Clearly, written references can be somewhat bland, but even in these cases they are better than nothing, and can be supported with a telephone call to the former employer. The most common practice is to follow up references after the selection interview, though some managers do ask for references before the interview. In the latter case, existing employers may be unaware of the applicant's intention to apply for a position with another firm, and this can cause difficulties. However, information from references can be useful when making a selection between candidates.

Whilst references are generally invaluable some caution needs to be shown, because references can be subject to bias.

- In the majority of cases, employers are loath to give explicitly damning criticism of employees.

- In some cases, they may even provide overly complimentary comments about an employee whom they wish get rid of.

- In other cases, the negative feelings created when an employee leaves may lead the employer to be unfairly critical of the employee.

Selection interviews

As shown earlier, the selection interview aims to obtain more information about candidates so that you are better able to make a satisfactory selection. In many ways people feel more comfortable with the judgements that they make in an interview than is justified by experience. There are several flaws with the interview:

- You are making judgements about people after only a short time.

- People give performances in a formal interview and these may not be a true reflection of their work performance.

- The formal situation may make people nervous and limit their performance.

- The interview relies on subjective judgement and may involve the 'halo effect' or a prejudice.

Some of these difficulties can be addressed through having several colleagues in the interview process, and by making the judgement through a wide range of sources of information.

Prior to the interview

1 You have identified and invited all other managers who will be involved in the interviews.

2 You have identified the interview process, test and role plays to be used in the selection of applicants.

3 Make sure you have read through all the candidate's application forms and identified issues that need to be explored with each candidate.

4 You have identified a quiet room for interview that will be free from interruptions.

5 You have allocated sufficient time for each interview and invited the candidates to attend at the appropriate time.

6 You have considered the room layout and style of the interview to be used.

During the interview

1 Stick strictly to the time allocated – poor timekeeping creates a bad impression.

2 First introduce yourself and other interviewers, and help the person to relax.

3 Explain the interview and selection process, particularly as to when they will hear the result.

4 Adopt a relaxed and friendly manner.

5 Start with easy general questions.

6 Ask open-ended questions – these encourage interviewees to talk.

7 Listen carefully to answers and pick up on issues that arise.

8 Always create the impression that you are interested in the candidate and are genuinely concerned to give the candidate a fair chance.

9 Provide an opportunity for the candidate to ask questions.

10 Recognize that the interview is a two-way process and that you want to leave each candidate with a good impression of the organization.

11 Close the interview on time and in an orderly manner, and ensure that the candidate understands what will happen next.

After the interview

1 Make notes about the candidate – again a scoring system can be used to help make the selection.

2 If more than one interviewer is involved confer with the others to decide on the candidate to be selected.

3 If you have not called for references earlier, arrange for references – when these have arrived confirm the candidate (or reconsider in the light of the references).

4 Write to successful applicant confirming the appointment and providing joining instructions.

The selection and recruitment process has to be conducted in a fair and legal manner. The following is a list of some of the laws that can apply during the process. This is not an exhaustive list, but includes the main legislation.

- The Asylum and Immigration Act, 1996

- The Disability Discrimination Act, 1995

- The Equal Pay Act, 1970

- The Employment Protection (Consolidation) Act, 1978

- The Employment Act, 1980

- The Race Relations Act, 1976

- The Sex Discrimination Act, 1975

Once the selected candidate starts you need to plan an induction programme so that the employee is eased into the new job and helped to be quickly effective.

New employee induction programmes

A surprising number of employers fail to provide induction training for new employees. The example of the Wise Owl Hotel in Chapter 5 is in many ways typical of many firms in the hospitality industry: poor selection and recruitment practices – no induction, no training, low-quality working practices and high levels of staff turnover. Induction training, in particular, can help to overcome one important feature of staff turnover, the induction crisis – the tendency for many new recruits to leave within a short period of joining the firm.

An induction programme:

- helps to overcome the early learning phase where the new employee feels incompetent

- assists the new employee to be accepted by existing staff and to make friends

- helps the new employee to feel part of the organization.

The benefits of providing induction training to the unit are that it:

- helps reduce customer service problems when new employees are learning

- increases productivity levels as new employee become effective more quickly

- demonstrates statutory duties for safe and hygienic working practices.

All new employees, irrespective of whether they are working full time, part time, temporarily or on a casual basis, need an induction programme. As individuals they still have the same needs to quickly be accepted by the organization, and as new employees you need to assist them to be effective as quickly as possible. When planning the induction programme it is necessary to consider the information and experiences needed to help them settle in and how to give the information. Generally, induction programmes are best planned over a period of time. It is a mistake to provide too much information on the first day. Good induction programmes occur over the first few weeks.

Before the new employee starts work ● ● ●

The interview should start the process, because the candidate should be told of the processes involved in recruitment – when the job will commence, where they will be working, the type of job, the hours, pay and conditions. All this can then be confirmed in writing in a letter of appointment. Many firms also provide staff handbooks that provide useful information including the company's various policies – health and safety, training and employee development, etc.

On the first day of work • • •

It is important to remember that all new recruits are likely to feel nervous about starting a new job, and the main aim is to put them at their ease. Too much pressure and inadequate preparation for work stresses are key reasons for staff turnover. Make sure the new person knows where the main facilities they will need are located. It is a good idea to provide the new recruit with a 'buddy', to help them fit in and show how things work. A basic programme on health and safety practices and basic hygiene is also useful at this stage. Though practice varies, induction is most effective when the new employee is timetabled as surplus to requirements for the first few days. The recruit may be working alongside a more experienced employee, but it is important to reduce the immediate work pressure in this early learning phase.

Within the first week • • •

In many cases, these initial training programmes will take several days, and the new recruit will continue to be timetabled alongside the experienced employee. Best practice involves a 'buddy' who is trained to train. Instead of just being an experienced employee, the person is trained to train the new recruit. Chapter 7 deals more fully with the business benefits of training, but at this stage it is important to recognize that induction training helps the new recruit to reach job competence more quickly and formal training is more effective than learning by trial and error. An interview with the new recruit during the first few days can help to identify any problems or difficulties and help you communicate to the individual his or her importance and value to the unit.

Within the first few weeks • • •

The induction programme may continue over several weeks. Apart from aiding the person to settle into the organization, this process will continue to build up the knowledge and skills needed for effective performance. As a general rule, it is a good idea to continue the induction process over a period, providing information in small amounts rather than cramming it all into the first few days. Another interview with the new recruit can again check on progress and begin to look forward to the individual's development needs and plans.

In summary, careful recruitment and selection involves planning the needs of the job before thinking about the sort of person most likely to be successful in the post. Once you have thought about the job to be done and the person who will do it, you need to think about where you are most likely to find the person needed, and the means by which you invite interested applicants to apply. The selection process by which you will select the candidate from the applications must be compatible with the person you are trying to recruit. Finally, a well-designed induction programme is required so as to ensure that the new recruit is quickly absorbed into the firm as an effective member of the team.

Approaches to recruitment and selection

As hinted at earlier, there is no single set way to go through the recruitment and selection process in hospitality retail operations. The type of person needed for different hospitality retail jobs varies according to the type of service offer being made to customers. In addition, the process of recruitment and selection varies to match the person required and the skills required for their contribution to the service encounter.

In hospitality retailing operations it is possible to identify three types of frontline staff needed in different operations. This leads to three different processes, which match with the ideal types. In Chapter 1 we identified the ideal types of service operations:

- uniformity dependent hospitality services
- choice dependent hospitality services
- relationship dependent hospitality services.

Uniformity dependent hospitality services

Uniformity dependent hospitality services involve tasks that are simple but highly structured. Work practices involve 'one best way' and employees exercise limited amounts of discretion in completing production tasks. Service encounters are also short and limited in scope, though service staff have to practise some skills and judgement in collating orders, taking money, socially interacting with customers and dealing with complaints. The job description lists simple production and service duties, and work is structured in such a way as to present few barriers to potential recruits – applicants who meet general requirements for employability and who do not have any health or legislative limitations on them. The interviewing process is generally simple and typically involves few sophisticated selection techniques because training and development programmes, and the management approach minimize the significance of individual skills and aptitudes.

Example 6.1

McDonald's Restaurants Limited

McDonald's Restaurants recruit crew through a process typical of uniformity dependent organizations. The jobs require few inherent skills other than those of general employability, discipline and basic levels of numeracy and literacy. Some attention is paid to customer service skills when the crew are being recruited for 'counter' duties, but only a small number of employees are 'non-rotatable'. Most are employed for functional flexibility and are trained in all elements of the job, including 'production' and 'service' roles. In most restaurants, numerical flexibility is achieved through the use of a high proportion of part-time staff. Typically, part-time staff work sixteen hours per week, though some crew, particularly school students, might be employed for busy weekend periods. Approximately 80 per cent of employees work on part-time contracts.

Vacancies are advertised within the restaurants and at Job Centres. In some cases, local managers make contacts with local schools and colleges to ensure supplies of recruits. Although significant recruitment has been from amongst young people in the past, the company has increasingly been recruiting middle and 'third' age employees.

The selection process consists of a single interview with one management person – in some cases an assistant manager, though the unit manager takes this responsibility in others. Levels of staff turnover in the company are low for this sector. Current national averages are around 90 per cent per annum.

All new employees – irrespective of their employment tenure – receive induction training which involves (a) Basic Orientation, a short taught programme on health and safety and basic food hygiene practices, and (b) a probation period during which they typically spend one to three weeks on basic induction training timetabled surplus to requirements. Once through this initial period all employees are trained and evaluated in their job performance.

Choice dependent hospitality services

Choice dependent hospitality services also involve simple tasks, though there are likely to be more of them. Production jobs may involve 'one best way' practices, but the service encounters are personalized to individual customers. Service employees have to be able to provide the service performance required by each customer. Service employees have to possess a range of personality and character traits that will enable them to be effective in 'performing' in front of customers. In these circumstances the job description will list simple duties but the staff specification might be much more elaborate in describing the personality which is require of the candidate. Selection and interviewing techniques are more complex, as managers are looking for people with the right 'personalities and skills'.

Example 6.2

TGI Friday Restaurants

Production jobs in TGI Friday Restaurants are similar to those in McDonald's in that the food to be prepared is cooked to set recipes and produced to 'one best way' methods. Some service aspects, too, are laid down and trained for as a way of standardizing service targets and performance. That said, frontline staff must be able to both advise customers about dishes and cocktail items, and provide the specific performance required by each customer or party. Frontline staff in the bar and restaurant need to be able to relate well to customers. In the words of the company, 'They need to be extraverts, but not too much'.

Most employees are recruited and trained for specific kitchen, restaurant or bar jobs. There is little functional flexibility where employees move between departments. Over 80 per cent of the employees are full time, and functional flexibility is achieved through timetabling people through a set number of busy and quiet shift periods. Part-time employment is often used as a way of getting to know an individual prior to long-term employment.

Advertising vacancies usually takes place through Job Centres and through contacts with existing employees. Selection processes involve several interviews – sometimes as many as four – and some role plays where applicants may be asked to tell jokes or give a performance. Many recruits have a higher education and most recruits are under thirty years of age.

All employees are trained prior to starting work in either a production or service capacity. They attend a one-week course that outlines the company's products and culture, and they have to successfully pass a test on the subjects taught. All staff are then trained in their respective roles and eased into their work situation. Usually they work alongside a more experienced employee, and restaurant staff, for example, will be given a quiet section of the restaurant to work for the first few shifts.

Relationship dependent hospitality services

Relationship dependent hospitality services involve simple but more frequent contacts between customers and frontline staff. Production jobs may range from simple 'one best way' approaches to more traditional food production operations. Service relationships need to be matched to customer social and ego needs. Hence service employees have to be capable of building a relationship with customers. The job descriptions may appear simple, but the staff specification will specify characteristics that focus on extraversion and stability. In some cases, the development of social relationships with customers is based on the establishment of sound social relationships amongst employees. Selection and recruitment procedures would typically be concerned with a person who fits in with other staff members and is the sort of person who can build relationships with customers. Word of mouth advertising through existing employees would typically help in building a team spirit and a shared culture.

Example 6.3

Harvester Restaurants

Harvester Restaurants has some features in common with both McDonald's and TGI Fridays in that there are standardized branded aspects to the customer offer that restrict and limit job autonomy. Whilst there are elements of 'one best way' in the kitchen, bar and service jobs, frontline staff need to develop good relationships with customers. Hence there is a need to select a person who can relate to the chain's customer base. In addition the organization of employees in empowered autonomous work groups means that new recruits must fit in with the existing workforce.

Employees are selected and trained for one of the three key departments – kitchen, bar or restaurant – and there is little functional flexibility. Approximately 40 per cent of employees are full time and numerical flexibility is achieved through the use of part-time staff who account for 60 per cent of employees.

Advertising is done through Job Centres but also, most importantly, through existing employees who recommend family and friends to apply for vacant posts. Interviews tend to be with several managers, though typically only one interview is used. In some cases, an existing employee is involved in the interview and advises managers on applicants. Most employees recruited tend to mirror the customer profile – traditional British with conservative tastes and thirty plus in age.

All employees go through an induction programme, though this is conducted concurrently with work on shift. Usually the new recruit works alongside a more experienced employee.

Conclusion

This chapter has outlined some of the important steps needed in recruiting and selecting employees to work in hospitality retail operations. Effective recruitment starts with consideration of the types of tenure required by the job. Recruiting people to full-time, part-time, temporary or casual employment has implications for both the sources of recruits and the levels of commitment that can be expected from jobholders. In situations where demand for hospitality retail services varies and has peaks and troughs, it is often necessary for you to plan ahead so employees are in place in time for the increased demand.

The first step in the recruitment process requires that you have a definition of the job you are trying to fill. A formal job description is useful because it helps you to think clearly about what the job entails, and leading from this the type of person capable of doing it. Again it is worth formalizing your thoughts by drawing up a staff specification. The staff specification helps you to identify the person, and their qualifications and experience, capable of being successful in the post.

Consideration of the ideal candidate helps you identify where that person may be found. Internal recruitment often can be

Hospitality, Leisure & Tourism Series

useful because you may have prior knowledge of the applicant. Recruiting from outside the existing workforce can have the benefit of bringing in new people and ideas. Whatever the source of applicants the selection process needs to be planned so as to give you enough information to make a sensible choice. It is likely, therefore, that there will be different approaches to recruitment and selection that are best matched to the type of employees you are trying to recruit.

Reflective practice

Answer these questions to check your understanding of this chapter:

1 Contrast and compare forms of numerical and functional flexibility in hospitality retail operations. What are the key benefits and limitations of each?
2 Critically describe the main steps in recruitment selection of staff in hospitality retail operations.
3 Contrast and compare, using internal and external sources, recruitment for a typical 'frontline' post in a hospitality retail operation.
4 Using a hospitality retail operation known to you devise a selection procedure for both production and service staff. Explain your answer.
5 Critically discuss the different approaches to recruitment and selection in hospitality retail operations. To what extent can there be a 'one best way' of recruiting staff?

Further reading

Beardwell, I. and Holden, L. (1994). *Human Resource Management: A Contemporary Perspective.* Pitman.

Biddle, D. and Evenden, R. (1993). *The Human Aspects of Management.* Institute of Personnel Management.

British Hospitality Association (1998). *Creating Hospitality's Virtuous Circle of Employment.* British Hospitality Association.

Maghurn, J. P. (1989). *A Manual of Staff Management in the Hotel and Catering Industry.* Heinemann.

Mullins, L. J (1998). *Hospitality Management: A Human Resource Approach.* Pitman.

CHAPTER 7

Employee development and training

After working through this chapter you should be able to:

- identify the key benefits of training and development

- plan and organize staff training

- plan and organize training sessions to meet various needs

- evaluate training undertaken.

Learning by trial and error always involves lots of error

Training and staff development are an important aspect of your work as unit manager. Many branded hospitality retailers recognize that staff training is a key business technique that impacts on service quality delivery, customer satisfaction, sales growth and profitability. Even in organizations that do not have a formal training policy it is important that *you* develop employees through formal training programmes. Most employees will learn by merely doing the job, but learning by experience is less effective than a formal training policy directed at either individual needs or at a collective need, undertaken by all staff. At its most minimal, training has to be provided to meet statutory obligations to employees and customers. All employers have an obligation to ensure employees work in safe environments with co-workers who understand safe working practices. Similarly, employers are obliged to ensure that employees work in a way that is hygienic, and handle food in a manner that reduces the risk to customers.

Training must go beyond these base-level legal obligations. Training *all* employees has direct impacts on business performance. Recent research for the Hospitality Training Foundation shows that training leads to:

- improvements in productivity

- improved sales per transaction

- reduced wastage

- lower levels of staff turnover

- improved service quality

- improved customer satisfaction

- improved employee satisfaction

- increased employee flexibility.

Apart from the benefits directly gained from training, it is also important to recognize that a *failure to train employees is not without cost*. If you allow people to learn the job by trial and error there is bound to be lots of error. This will involve problems in service quality, employee dissatisfaction, higher levels of wastage, lower productivity and reduced employee flexibility.

All training must start with a clear understanding of the aims and objectives of what you expect to achieve from the training activity. Adopt a systematic approach that focuses clearly on the needs of the person to be trained, the materials needed, and how the training will be evaluated.

The benefits of training

Estimating the benefits of training – particularly in the context of potential contributions to improved business performance – is clearly difficult to gauge. This is not surprising given the variety of forms of training undertaken within the hospitality industry and because other variables impact upon training activity, for example, the quality of the training provided, the existing skills and capabilities of trainees, and the duration of training programmes.

In addition, it is self-evident that a wide array of influences impact upon the business performance of an organization, for example:

- economic climate

- levels of investment

- marketing and promotional activities.

The main themes identified in the literature are listed below. It is interesting that some people have called these the 'costs of not training'.

- improved productivity

- increased sales

- reductions in labour turnover

- reductions in waste

- quality improvements

- greater organizational commitment

- reductions in accidents

- greater flexibility.

When considering the aims and objectives of employee training it is important to remember that training:

- primarily changes individual behaviour

- through changes in behaviour direct benefits are about employee performance

- improves employee performance, which may then lead to desired financial benefits, that is, reduced costs, increased sales and improved profitability.

Improved productivity

In this context, improving productivity is about improving employees' output. Output is

- the number of meals produced
- customers served
- rooms cleaned
- sales made
- cash value taken, etc.

measured against some indicator of the staff involved. Usually the latter is staff hours, because the time period is fixed. Where measures are set against shifts or staff on duty, the precise time involved is likely to vary. To calculate the productivity rate:

$$\frac{\text{Output over the period}}{\text{Labour inputs}} \qquad (7.1)$$

Thus if staff behind a bar serve 750 customers over a five-hour period, and there are five members of staff on duty (twenty-five staff hours in total) the calculation is:

$$\frac{750}{25} = 30 \text{ transactions per staff hour} \qquad (7.2)$$

Table 7.1 shows how productivity can be compared using both numbers of customers served and the value of sales for employees who were untrained and those who were trained. The comparisons use both indicators because 'up-selling' (increasing the value of average sales) is an important additional source of revenue and profit.

In Table 7.1 formally trained employees are more productive in transactions, numbers of sales by an average of 33 per cent and take more money by both serving more customers and selling more per transaction. Trained staff take on average £3.43 per transaction whilst informally trained staff take £3.06 per transaction.

	Trained trans	Untrained trans	Difference	Trained sales	Untrained sales	Difference
Shift	1434	1137	297	£4920	£3485	£1435
Hours	38	40	−2	38	40	−2
Rate per hour	37.73	28.4	+ 33%	£129.47	£87.12	+ 48.6%

Table 7.1 Comparison of trained and untrained employees in a bar

Clearly different businesses may restrict the value of transactions because some business or service periods involve more single customer transactions whereas in other cases each transaction involves more customers – in parties, groups or families. You need to keep a record of these matters because they help to track sales and will also help evaluate the impact of various training initiatives.

A structured approach to training helps new employees to become effective more quickly than just allowing staff to learn by experience. Figure 7.1 shows that training new employees, either before work or as part of an induction programme, has two overall effects:

1 New, trained employees quickly reach their optimum output level.

2 They have a higher optimum level output than staff who are not formally trained.

We can see from Figure 7.1 the effects of training on both the speed at which staff learn to become effective and the level of effectiveness reached. Some organizations see the benefit of training prior to the first shift as helping new recruits to develop basic skills before they are put in front of customers. Their thinking is that employee effectiveness and the impact of sales and customer satisfaction are too important to allow new staff to learn by trial and error.

Finally, before we move on from considerations of output, it is important to think about the effects of service quality. There is no point in serving lots of customers if many of them receive

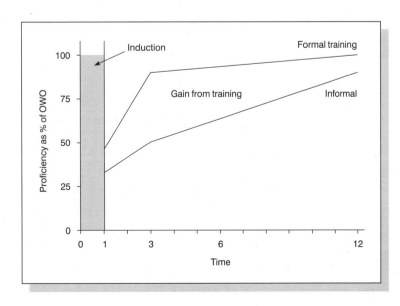

Figure 7.1
Proficiency and time taken to reach optimum work output (OWO)

unsatisfactory service. Any calculation of productivity must therefore consider the impact of customer complaints and lost business. As we shall see later, employee training has an impact on service quality and levels of customer satisfaction.

In conclusion, training can have a dramatic impact on employee productivity. Trained employees:

- have higher levels of output than untrained employees
- reach optimum levels more quickly
- reach higher optimum levels than those who learn from experience
- produce better service quality at any given level of output.

Increased sales

As we saw in Table 7.1, experienced staff sell more product per head than employees who are untrained or inexperienced. The potential increase in sales per labour hour, or per transaction is very important in many hospitality retail units. The ability to *up-sell* by persuading the customer to buy a larger drink, an extra portion, or a better quality room can increase both revenue per sale and profitability. An unpublished study undertaken by one major licensed retailer showed that trained employees could increase the value of sales per transaction by between 25 and 30 per cent.

Staff turnover

As we have seen in Chapter 5, sometimes the causes of staff losses are beyond the control of the unit manager. Local levels of employment and competition for staff may create difficulties that affect staff retention. However, staff turnover is something you must attempt to manage, and providing staff with training is an important way of keeping them with you. Well-structured training helps:

- new employees to quickly understand what is expected of them
- employees develop confidence in their job
- employees feel effective
- establish that employees are important and worthy of investment
- see a path of opportunities open to them
- create a learning environment committed to improvement.

All the above are reasons why employees should stay with an employer, rather than having an environment of low trust and low investment where employees feel undervalued and leave.

The relationship between staff turnover and training is complicated because it is not a simple process. As we have seen, training provides employees with reasons to stay with an organization, however, units with high levels of staff turnover are also likely to have fewer trained employees because employees do not stay long enough to be trained.

Reductions in waste and equipment damage

In many hospitality businesses, food costs would range between 25 and 40 per cent of revenue. Similarly, alcoholic beverages frequently account for a significant proportion of costs.

Loss or damage, accidental handling, making up the wrong order and the replacement of items which customers find unsatisfactory all add to costs, and the problems are made worse by ill-trained staff. Trained workers make fewer errors during production and this minimizes waste.

Training can have a positive impact on theft, pilfering and 'give aways' to friends. Poor or lack of training impacts on the professional behaviour of employees. A value often stressed in employee training programmes is the need for honest practice. In hospitality retail operations many of the items which employees handle are highly consumable – food, drink and money – and levels of training impact on the amount of these stolen by staff.

Quality improvements

It is now widely recognized that the management of quality is a vital challenge if hospitality retailers are to strengthen their competitiveness. Employee performance has a direct influence on employee experiences and service quality. Service employee training can be directed at the employees' delivery of the service, ensuring that they 'get it right first time'. Training employees in what to do if errors occur is also important. Most research shows that when complaints and faults are dealt with immediately, customers are more likely to stay loyal to the organization. Chapter 8 highlights some ways employees can deal with customer complaints. Training employees how best to respond is an essential feature of complaint management.

Reducing customer complaints and increasing customer satisfaction are necessary elements in retaining customers. Most hospitality retail organizations are well aware that it is much more expensive to attract new customers to the business than to retain existing customers. Training results in improved levels of retained customers.

Organizational commitment

Most hospitality retailers now conduct regular surveys of employee satisfaction, because they recognize that *internal customers* have to be committed to the organization's service values to external customers. All things being equal, training has an impact on employee satisfaction and commitment. Whilst employee commitment can be measured, it cannot be given a financial value, but it is none the less a benefit of training that can be measured through changes in employee satisfaction score.

Greater flexibility

Greater employee flexibility brings benefits to an organization because managers are able to schedule the same individuals to undertake a variety of tasks. In part, additional training means that employees are:

- able to undertake a variety of different jobs
- more flexible to do other jobs
- cheaper because they can be used as and where needed.

This *functional flexibility* also enables employees to take on more interesting jobs and, in some cases, training empowers employees to make decisions which had been formerly been undertaken by managers.

Improved ability to accept change

Overlapping but distinct from functional flexibility, an investment in training can produce benefits in the extent to which employees are willing to accept change. An investment in training employees with a wide range of generic skills, or in the specific need for change, are likely to reduce resistance to change and to aid transition from one form to another. For example, studies of empowerment initiatives show that the defining feature of the success of an initiative is the extent to which employees are prepared for new responsibilities and feel empowered.

In summary, training is undertaken to achieve business objectives and it is important that you monitor the effectiveness of training to measure the extent that it has achieved the objective set, for example:

- improve performance
- increase productivity
- increase sales per transaction
- reduce staff turnover
- reduced wastage and equipment damage
- improve service quality
- improve customer satisfaction
- improve employee satisfaction
- increase staff flexibility
- improve the ability to accept change.

Example 7.1

McDonald's Restaurants Limited

The approach to crew training by McDonald's Restaurants has several features that exemplify best practice in the hospitality industry:

- All crew are trained including full and part-time employees.
- Training is competence based.
- Ultimately training aims to develop a flexible workforce capable of undertaking all crew jobs.
- Much crew training involves learning to do the job in 'the one best way'.
- Competencies are defined for each task on *observation checklists* (OCLs).
- Completed training is rewarded with the *five star badge* and a pay increase.
- Training is delivered primarily through a *training squad* (crew members trained to train).
- Observation checklists are also used to monitor ongoing employee performance.
- Unit managers are accountable for training and are monitored through a *training log* and training audits to ensure that crew training is being administered correctly and OCLs are being completed to plan.

Training activity

In a recent case study, detailed analysis of the training activities in two sets of McDonald's Restaurants confirmed a lower level of training activity in the second group of restaurants. Specifically, lower than average training restaurants had:

- a lower proportion of fully trained staff
- a larger backlog of OCLs
- registered below average responses to the training section on employee satisfaction survey
- more critical employee comments about training on RAP Session reports
- managers who seemed to give employee training lower priority.

The results of this study of two sets of restaurants in the same company (McDonald's) showed considerable business benefits for the restaurants that applied the company's approach thoroughly:

- on average 728 more transactions per annum per restaurant
- consistently lower staff turnover at £450 per head minimum – average £19 500 lower per restaurant
- better than average service quality grades – mystery customer service score averaged 10 percentage points better
- better than average employee satisfaction grades and ratings of employee attitudes – averaged 27 per cent better on the company's survey
- more flexible workforce to plan the restaurant's activities
- reduced wastage estimated at £10 per head.

Training your staff

As the immediate manager accountable for the business performance of the unit you are responsible for ensuring that employees are adequately trained to meet the service needs of customers. Even in a situation where your line manager does not ask you to account for staff training undertaken, you must recognize that staff training is key to ensuring effective unit performance. It is essential that you adopt a systematic approach:

- Decide your training policy.
- Identify what training is needed.
- Plan the training to meet the needs identified.
- Prepare programmes to achieve training plans.
- Carry out the training programme.
- Evaluate the training undertaken.

Planning and systematic organization of training in this way will yield many benefits, as we have seen, not the least of which is that it will communicate to employees their key role in service delivery and that you are prepared to invest time and effort in them.

Deciding the training policy

A declared policy about the aims and objectives of training is essential. In fact many large branded hospitality retail organizations have written policy statements that are included in staff handbooks. In these cases, you will not have to write the policy, but you will be expected to make the policy work in the unit. The McDonald's case study in Example 7.1 confirms that even in organizations with highly systematic and structured approaches to training, unit managers make a significant impact on the quality of training delivered at unit level.

If you do not have a brand or organization policy, you will need to write one yourself. A formal written statement assists both you and staff to clearly understand the aims and objectives of your approach to training. There are a number of issues that the policy might consider:

- Is the policy aimed at merely improving job competence or at individual development?
- Are all employees – full-time, part-time and temporary – included and covered by the policy?
- How does this relate to your appraisal policy? Do you follow through with plans for employee development?

- Is the policy related to a wider commitment to being a *learning organization*?

- What support will you make available to 'off-the-job' training and educational qualifications? How would you deal with requests for educational programmes not immediately related to job competence or workplace performance?

- Who will be responsible for training management and delivery, and what resources are available in the form of people and cash?

Most importantly, you must ensure a degree of consistency and integrity in following through on the policy. Fine-sounding policies that are not followed through, or that are set aside when trading times are difficult, will soon be seen for what they are, and people will not take you or the policy seriously.

Identifying training needs

The identification of training needs usually flows from your staff appraisal process. Essentially you are attempting to identify the knowledge, work skills and social skills that employees need for both their present and future jobs. There are several broad areas that need to be considered:

- where individual performance of staff is not up to the standard you require

- where an identified business objective requires all staff to be trained to be more effective – say, to improve productivity or to increase up-selling

- new staff need induction training

- when planned changes require new skills or knowledge

- when individuals or teams will be changing jobs in the future and training builds their personal development.

It is good idea to consider all the types of jobs in the unit. Make a list of these and then think about the relationships between them. Where are there overlaps and relationships? Remember you are thinking about job titles not the current jobholders.

1 Consider flexibility, to what extent is it desirable to have people specialized in departments? For example, many staff specialize in one job or type of job (kitchen, bar, restaurant) because of a combination of personal preferences and effectiveness. Specialization frequently improves job skills and productivity, but at the expense of flexibility.

2 Does specialization lead to rigidities in the workforce? Is it desirable to train staff to be functionally flexible and who can then be employed in different roles?

Once you have listed the job types, make a list of the duties to be undertaken in each job. This process of drawing up *job descriptions* helps you think carefully about the range of tasks to be undertaken and, flowing from this, the skills, knowledge and social skills needed to undertake them.

Next compare the performance of individual jobholders against the requirements of the job both as needed now, and for the future.

1 Consider changes that may be needed because of expansion, new equipment, new products or new services.

2 Think about the personal development of existing employees and the implications for training and development and further education.

Bring together all the training needs you have identified and arrange these in priority order bearing in mind their importance to your overall unit objectives and the ease with which they can be achieved. In some cases, short training activities during a quiet period may help you to address problems that can be of great benefit.

Contrast and compare the training needs and resources needed against the resources available to you. Obviously, there may be extra resources you can call on and a prior investment in building a base of staff or managers who are 'trained to train' will help because they give you a better resource base. Like McDonald's in Example 7.1, an investment in a training squad helps to establish the resources need for an ongoing commitment to training and the establishment of a training culture. Most importantly, the more people are trained to train others, the fewer constraints there are on delivering training.

The training plan

The plan of action flows from the identification of training needs and priorities. You have to make judgements about whether an identified need has to be met immediately and, bearing in mind the comments about the costs of not training mentioned earlier, you need to consider the implications of delaying the delivery of an identified training need.

Again a written plan may seem overly formal, but it is an investment in time that is well worth making;

1 Decide the timescale of the plan. You may have a broad plan covering twelve months, but there may well be shorter-term

objectives – say, to increase average sales per transaction. A realistic target helps you to evaluate the training.

2 Plan the resources needed and available to help you achieve your plan, and budget for them – remember you need to make the policy and plans work.

3 There is no point in being overambitious. Be realistic. Even if you have identified more training activities than you can resource, do not try to do everything; start with what you can and must achieve.

4 Set down the numbers to be trained and the various targets to be achieved.

5 Remember to include induction training, and the training needs of new staff. Where staff turnover is high, or where you are recruiting new employees for an anticipated busy period, you must allow time for new employee training.

6 Against each item on the training plan, identify where, when, how and by whom the training will be carried out.

7 Where appropriate fix dates against the training events.

8 Build in processes of monitoring and evaluation – has the training been effective?

Carry out the training programme

It is likely that there will be a number of different training needs identified in your unit. Some will be aimed at all or a significant group of your staff, in other cases, you may want to train individuals.

- In some cases the sessions might be short sessions taking no more than 20 minutes.

- In others, the training may require a series of different sessions building an integrated set of skills – you may want to train the individual in how to complete a different task in each session.

- In yet others, you may want to train the person in knowledge and social skills.

It is essential that you plan these sessions very carefully and remember that you are intending to achieve specific outcomes:

1 What do you expect the trainees to be able to do after the session? Remember this is likely to be expressed in active verbs – make a *Manhattan*, wash down the counter, change the till roll, etc.

2 Decide where and when the training will take place – in the workplace before service, during service but in a quiet period or during normal service. Remember that it is easier to learn knowledge, say, recipes or legal issues, away from the pressures of service. Learning a skill requires practice, so this may be best done during service, though you may need to work alongside the trainee, and issues about planning the time period and choosing the right sessions may be relevant.

3 Draw up a list of the training events and stages needed, and the time each will typically take.

4 Specify the subjects to be covered.

5 Decide on the learning and teaching methods to be used – will the training involve materials, say, when you are training a person to make a cocktail? Highlight and list the materials you will require. Will you be using a video or on-line service?

6 Identify who will carry out the training.

7 Identify the means by which you will assess the trainee's achievement of the objective set. Will this be via demonstration, or observation whilst doing the job? Will it involve tests? Remember, the means by which you assess the trainee will be a by-product of the objectives set.

Some training tips

Training is ultimately about changing behaviour, so make sure that you are clearly focused on the behaviours that you wish to develop.

- Learning and training are likely to be most effective when the trainee wants to learn and can see the benefit of the training.

- People will learn most effectively when they are told what they are going to learn.

- People learn at different rates, and staff will have different knowledge and experiences on which the training will be built. Make allowance for this.

- Learning is made difficult when the trainee is frightened or anxious. Similarly, hurried or interrupted sessions can also create learning difficulties.

- People have different learning styles, but in the main people attracted to hospitality retail occupations are Activist learners, and learn best by doing. In other words, practical involvement and completing tasks is most effective.

- People cannot remember long strings of information or actions. You may need to break the training into steps during which time you provide short sets of inputs.

- Learning is most effective when the training sessions are entertaining and use varied techniques.

- Trainees need targets and they like to be able to monitor their own progress. The more the trainee has a sense of ownership of the training, the more effective it will be.

- Build up the trainee's confidence by focusing on achievements. Reprimands for faults will create a climate of fear or reduced confidence that can present a barrier to learning.

- Trainees will make mistakes, it is almost impossible to learn any new skill or technique without making mistakes, so expect these and treat them as positive learning opportunities.

- All skill learning goes through a learning curve during which trainees progress quickly, slow up or slip back and make progress again. It is essential that you understand that this is part of the normal learning process.

Remember that training someone is most effective when they have a chance to practise close to the training session what they have learnt. So make sure that this is part of your planning process.

Finally, keep a record of the training that has been undertaken, and continue to monitor performance on a regular basis. It is very easy for people to slip back into old ways of doing things, particularly under pressure of service.

Evaluating the training undertaken

When the training programme has been completed you need to evaluate its impact on the objectives that you set:

- Were you able to carry out the entire plan? Were there difficulties and problems? How might these be overcome in future?

- Consider the elements of the training programme that worked best and worst. What can you learn from this?

- Consider the training undertaken in detail. Were some techniques more successful than others?

- What are the priorities for the next period? Can you now concentrate on things that you identified but were not able to achieve in the earlier period?

- Finally, using the objectives set out earlier, what business benefits have been achieved through the training activities?

Example 7.2

TGI Fridays Bars and Restaurants

Employee performance, particularly of frontline staff, has a crucial role to play. The success of the service depends 'on the worker's ability to construct particular kinds of interactions'. 'Dub-Dubs', as the waiting staff are called, have to advise customers on the menu and how best to structure their meal. They also have to identify the customer's service requirements and deliver what is needed. In some cases, 'having a good laugh with the customers is needed', in others, they need to leave the guests to their own devices or create the necessary celebratory atmosphere to match with a birthday or other party occasion. At other times they have to entertain restless children. Employee performance requires, therefore, more than the traditional acts of greeting, seating and serving customers. Employees have to be able to provide both the behaviours, and the emotional displays, to match with customer wants and feelings. Similarly, bar staff provide both the flair needed to command a premium price, and the personalized service needed to 'connect with others'.

The organization structure within restaurants is somewhat traditional and typical of this kind of business. Each unit has a Restaurant Manager responsible for the overall running and performance of the unit. A junior manager then heads up each of the two key elements of the operation. The Senior Service Manager is responsible for the front of house operations (restaurant and bars). The Quality Manager is responsible for the back of house operations (kitchen and stores).

Individuals are trained for specific jobs: bar, restaurant and kitchen. There was some evidence of staff moving from one department to another, but this was not a formal feature of the training, nor was it a widespread experience. Some employees play a supervisory role as Shift Leader and are given extra pay, in the form of extra hours, when they take on the role. The other positions of note were: hosts, who were responsible for receiving guests, and the expediter who is responsible for ensuring the speedy production of meals from the kitchen and appropriate garnish of dishes prior to service to customers.

The training starts before the new recruit is put to work. A one-week course 'frontloads' training for every new employee. The course focuses on the nature of the brand and service offer to customers as well as specific product knowledge – recipes for the 100 food and cocktail menu items. This programme ends with a test on the content of the course. Those who pass the induction programme examination move to the specific job training in the bar, restaurant and kitchen. In the kitchen, a recruit would be trained at a specific 'corner' and supported by a training manual and a more experienced employee. The new bar recruit also works alongside an experienced employee who takes the recruit through various cocktail recipes and drinks service. In the restaurant, the new recruit is put to work in a quiet section of the restaurant and given just two tables to serve. As the recruit becomes more experienced, this is increased until they are able to take on a full station of four tables in a busy part of the restaurant.

In all cases quarterly staff appraisals are undertaken by the restaurant's management. Future training and development needs are then identified and plans put in place to action them.

The ABC of training

The following section provides you with a simple step-by-step set of practical tips when undertaking a training session. Remember, the training session may be either a short session undertaken during a quiet period or a more detailed session prior to the shift. In all cases the following steps will help both you and the trainees gain the most benefit from the session.

Preparation

Although training might be undertaken during periods of a service shift, *it should never be unplanned.* You must ensure that:

- you will be uninterrupted during the session – it is difficult to concentrate on the training when there are interruptions

- you are prepared and have all the materials and knowledge needed to conduct the session effectively – a lack of preparation or knowledge makes it difficult for the trainees to learn

- all the materials and equipment you need are also working – nothing can be more off-putting than a training session where the things needed are not available or not working.

Effective training is totally dependent on effective preparation and planning.

Attention

You need to gain the trainees' attention before starting. Effective training will depend on the trainees wanting to learn and being attentive and responsive to the trainer. Here are some steps that you might take when setting up the trainees and gaining their attention.

What ● ● ●

You must state clearly and simply what the trainee is going to learn. Try to avoid jargon. Explain it in terms that trainees will understand. Work from the principle that *'if they can get it wrong, they will get it wrong'.* Clear explanation is the key.

Interest ● ● ●

The second aspect of gaining the trainees' attention is in creating interest in what is to be learnt. Being motivated to learn is dependent on the trainees feeling that they will be learning something that they are interested in and a task they want to be able to do:

- Show the finished product.

- Give a brief background of the product or task.

- Recount a positive personal story about the task.

- Relate the task to the trainees' own interests.

- Ask a question.

Avoid long and complicated explanations, because the trainee will become bored. Your purpose is to develop the trainee's interest in learning.

Need

The third aspect of building the trainees' attention and motives to learn is to establish the benefits to them. In other words you are trying to answer their, 'What's in it for me?' question. Trainees who see the benefit to themselves are more likely to learn more quickly and effectively. These benefits include:

- safer, easier working

- respect from other staff members

- better relationship with customers

- pride in doing a good job

- any material rewards paid to trained employees.

Breakdown

Training is communicated by you demonstrating the task. This should be planned and undertaken in stages. This is where the planning and preparation stages are important because ill thought through training programmes often result in trainees being given 'only part of the story'. It is very easy for the experienced trainer who does the task automatically, to miss out some key fact or judgement.

The task needs to be broken down into all its key steps. Complicated tasks may be learnt in a series of stages. In other cases, the whole task is demonstrated in sequence

Explaining each step as you go, picking out key points or stages where things can go wrong. Asking and inviting questions are important parts of this step. You are trying to make it as clear as possible.

Again, remember that ' if they can get it wrong, they will get it wrong'. This is not a comment on the skills of the trainees, but a fact of training life.

Check

This stage is concerned to ensure that both the trainer has trained the trainee to the required standard and the trainee is capable of undertaking the task to the required standard. There are two aspects to the check stage.

Verbal check ● ● ●

The trainer uses testing questions to ensure that all the information has been understood and all the new information can be recalled. Factual questions might be asked about specific knowledge about the task or service being taught, for example, 'What temperature should raw meat be stored at?' More open-ended questions are relevant to understanding the general reasons why some things are done, for example, 'Why is correct food storage an important aspect of safe food handling?'

Practical check ● ● ●

This is the most important part of the training. The trainee works though the task and shows they can complete the task to the required standard. The trainee completes the task uninterrupted. Frequent interruptions and comments from you can cause the trainee to lose concentration and confidence.

When evaluating the trainee's performance, focus on the strengths and positive aspects, and discuss those aspects that were not done correctly in an unthreatening and non-blaming manner. Everyone makes mistakes when learning something for the first time. Remember, trainees often go through a learning curve that includes downs as well as ups. So expect that people need to practise a new task several times, and that they will make errors even about tasks they seemed to have mastered at an earlier stage.

When the trainee has reached the appropriate standard, praise them and leave them to get on with it. They will need to work on the task for a while before their output and performance is at its best. Go back and check with the trainee every now and again.

A performance review and appraisal process is essential. It is not good enough to just train staff and leave it there. If you want to sustain high levels of performance you must continue to monitor and evaluate that performance. You will have to retrain staff if their performance slips away from the standard expected.

Conclusions

Employee training is one of the key elements in successful unit management in hospitality retail operations. Through training production and service staff you are able to deliver consistent brand performance to customers. In most hospitality retail brands there will be some element of training employees in the 'one best way' to perform tasks. This is in many cases the means by which the brand consistency is achieved. Obviously this aspect of training takes on added significance in *uniformity dependent* brands like McDonald's. Even in these brands, however, there is also an aspect of customer service training that has to go beyond the 'one best way', and some customer service needs will be difficult to predict and script. Service staff need to be trained in how to respond to unusual requests, and this aspect of training takes on more significance in *choice dependent* and *relationship dependent* services. In these services staff training is likely to involve more role-modelling, critical incident acting and values learning than when learning to do things in a set way.

An investment in training will help you achieve wider business benefits. Though it is important to remember that training is aimed at changing employee behaviour, financial benefits flow from these changes. So improving employee productivity, increasing sales revenue, reducing staff turnover, and reducing wastage and equipment damage have an impact on sales revenue and costs. This in turn impacts on operating profits. Staff training improves service quality, increases customer satisfaction and leads to the greater likelihood of customers returning to the unit. Similarly, staff training impacts on employee satisfaction, increased flexibility and willingness to accept change, and these produce more intangible but none the less real benefits.

Finally, your approach to training needs to be systematic, planned and ongoing. It should be part of a general commitment to being a *learning organization* – an organization that gives complete commitment to developing both managers and employees. In these circumstances, training and development needs flow from staff appraisals and performance review processes. Employees' future development needs and their current work performance enable you to come up with a plan of what has to be achieved and the priorities for action. Benchmark training organizations like McDonald's set standards of excellence that many hospitality retailers could follow. In this company, not only is the training provision made available, it is made an important business performance indicator, and managers are made accountable for the training taking place.

Reflective practice

Answer these questions to check your understanding of this chapter:

1 Critically discuss the business benefits of training in hospitality retail operations. Make the case for and against an investment in training.
2 Describe the steps you will take in identifying training needs in a hospitality retail operation.
3 Contrast and compare different approaches to training and show how you might evaluate training effectiveness.
4 Using a hospitality retail operation known to you devise a training plan for both production and service staff. Explain your answer.
5 Critically discuss the different approaches to training and employee development in hospitality retail operations. To what extent can there be 'one best way' of training staff.

Further reading

Beardwell, I. and Holden, L. (1994). *Human Resource Management: A Contemporary Perspective*. Pitman.

British Hospitality Association (1998). *Creating Hospitality's Virtuous Circle of Employment*. British Hospitality Association.

Maghurn, J. P. (1989). *A Manual of Staff Management in the Hotel and Catering Industry*. Heinemann.

Mullins, L. J. (1998). *Hospitality Management: A Human Resource Approach*. Pitman.

Managing service quality

After working through this chapter you should be able to:

- identify the key problems in managing service quality in hospitality retail operations

- critically discuss different approaches to service quality management

- operate a suitable service quality management system

- evaluate service quality and create correction strategies.

You serve hot food hot, and cold food cold, and everybody smiles

The major underlying theme of this book is that service quality is an important business strategy that is fundamental to success in competitive hospitality retail operations. Customer retention and the attraction of new customers depends on ensuring that customers have a clear idea about what to expect from the hospitality retailer and ensuring that they get it. This theme is developed more fully in Chapter 12, but 'You serve hot food hot, and cold food cold, and everybody smiles', from the *My Kinda Town* training manual, sums up the key issues for hospitality retail operators: you deliver what you say you will deliver, you supply both products and services, and employee performance is a fundamental element of successful service delivery.

Though managing successful hospitality service quality is not 'rocket science', there are some important difficulties and tensions for you to manage. As we have seen in Chapter 1 hospitality services differ and require different forms of standardization and control. The varying combinations of products and services and the importance of employee performance, together with different customer expectations and evaluations of successful service encounters, all make for complexities in managing service organizations that are not found in the management of manufacturing organizations.

For these and other reasons, several systems of service quality management and performance monitoring have been introduced. Investors in People, ISO 9000, total quality management and other systems were all devised so internal management processes would ensure quality is delivered 'right first time'. In addition, these systems certificate individual businesses and units as a message to external customers and clients. This matter should not be dismissed lightly because,

- customers are often uncertain about the quality of experience they will receive

- benchmark labels help customers feel more secure about the service they will get

- when applied properly these systems can assist in delivering real benefits in the management of service quality.

Different systems deliver different benefits, so you need to select the system most closely suited to your needs. The following chapter explores some of the problems associated with defining and managing hospitality retail service quality. The chapter briefly outlines some of the more widely applied approaches to quality management, and details steps that you can take to ensure that your unit achieves high levels of customer satisfaction.

Hospitality retail service quality

As indicated in Chapter 1 the core features of services are intangibility, inseparability, variability and perishability, leaving hospitality retail organizations with some difficulties and dilemmas to manage in the delivery of services.

The *intangible* elements of services make it difficult for customers to establish the benefits to be gained from a service prior to the purchase. This can only be done as a result of receiving the service.

- It is difficult to measure and define the expectations of customers, service employees, and managers in what the intangible benefits should deliver.

- Successful service delivery frequently depends on customers developing feelings of comfort or belonging that are difficult to generate.

The *variability* of services is also a feature that distinguishes them from typical manufacturing production. Service delivery is frequently variable and difficult to standardize owing to the personal nature of the contact between the customer and the service deliverer (the staff member).

- Individuals may well vary in their interpretation of customer needs.

- Elements of human 'chemistry' may interfere with performance; some individuals may be more personally committed to successful service encounters.

- Customer expectations of satisfactory service may well vary and be difficult to predict.

Hence it is difficult to say the service delivery is homogeneous, even where the service is relatively simple.

The third important feature of services is that the production and consumption of the service are *inseparable*. This creates a number of differences with typical manufacturing firms.

- Consumers of the service are themselves participants in the service delivery, say, as customers in a restaurant or a bar.

- They interact with the service deliverer, the environment and other consumers.

- Customers are party to the service interaction and will partially shape it – through their own perceptions of the service environment and the perceptions of fellow customers.

Typically services are subject to *perishability* because they are temporal. Bed spaces in hotels or seats in restaurants represent capacity for a given period.

- It is not possible to store up sales and satisfy them at another time.

- Nor can any loss of service output be made up at a later date. In many cases, the service is time specific and once lost is gone forever.

- Hence the empty hotel bed or unsold restaurant meal represents revenue never to be regained.

- Hospitality retailer service deliverers are not able to stockpile services, or make up for lost service production by working overtime, or multisource services to allow for fluctuations in the demand and supply of services.

- Service quality faults cannot easily be reworked and given back to the customer, as might happen with a manufactured product.

- Service demand has to be satisfied as and when it is required, so there is difficulty in planning service delivery to meet service demand.

Finally, most hospitality retail services are supplied to customers who do not 'own' the service as supplied, they cannot take it away or return it if unsatisfactory. Because of the intangibility and perishability features, customers are frequently buying the right to a service, or an experience. This creates problems of loyalty and memory, unlike the possessors of a tangible product that is taken home, hospitality retail consumers rarely have permanent reminders of the product's features or benefits. Repeat purchases will be based on a bundle of memories, experiences and expectations. Individual perceptions and differences become important issues.

Hospitality retail products and services

Hospitality retailers supply a combination of products and services and, as we saw in Chapter 1, there are differences between various types of offers made to customers. In some cases, the service offer is:

1 *Uniformity dependent*: customers expect that the product and services delivered will be uniform and standardized. Customer evaluations of service quality in these cases will be largely concerned with the consistent delivery of standardized products and services, delivering 'good value' for money.

2 *Relationship dependent*: customers experience more contact with service personnel and evaluate service quality in terms of the intangible aspects of the service encounter. The relationship with service personnel in particular produces appropriate feelings in the customer.

3 *Choice dependent*: customers want security of the branded product but also want a wide choice so they can make the occasion suit their mood and needs. The product range in both food and drink items is usually extensive. In addition, the service personnel have to be flexible enough and capable of giving the performance to match the customer occasion.

In each of these types of hospitality retail operation customer evaluations of the quality of the experience will vary, because customers are seeking different types of experiences and using the outlets for different occasions and with different expectations of a successful service encounter. In all cases, however, hospitality retailers are supplying a bundle of *products* and *services*. In both cases, they include *tangible* and, therefore, measurable benefits as well as *intangible* benefits, the latter being more difficult to evaluate. Table 8.1 provides some examples of the tangible and intangible aspects of products and services.

The matrix in Table 8.1 is not an exhaustive list of product and service tangibles and intangibles (Figure 1.2 in Chapter 1 provides a more in-depth list). It does show, however, that some aspects of hospitality retail operations are more measurable and capable of being monitored than others. Given the variations in service types noted above, the significance of different features will vary between different types of hospitality retail operations, and the nature of how the characteristics are defined will also vary. For example, *speed* is one of the tangible aspects of the service provided. In most hospitality retail brands, operational standards lay down target times that the customer should be waiting to be greeted, or for their meals and drinks to be served. In McDonald's Restaurants, for example, the service standard

	Tangible	Intangible
Nature of product	The food and drink product	Atmosphere
	Serving goods: plates, glasses, cutlery, linen, etc.	Décor and furnishings
	Information: menu	Feelings
	Process, e.g. credit cards	Comfort
The contact service	Actions	Warmth
	Process	Friendliness
	Speed	Care
	Script	Service
	Corrective action	Hospitableness

Source: Adapted from Lockwood, Baker and Ghillyer (1996).

Table 8.1 The quality characteristics matrix

states that customers should not be queuing for more than ninety seconds, and customer orders should take no more than three minutes to complete. Speed of service is one of the key elements of the company's offer to customers, and is very consistent with the customer occasion based on *refuelling*. For other customer occasions, overly speedy service would not be appreciated by customers. When customers are having a *special meal out*, for example, more leisurely service times are required, and hurried service would be seen as a service fault.

Active learning point

In three brands known to you describe the key characteristics of service quality in each brand. Contrast and compare the similarities and differences between them.

Characteristics	Brand A	Brand B	Brand C
1			
2			
3			
4			
5			
6			
7			
8			
9			
10			
11			
12			

As unit manager your problem is in understanding what these expectations are and then sharing them with employees on the front line who will deliver the service in a way that matches with customer expectations.

- Consumer expectations of service quality become an important definitive feature of service quality when set against experiences of the service.

- Customers have a base level of expectations of the service – the minimum they expect. They have a level of expectation about what the service should be like versus what they want.

- Customers also predict what they expect the quality to be like.

- Customers may vary in their expectations; those with more experience of a service may well have higher expectations than those who have less experience of it.

- Hospitality retailers have a role in shaping expectations; advertising and other promotional activities may influence consumer expectations.

- It is important that the service delivered in your unit matches these expectations.

The key aim is to ensure that you meet customer expectations in such a way as to ensure that customers are not just satisfied that their expectations have been met, but also that they are satisfied to ensure a return. It is worth considering Herzberg's motivation model here. Herzberg suggested that there are two sets of factors that people potentially evaluate when considering positive and negative response to service.

1 Hygiene factors are exactly those characteristics – like the cleanliness of the toilets. Customers have an expectation of the required standards, and will be dissatisfied if they do not meet these standards. However, when these standards are met customers are not motivated to return.

2 Motivators, on the other hand, are those characteristics of service that customers value highly – mostly intangibles like being made to feel important and valued, and hospitableness that will motivate customer loyalty.

Herzberg's model is valuable because it suggests that there are some characteristics which, if they do not meet expectations, will cause customer dissatisfaction. On the other hand, meeting customer expectations in these characteristics is no guarantee of customer loyalty – just an absence of dissatisfaction. Real customer motivators are those characteristics of the service that customers value most.

As unit manager you have to ensure that you understand customer expectations, particularly:

- the hygiene factors that might cause dissatisfaction

- the motivators that will motivate customers to return.

SERVQUAL is used by some hospitality retailers to compare customer's expectations with their experiences and, thereby, show the strengths and weaknesses of the service delivery. The performance of different competitors can be compared with the service organization's own performance. In particular it reveals 'five service 'gaps' where there may be a mismatch been the expectation of the service level and the perception of the service delivered. Table 8.2 highlights the five dimensions that have been identified and on which the SERVQUAL system of quality evaluation is based.

Dimension	Definition
Reliability	The ability to perform the promised service dependably and accurately
Tangibles	The appearance of physical facilities, equipment, personnel and communication materials
Responsiveness	The willingness to help customers and provide prompt service
Assurance	The knowledge and courtesy of employees and their ability to convey trust and confidence
Empathy	The caring individualized attention paid to the customer

Table 8.2
The five dimensions of service

These gaps focus on the points at which expectations of service requirements by management, the standards set, the standards achieved or the service standards communicated to customers produce a situation where customers' perceptions of the service delivered do not match with the expected service.

Responsiveness, assurance and empathy are elements of this model that underscore the importance of employee performance in the service encounter. Given the nature of services, it is often difficult to predict what employees have to say or do in given service encounters. Although some employee tasks can be

Hospitality, Leisure & Tourism Series

predicted, standardized and trained, frontline staff are often required to respond to unforeseen situations even in typical uniformity dependent operations like McDonald's. Some writers look to *critical incidents* in which employee responses can be shown to either save a situation and create customer satisfaction or can create dissatisfaction. Their findings suggested three broad groups of incidents:

- employee responses to service delivery system failures
- employee reactions to customer needs and requests
- unprompted and unsolicited employee actions.

Each group represents a cluster of incidents in which employee response behaviour could result in customer satisfaction or dissatisfaction (Table 8.3).

Critical incident	Customer satisfaction	Customer dissatisfaction
Employee responses to service delivery failure	Could be turned into incidents that employees use to advantage and generate customer satisfaction: an employee reacts quickly to service failure by responding sensitively to customer experiences – say, by compensating the customer or upgrading a customer to a higher status service.	More frequently, however, staff responses are likely to be source of a dissatisfaction – where the employee fails to provide an apology or an adequate explanation, or argues with the customer.
Employee responses to customer needs and requests	Employee responsiveness, flexibility and confidence that they can match whatever is required by the customer are important sources of positive customer responses.	Employee intransigence, inflexibility and perceived incompetence are all likely sources of customer dissatisfaction.
Unprompted and unsolicited employee actions	This might involve employee behaviours that made the customer feel special, or where an act of unexpected generosity takes the customer by surprise.	Customer dissatisfaction could be the result of a failure to give the customer the level of attention expected or inadequate information, or might involve inappropriate behaviour such as the use of bad language, etc.

Table 8.3 Positive and negative response to critical service incidents

Employee responses to service delivery system failures can be critical, because customers are more likely to excuse a service failure if the fault is acknowledged and quickly corrected. Any problem that is not corrected at the unit may result in complaints to head office and, more importantly, a lost customer. Taking into account that each customer tells friends and relatives, the lost custom can cost far in excess of the replaced meal or free bottle of wine.

Similarly, employee reactions to customer needs and requests are important in all service situations because there are bound to be occasions when customers want something that is not normally sold via the brand, or where they make a mistake and want some assistance in correcting their fault. Customers are much more likely to respond positively if they are treated with flexibility and the service employee makes every effort to meet their needs.

Unprompted and unsolicited employee actions incorporated those that exceeded the customer's expectation of the service encounter. Where employee performance is beyond the customer's expectation the incident can produce satisfaction. Exceeding customer expectations may involve the detail of their performance. Employees in TGI Fridays are encouraged to perform in a way that underpins the brand's offer to customers, which involves humour and a 'fun' atmosphere. Often this might include providing balloons or singing songs at a birthday celebration.

The issue of employee performance and customer satisfaction takes on added urgency when firms begin to consider the costs of lost business and the benefits of generating customer loyalty.

1 In a pub context one firm estimates that every pub customer spends an average of £785 per annum in public houses. A customer lost due to an unresolved complaint directly loses the business that amount. In addition it is estimated that a dissatisfied customer tells another thirteen people about their experience. The potential cost of one unresolved complaint is, therefore, fourteen times this amount – £11 032.

2 In a restaurant context it has been estimated that if an organization lost one customer per day for a year, the total cost to the business could be over £94 000 per annum, even if customers only spent on average £5 per week with the organization.

3 Similarly it was estimated that repeat custom only cost one-fifth the amount needed to generate new customers. Within a hotel context the ratio was closer to 1:7 – in other words, attracting a new customer costs seven times what it costs to get an existing customer to repeat.

Hospitality, Leisure & Tourism Series

The financial implications of customer satisfaction, and the key role employees play in the service encounter, has caused concern to ensure employees are equipped to maximize their effectiveness. It is essential that you *invest in your staff*. Figure 8.1 shows the links that are made between customer satisfaction, customer turnover, employee satisfaction and employee turnover. In the upper part of the diagram a virtuous cycle results in a continuous improvements in all the elements. The lower portion of the diagram, on the other hand, presents a vicious cycle in which declining customer satisfaction results in reduced customer retention; that results in employees having to work harder to recruit new customers, which reduces employee satisfaction and increases employee turnover, and in turn impacts on customer satisfaction.

This section has attempted to show that hospitality retail unit managers have problems in the management of service quality. The very nature of the service encounter is difficult, because it involves subjective assessments of what is expected on behalf of customers, frontline staff, and management. Branded hospitality retailers have attempted to simplify some of the problems by sending clear messages to customers as to what to expect and then adopting systematic approaches to service delivery so that

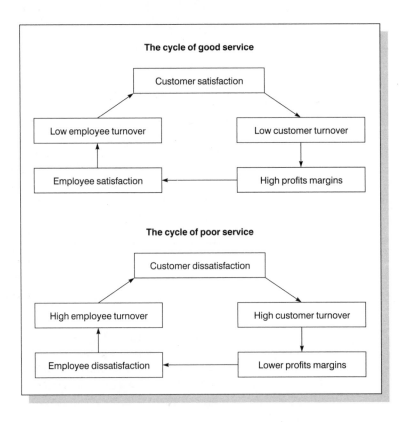

Figure 8.1
Customer satisfaction and employee satisfaction

these expectations are met. The section suggests several key concepts in managing service quality.

1 Hospitality retail operations supply both products and services to customers and these result in tangible and intangible benefits. It is easier to manage the tangible aspects of the offer but both are important and need careful monitoring.

2 As a unit manager you need to understand that customers use the same restaurant and bar on different occasions with different expectations and motives. You need to understand these different requirements and expectations so that you are able to focus on what customers consider important.

3 Customers have different expectations of the service characteristics supplied and rank these differently. For some aspects expectations are that the service will be up to a basic standard, though overprovision of these things will not always motivate customers to return. You need to understand the *motivators* – those aspects of service that will build real customer loyalty.

4 Employee performance in the service encounter is seen to be key to much of the customers' experience. Employee responsiveness, assurance and empathy when dealing with customers, and their ability to manage critical incidents, are crucial to the encounter. Appropriate human resource management techniques – recruitment and selection, training, motivation and empowerment – are all fundamental.

Quality management and hospitality retail operations

The earliest developments in quality stem from the manufacturing industry, and hospitality organizations have adopted and adapted these different approaches, though they do not always match the needs of the organization and need to be linked to their service offer to customers. The following provides a brief overview of different systems and terms used:

1 *Quality inspection*: actual output of a product or service is checked against a standard specification. Defects are then reworked or sent for scrap. Whilst quality inspection is undertaken via line managers, quality inspectors and mystery customers, the approach is frequently limited by the nature of the hospitality products and services. It is not always possible to rework a faulty product or service. Also there is no way of identifying the cause of the fault.

2 *Quality control*: quality is designed into the detailed specification in the production of products and services through detailed standards. Quality checks are introduced through the

various stages of the process, say between departments. At root, the approach is still concerned with the detection and correction of faults. It will not improve quality but it does show when quality is not present

3 *Quality assurance*: rather than waiting for faults to occur, quality is designed into the process in such a way that faults cannot occur. If faults do occur they are corrected as they happen. The approach involves developing a documented and planned quality system. Quality assurance requires total organization commitment and involvement of all employees in the process. A key problem is that although quality assurance may deliver consistently faultless products and services, but the standard may not be what customers want.

4 *Total quality management*: the focus is on customers and the satisfaction of customer needs. The system is totally directed at customer satisfaction and the removal of any barriers to delivering customer satisfaction. People in the organization are key to successfully achieving customer satisfaction; employee training, motivation and empowerment are important. Again successful implementation requires total cultural commitment and this can be difficult to achieve because it is often hard to change the organization's culture.

The approaches listed above are not of themselves mutually exclusive; one approach builds on another and, as we will see later, effective quality programmes often incorporate aspects of all these approaches. So systems based on total quality management still need to involve quality inspection and quality control, though the number of faults and problems should be greatly reduced.

Although hospitality retail organizations can develop their own quality systems, many find that national and internationally recognized systems are helpful as a way of providing a framework in which to work. As stated earlier, many of these systems are also recognized by customers and clients, and help to reassure them about the quality of service they will receive. In addition, in some markets – workplace retailing for example – many firms will only deal with companies who are themselves recognized quality suppliers.

Quality standard awards in hospitality operations

ISO 9000 series

A system of quality assurance developed initially in the defence industry, this has been adopted by several hospitality organizations – particularly in contract catering and workplace retailing. The approach sets out a standard through which a company can document an effective system that demonstrates the organization's commitment to quality and the systems that ensure quality is delivered. Once an organization has set up and documented the system, they are then assessed by one of several independent assessor agencies. Registration usually lasts for three years but the company is subject to inspection to ensure that the systems are still being applied.

There are several variants within the ISO 9000 series and ISO 9002 is considered to be the most suitable for hospitality firms. The elements covered by the system include items that demonstrate responsibilities for quality management, the definition and management of standards, and the monitoring and inspection system.

As a system of quality assurance ISO 9000 and its predecessor BS 5750 have been successful in manufacturing industry, but there are problems when applying this approach to dynamic hospitality service operations:

- Although there is consistent quality, this may not be what the customer wants.

- Standard procedures and systems have limited use when applied to the quality of human interactions in the service encounter.

- The approach may work well in predictable service encounters, but is more difficult in service situations where employee performance requires high levels of employee discretion.

As stated earlier, the approach has been most widely adopted in contract catering operations where many potential clients are themselves ISO 9000 accredited and are required to deal only with suppliers who are also so registered.

Investors in People

Whereas ISO 9000 is an international system of quality accreditation, Investors in People is a UK-based award for companies that are committed to business growth and success through the development of managers and employees. The focus is on the development of people, though there is a recognition that service quality will improve as a result of improved training and other human resource management techniques. The standards stress the importance of customers and the need to prioritize customer needs. The award of accreditation brings with it public recognition of the commitment to developing employees, which has benefits both potential customers and employees.

The standard provides twenty-four indicators in assessing the company's commitment to investing in their people. For each indicator there are guidance notes that describe what each indicator should demonstrate. The system is not prescriptive and companies can interpret the indicators in their own way There are four key stages in process – commitment, planning, action and evaluation. Once a company has these stages in place, the company is assessed by the local Training and Enterprise Council. Assessment includes inspection of documents and, most importantly, site visits to interview managers and staff – the recipients of the training.

Given the nature of hospitality services it is perhaps not surprising that Investors in People has been widely accepted across the industry and hotels in particular. Registration is on a unit by unit basis and lasts for three years. Companies such Queens Moat House, DeVere Hotels, Friendly Hotels and Centre Parcs have all achieved the award in their units.

The key weakness with the award is that it represents only part of a quality management system. People skills are essential to service quality delivery but these need to be developed as part of an overall quality approach.

As a consequence many are now looking to a specific hospitality award systems introduced by the Hotel Catering and International Management Association.

Total quality unit management

As a unit manager in a branded hospitality retail unit, you may be involved in managing service quality in compliance with another of the above award schemes. However, you may also be managing a unit where there is no imposed system. In these cases, the philosophy of total quality management will be very helpful to you.

Hospitality retail organizations require quality systems that are holistic enough to allow for the characteristics of services and the varied perceptions of customers. Total quality management appeared to offer service organizations the system needed.

Even though there are several forms of total quality management the following list of principles covers several broad features which are found in most descriptions of this initiative:

- The initiative locates a commitment to quality services as a core organizational concern. The commitment of senior management is crucial and the approach has to permeate every aspect of the organization.

- The approach has been particularly attractive to hospitality retail organizations because it aims to create a cultural environment in which employees, operating independently, are guided by a commitment to delighting customers because they have internalized the organization's objectives and values.

- These internalized values, beliefs and objectives ensure employees aspire to customer satisfaction and quality improvement, without extrinsic controls or inducements.

The principles of total quality management (TQM) are:

1 Highest priority given to quality throughout the organization.

2 Quality is defined in terms of customer satisfaction.

3 Customers are defined as those who have both internal and external relationships with the organization – including employees, shareholders, the wider community.

4 Customer satisfaction and the building of long-term relationships are at the nub of the organization.

5 The organization's aims will be clearly stated and accessible to all.

6 The principles, beliefs, values and quality are communicated throughout the organization.

7 TQM creates an ethos that pervades all aspects of the organization's activities.

8 Core values of honesty, integrity, trust and openness are essential ingredients of TQM.

9 The total quality organization is intended to be mutually beneficial to all concerned and operates in a climate of mutual respect for all stakeholders.

10 The health and safety of all organization members and customers are given priority.

11 Total quality offers individuals the chance to participate in and feel ownership of the success of the enterprise.

12 Commitment is generated in individuals and teams through leadership from senior management.

13 TQM results in an organization-wide commitment to continuous improvement.

14 Performance measurement, assessment and auditing of the organization's activities is a common feature of TQM.

15 TQM aims to use resources more effectively and members are encouraged to consider ways of doing this.

16 TQM require appropriate investment to ensure that planned activity can occur.

The similarities between TQM and empowerment are not accidental because many of those writing about the benefits of TQM as an approach for managing service organizations also advocate the need to empower staff with authority to correct defects and to respond to service failures as they occur. Furthermore, employee empowerment is necessary so employees can respond to unusual customer requests, or use their experience and creativity to look for ways of 'delighting the customer'. These aspirations for TQM and empowerment are relevant to the three critical incidents that could create, or damage, customer satisfaction.

- Dealing with service failures.
- Responding to request for unusual service.
- Providing extraordinary interactions.

The three occurrences listed above are all occasions when employee behaviour impacts either positively or negatively on customer satisfaction and perceptions of service quality. Total quality management provides an organizational setting in which empowered employees, through a heightened sense of their own personal efficacy, will respond in the desired way.

Forms of TQM

All the companies that have been used as examples in this book have their own ways of dealing with the management of service quality which incorporate many of the concepts of TQM, even though they have not called it by that name. The following three forms of TQM provide you with some options, though there is likely to be an ideal match to the three hospitality retail types that we identified earlier.

The 'hard' version of TQM

This definition, places emphasis on the production aspects such as systematic measurement and control of work, setting standards of performance, using statistical procedures to assess quality. It is this the hard production/operations management type of view which, arguably, leads to less discretion for employees. This approach has compatibility with *uniformity dependent* hospitality retail services. Using the terms in Table 8.1 the service offer depends on products and service that are largely tangible and thereby measurable.

Example 8.1

McDonald's Restaurants Limited

McDonald's Restaurants use *quality, service, cleanliness* and *value* (QSCV) as core organizational aspirations. All the company's service quality monitoring processes assess QSCV though, recognizing that *value* is a psychological concept, this is assessed using different techniques from the other three. Quality measures consider the physical food and drink product against standard specifications and appropriate temperature checks. Service includes waiting and queuing times as well as the time taken to process orders, and the correct delivery of items. Cleanliness relates to the appearance of staff and premises including front and back areas as well external approaches – car parks and surrounding pavement areas.

All restaurants are assessed on a regular basis using 'mystery diners' who represent a form of quality inspection – again using all the key quality, service and cleanliness (QS&C) measures. Area Supervisor audits, and manager-conducted assessments perform quality control checks. Customer comment cards are for all customers to comment on immediate service experience, though these are further supported by customer surveys that are given out to customers and entitle the customer to a discounted meal when they are returned. Customer complaints or praise received at head office also detract from or add to the quality score. All the sources of assessment are brought together in a series of grades that are used to evaluate unit performance. These quality assessments are used as points of entry for manager bonus schemes. Thus if a restaurant is increasing turnover and profits but failing to match quality targets, the manager will not be eligible for bonus payments. Only when service quality markers have been met will bonuses be paid.

Standardization and the accompanying psychological benefits, are important features of the offer made by the company to its customers, and this shapes much of its management of human resources. Its brand values are tightly drawn and closely managed. Even franchise businesses are bound by the disciplines of the brand. The service dimension is largely shaped by concepts and practices developed in manufacturing industry. The approach draws on principles and techniques such as the standard procedures manuals, division of labour, scientific management and the use of technology to minimize the need for much employee discretion. Employees are trained to perform the various production processes in the 'one best way' and their performance is monitored through Observation Checklists. The McDonald's approach has much in common with the hard form of TQM and empowerment that is largely associated with winning commitment and developing the sense of personal efficacy. Little decision-making authority passed to employees.

The soft approach to TQM

The soft approach incorporates the characteristics identified by Peters, 'customer orientation, culture of excellence, removal of performance barriers, team working, training, employee participation, competitive edge'. From this perspective TQM is seen as consistent with open management styles, delegated responsibility and increased autonomy of staff. Quality auditing is carried out by employees or management, and through consideration of customer feedback. The approach to employee empowerment is through participation, particularly through the working of autonomous work teams or individual targets for the service encounter, as in Marriott Hotels. Teams play an important role in both controlling individual performance, and delivering employee commitment to organizational quality service targets.

The offer to customers, though still incorporating tangible benefits via products and services, relies more on intangible benefits from the service element. The approach is consistent with *relationship dependent* hospitality retail services.

Example 8.2

Harvester Restaurants

Harvester Restaurants has some features that depend on tangible aspects of product and service. Standard recipes and operational manuals, and standard décor and service processes provide measurable aspects of the service offer to customers, however, the approach relies heavily on service relationships. The service values expressed in the phrase of 'treating customers as though they were guests in your own home' provides a core value of homeliness, hospitality, tradition and naturalness.

Employees work in autonomous work teams that self-manage the service quality to customers. Each team is empowered to deal with customer complaints and whatever it takes to ensure customer satisfaction. This includes replacing meals, providing free bottles of wine and other 'give-aways' to customers. Frontline teams in the restaurant and bar area were actively encouraged to deal with the complaints without recourse to a manager. Complaints and difficulties were recorded after service through the use of representative meetings. All team members who acted as Shift Co-ordinator at some point in the week attended a weekly co-ordinating meeting. Customer comments and experiences are discussed at these meetings. A record of these meetings is made available to staff through a record book freely accessible to all full- and part-time staff.

Recurring problems or difficulties are discussed with the immediate teams prior to each service occasion and employees are able to make suggestions, or make immediate tactical decisions, that positively impact on service quality. In the case of customer complaints to head office, employees and the Team Manager thoroughly investigate the problem together. Where the system works properly, complaints are dealt with in the unit and many restaurants report no formal complaints to head office over a whole year.

A combined 'hard' and 'soft' approach

A third approach to TQM is defined as a mixture of 'hard' and 'soft', comprising three features: an obsession with quality, the need for a scientific approach and the view that all employees are part of one team. Empowerment is through employee involvement, in that employees are encouraged to engage in and identify with the performance of the unit.

Hard measures are used on the tangible aspects of the product and service. Standard procedures manuals specify dish and drink recipes and presentation. Service times and procedures are also specified. Staff are engaged in the activities through teamwork, careful recruitment and training. Team briefings and appropriate motivation and rewards are also an important aspect of the approach.

This approach is consistent with service styles that are *choice dependent*. Services that rely on a highly standardized tangible offer in products and services, but that also require employees to delivery a quality experience, will match with this approach to quality management.

Example 8.3

TGI Friday Restaurants

In many ways, TGI Fridays incorporated elements of both hard and soft approaches. Standard procedures manuals laid down production and presentation specifications, and service times are much more prescriptive than are Harvesters'. Employee performance is not quite so prescribed as at McDonald's, though tests on product knowledge are used to ensure that frontline employees have the requisite technical knowledge to be able to advise customers. Employee performance is judged against time and behavioural service requirements such as checking customers are happy with the dish served. On the other hand, employee performance and the ability to identify customer service needs are evaluated at a more evaluative level. Ultimately, the company aims to create a cultural environment through which employees can provide a performance to which customers will respond favourably. A mixture of both personal material rewards – sales-related bonuses and tips – and appeals to teamworking were elements by which individuals were encouraged to deliver the quality experience. Careful staff selection and prework training are also key elements to the approach.

Prior to all service periods, employees attend a team briefing session that is formally organized by a senior member of the team. These sessions encourage staff to make suggestions and promote ideas for good service. They are also encouraged to tell jokes and even perform tricks and contribute to a 'fun' atmosphere.

Service quality management includes formal monitoring of service times through a computer programme that manages the delivery time for starters and main courses, and through formal quality checkers (Expeditors) who stand at the service hatch and check that dishes are presented correctly before being served to customers. Employees are required to contribute the customer's celebration of party atmosphere. Their performance is therefore key to the success of the brand. Their performance is monitored by managers on a quarterly basis, and 'best' staff are given choice over shifts and restaurant service areas.

Customer complaints are generally dealt with by the managers, who monitor difficulties and general problems. Where there are general difficulties these might be raised at the briefing sessions.

The names of initiatives that prioritize customer service quality vary. Total quality management, customer service organization and total quality organization are all variations of an approach which have similar intentions, conceptual origins and ideological roots.

- All suggest that service organizations can benefit from an organization-wide commitment to quality, the development of a customer quality dominated culture, employee empowerment, etc.

- Many of these approaches recognize that competitive advantage can be gained from delivering consistent service quality and ensuring customer satisfaction.

- Each identifies employee performance as playing a crucial role in identifying potential faults and thereby continuously improving performance, and in interacting with customers in ways that can either deliver customer satisfaction or dissatisfaction.

Conclusion

This chapter has shown that customer service quality management is an important, if not vital, aspect of your role as unit manager. The retention of existing customers and the attraction of new customers to the business are essential for sales growth. Certainly the loss of regular customers has a material impact on turnover and sales. In addition, dissatisfied customers rarely keep their experiences to themselves, and by the time they tell friends and acquaintances, the lost business can run into thousands of pounds.

Service quality management is difficult because customer satisfaction is associated with customer expectations. Not all customers use the unit for the same occasions and their expectations and assessment of incidents critical to service success vary. Employee assessments of customer needs may also not match the customer expectation. The nature of the service encounter itself is difficult because of the intangible aspect of service and the difficulties caused by the perishable nature of services. You cannot rework a smile or a false greeting.

Given these difficulties many hospitality retail organizations have explored a number of national and international award schemes that both provide a framework for designing and delivering quality and provide a 'kite mark' for customers and clients. Even in situations where there is no award system, TQM provides a useful philosophical model for you to apply in your unit. Different types of service offer will require different TQM approaches, but all depend on a cultural commitment to delivering high-quality service, and employee skills and performance are essential to successfully meeting customer expectations.

Reflective practice

Answer the questions to check your understanding of this chapter:

1 For a hospitality retail unit known to you, describe the key elements of the product and service offer to customers. What importance do the tangible and intangible aspects of the goods and service play?
2 In the same business consider the main customer occasions which are served by the unit. Describe different customer expectations of successful experiences? Do they use different critical success factors?
3 Would one of the quality award schemes benefit this unit? What do you see as the key benefits and limitations on the award schemes?
4 Highlight the steps needed to introduce a total quality management programme in your unit.
5 Critically discuss the various approaches to total quality management and identify the approach that best matches the needs of the business unit you have in mind. Explain your answer.

References

Herzberg, F. (1966). *Work and the Nature of Man.* Staple Press.
Lockwood, A., Baker, M. and Ghillyer, A. (1996). *Quality Management in Hospitality.* Cassell.
Peters, T. (1992). *Liberation Management.* Harper & Row.

Further reading

Lockwood, A., Baker, M. and Ghillyer, A. (1996). *Quality Management in Hospitality.* Cassell.

CHAPTER 9

Time management and activity planning

After working through this chapter you should be able to:

- plan your time and priorities for action
- develop objectives and action plans
- use a planned approach to delegation and scheduling
- follow up actions and evaluate performance.

What sets you apart from others is how you use your time

Your role as unit manager requires that you set priorities and actions for the rest of the team in the restaurant. Both the management team and the wider team of employees require a systematic approach to steering and guiding their efforts in a way that achieves the overall objectives you have set. Initially this requires that you understand how to identify priorities that make effective use of each person's time.

You have an array of conflicting pressures that require you to put your efforts into the right set of priorities. A common mistake made by many managers in the hospitality industry is that they spend their time being very active, but are doing jobs that other people in the team could, and should, be doing.

In part this error flows from the personality of the people concerned. Chapter 4 showed that people with extrovert personalities are prone to be active and find difficulty with planning and thinking. *Working smart is more important than working hard.*

It is essential, therefore, that you understand and apply the techniques of time planning to your timetable and the working time of the people in the unit team. To be effective you need to apply a systematic approach to setting objectives:

- devising action plans
- delegating the actions needed to achieving the objectives
- agreeing schedules and providing support training, where needed
- following up the actions and appraising performance.

Time management

As unit manager you have more freedom to use your time as you see fit than most of the team. At the same time the number of demands on your time increases as your responsibilities increase. In these circumstances it easy for you to be less effective, in one of the following ways:

- You concentrate on tasks rather than planning because you prefer to be active.
- You give priority to areas of work that you enjoy best, say dealing with people, rather than on some essential technical or administrative tasks.
- You spend time working on tasks that other members of the team could do.
- You spend time on tasks that are not important to the unit's success.
- You spend time on activities that are not urgent.

In all these examples you might be busy, perhaps even over-worked and stressed, but you are not using your time to maximum effect. Time is a limited resource. No matter what you do there are only twenty-four hours in each day. Given the many demands on your time, you need to plan how to use your time to best effect.

Because you will have limited contact with your line manager, it is important that you know how to plan and schedule your own time effectively. Time planning and time management will allow you to achieve more each day, each week, each month, each year. *Just think what you could achieve over twelve months if you were able to be 10 per cent more effective on each day of the year.*

Time planning allows you to be proactive, to foresee events and deal with them before they occur – for example, planning to recruit more staff before a busy trading period. Planning ahead will also help you to explore new markets and continually build the business.

On a daily basis, planning for each upcoming shift allows you to run the unit effectively by:

- ensuring that there are enough staff on duty with the right balance of skills to meet the needs of the service period

- having enough product available to serve the sales of meals and drinks that are likely to occur on the shift

- making sure that all the equipment needed is in working order.

In the longer term, time management allows you to devote time to those activities that will develop the business. Managers who are poor time managers frequently rush from one crisis to the next, never able to see their way out of their difficulties. They react to situations and events by acting on these rather than acting on events.

The way you spend your time can be divided into three main areas:

1 *Boss-imposed time* is the time you spend on activities that have been requested by your bosses.

2 *System-imposed time* is the time you spend responding to issues that come from the normal working of the unit – dealing with employees, dealing with customers, responding to issues raised by your management team, meeting and dealing with suppliers and the local community.

3 *Self-imposed time* is the time you spend proactively developing the business.

Boss-imposed time and system-imposed time are likely to be reactive, but they cannot be ignored. Long-term proactive measures you put in place through your self-imposed time can lead to a reduction in the amount of time spent on these issues. For example, time spent planning for and reducing the amount of staff turnover can ultimately result in less time spent recruiting and training new staff, and dealing with customer complaints arising from poor quality work.

If the majority of your time is spent on reacting to problems, then *the unit is managing you.* On the other hand, if you spend most of your time in a proactive way, *you are managing the unit.*

Proactive, reactive and passive time

As well as boss-, system- or self-imposed time, the way you use your time can be classified as proactive, reactive or passive.

1 *Proactive tasks* are those that you have chosen to undertake in order to develop the business. You may be working on one of the unit's objectives or dealing with an individual employee's development needs. There may be little noticeable difference in the short-term effects, but the unit benefits in the long run.

2 *Reactive tasks* are those that you have to undertake to avoid serious consequences. This will usually include tasks that you had not planned to do, say dealing with a customer complaint or an employee-related problem. Here the consequences might be negative for the unit, if nothing is done, but dealing with the issues does not positively benefit the business.

3 *Passive tasks* cover situations where you are not taking action. It may be classified as wasted time, though some passive time is necessary – taking breaks, social conversation with team members, measuring tracking performance. The key issue is whether this ultimately leads to proactive tasks and contributes to long-term benefits to the unit.

As unit manager you should be aiming to spend the majority of your time in a proactive manner, because you are then managing the restaurant. If you are spending your time in mostly reactive tasks, then you are in danger of getting into a vicious cycle that can be difficult of break out of, because you are often beset by problems that are urgent, and you have few opportunities to stand back and plan.

Active learning point

The following exercise will help you plan your time effectively by analysing the work that you currently do.

Exercise 9.1

Work analysis

Keep a detailed record of the way you spend your time at work. You should include every activity, even your time in the restaurant. Avoid nothing, even whether your work is planned or not, whether productive or not. Keep this record for one week, and be as honest as possible.

Record all the ways you spend your time in the first column, using a chart similar to that in Table 9.1. Categorize these as being boss-imposed, system-imposed or self-imposed time. Then categorize them as being proactive, reactive or passive.

Urgent or important tasks

When you analyse the way you spend your time, you should recognize the need to spend your time proactively and to reduce the time spent on reactive and passive tasks. Furthermore, you will be able to reduce the time you spend on activities that are of little benefit. Another way of improving your productivity is to consider tasks in order of the urgency and importance.

Urgent means those tasks that have to be done quickly. They are not necessarily tasks of great relevance but they have to be done now. A task that can be left for a week or two is not urgent.

Importance refers to tasks that make a significant impact on improving the unit and its performance. Activities that do not impact positively on the unit's performance are usually not important.

Bringing these two considerations together it is possible to construct a four-quadrant box that can be useful in time management planning. Figure 9.1 shows these four quadrants.

	Activity/task	Time spent	Boss/system/ self-imposed	Proactive/reactive/ passive
1				
2				
3				
4				
5				
6				
7				
8				
9				
10				
11				
12				
13				
14				
15				

Table 9.1 Time analysis chart

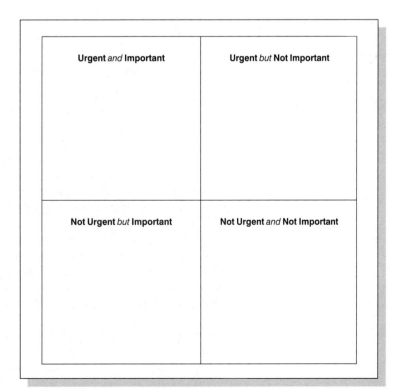

Figure 9.1
Urgent/important theory

Hospitality, Leisure & Tourism Series

Active learning point

Using the activities listed in the earlier exercise, arrange them under the headings given in Figure 9.1.

- *Urgent and important* activities that must be done now and that will benefit the unit fall into this category. Dealing with a customer complaint or an employee matter are examples of situations like this. The key issue here is that the activity must be dealt with in a way that produces a long-term benefit by correcting the problem for the future. For example, if one of the assistant managers is involved in selecting and recruiting staff who subsequently leave quickly and you provide the manager with support in better recruitment and selection techniques that reduces problem recruitment and staff turnover in future, this was an action that was both urgent and important.

- *Urgent but not important* activities that must be done now but do not directly benefit the unit fit into this category. Examples might include tracking and monitoring information that will not necessarily improve the business. In some cases you are being asked to provide information, or are doing things because they have always been done this way. Ideally you should not be wasting time on these activities. Where possible the tasks should be eradicated or at least delegated to someone else.

- *Not urgent but important* activities will directly benefit your or the unit but there may be no immediate negative impact if they are not done. There is a danger that you will be lulled into taking no action. In the long run these activities benefit the business. Examples are planning, training, communication events and working on building employee morale.

- *Not urgent and not important* activities are when you find yourself doing things that are nice to do but which yield few benefits. If something has been on your list of things to do for several weeks, it probably falls into this category. These should be the first things to drop.

Now that you have analysed the way you spend your time, you should be in a position to take action to remove wasted time and to work on improving your productivity. The following are some actions that might be of benefit to you:

1 *Delegation*: one of the main ways to improving the use of your time is in delegating work to colleagues. To be effective delegation must involve an investment in training and development of the person who will be empowered.

2 *Causes not symptoms*: for example, if you are constantly bringing in agency or other temporary staff to cover high levels of staff turnover, you are dealing with the symptom not the cause. This might require a more thorough investigation and retraining of some of your team.

3 *Communication*: successful unit management requires that you get all your team to understand and work towards the objectives set. To do this you need to spend a large amount of time communicating with your team so that future problems and difficulties are avoided.

4 *Proactive changes*: a recurring problem needs a long-term fix. If you find yourself having to repeat the same actions to overcome the same problems, you need a long-term systematic response that will stop the problem occurring in the first place.

5 *Records and actions*: successful unit management is based on active involvement in the operation out on the floor of the unit, but some record-keeping, auditing, tracking, weekly statistics and daily reports inform decisions and actions in the future. You need to keep the right balance, so that records result in actions.

6 *Information technology*; most units now have access to information technology systems that can greatly reduce your time-keeping records and time taken to respond to messages. E-mails, word processing and spreadsheet packages are examples.

7 *Personal organization*: your personal organization – recording and noting the tasks that you need to do and achieving your own targets and commitments to others – require you to adopt effective reminder systems for both routine and one-off tasks.

8 *Improving personal performance*: because of the large and wide range of commitments on your time, there are no easy answers to time management. You have to keep working at it and always be committed to using your own time effectively.

This latter point cannot be stressed enough, because time management requires a long-term commitment to working more effectively and focusing your efforts on those tasks that give priority to the development and progress of the unit – those activities that result in one or more of the following outcomes:

- sales growth
- increased market share
- increased profitability
- improved service quality
- better customer satisfaction

- improved staff retention

- better employee satisfaction

- other objectives set.

Managing your time is clearly an important, if not vital, starting point but you also need to pay attention to managing the time of your team. A systematic approach will help you ensure managers and employees are given the right direction and support so that they also grow and positively contribute to the development of the unit.

Activity planning and management

Chapter 3 provided you with some guidance on the skills and approaches needed to be an effective team leader. In order to be a good manager you need to be a good leader, because these skills enable and encourage people to make a positive contribution to the work environment, responding to the changing needs of everyone in the unit. Management is different; it is about providing the systems and direction through which results will be achieved.

Figure 9.2 suggests an approach to systematic unit management that should be applied in each unit. It is up to you, as unit manager, to ensure that the systems and environment are created so that all members of the team:

- understand what is expected of them

- are given the support to achieve the tasks set

- are given feedback on their activities.

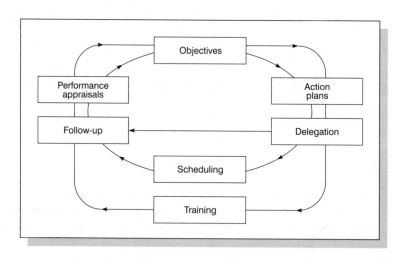

Figure 9.2
The unit management system

This approach also recognizes two different parts to the activity:

- developing your plan
- implementing your plan.

In the following sections this approach will be explored stage by stage.

Unit goals

All hospitality retail operations have business goals. These are what give the business strategic direction on a national or, even, international basis. As a unit manager you will be expected to understand these goals and manage your unit in a way that achieves the goals in your section of the business. Thus you may not be expected to write business goals at unit management level, but will be expected to decide the most relevant priorities for your unit.

Example 9.1

McDonald's Restaurants Limited

McDonald's Restaurants have company goals that relate to the company's mission to make the company 'the number one restaurant choice'. These goals stress:

- delivering 100 per cent customer satisfaction
- increasing market share
- increasing profitability.

Each restaurant will be aiming to contribute to achieving these goals. However, they are not the only goals set by the company, and national company management may also decide on priorities that will focus each restaurant's management team over the next six to twelve months. These might include:

- 'A' grade food safety audit scores
- hourly paid employee turnover below 100 per cent
- gross profit at 68 per cent
- minimum B grade on training audit scores.

A manager in a restaurant who had grade A on food safety and training audit grades, and staff turnover at 66 per cent, with gross profit at 63 per cent might focus on gross profit improvement as the key business goal in addition to the major strategic goals.

A unit manager needs to assess the priorities and goals, and ensure the priorities are relevant and will have maximum impact on the business.

As part of the marketing and business planning activities (Chapters 12 and 13) you will identify the *strengths, weaknesses, opportunities* and *threats* that you will use to further develop your goals. These will help you to shape your unit's direction for the next six months to a year.

Active learning point

1 List the various goals that have been set by the national or regional management team and from your own analysis of the business needs.

2 Prioritize the goals that will have the biggest impact on the business. The following questions may help you to draw up your list of priorities:

(a) What is the unit's weakest area?
(b) What is the unit's greatest opportunity or potential for development?
(c) Which areas need to be focused on urgently?
(d) What will happen if these areas are not focused on?
(e) How will focusing on the issue impact on the unit's performance?
(f) Are there too many issues to be realistically achievable?

Once you arrive at a list of goals that give the unit long-term direction, you need to develop objectives that will help to achieve the goals.

Objectives

An objective must be about specific actions and accomplishments over a known time period. It must be measurable, so that you know whether or not you have achieved it. Objectives are steps to take towards the achievement of a goal. Each goal is likely to require a number of objectives.

For example, a goal to increase staff retention and reduce staff turnover is likely to involve objectives related to training, team meetings, communications, and employee satisfaction.

Objectives should also be the responsibility of named individuals. Individual members of the management team, or hourly paid employees may be delegated individual projects that contribute to the achievement of the goal. Thus, in the above example, different members of the management team may be dealing with separate issues that contribute to the reduction of staff turnover.

For effective delegation it is essential, first, that the individual has the skills necessary to complete the task successfully. The objective must be clearly defined, and so that the person knows what is expected of them, how success will be measured and when.

The acronym RIMS is useful as a guide to writing effective objectives:

- *Realistic*: the objective must be challenging to the individual, but it must also be achievable. Nothing is more demoralizing than being set unachievable targets. Both the objective itself and the capabilities of the individual have to be considered here.

- *Individual*: one individual must be accountable for the objective so that he or she will be responsible for achieving the objective. The individual may work with a team of other people, but ultimately this person is accountable to you as manager.

- *Measurable*: describes in detail the time frame and means by which the objective will be measured.

- *Specific*: the statement has to be clearly expressed and should use action words – *increase* employee training, *organize* team briefings. For example:

  - Unit goal: Reduce staff turnover to the company average of 70 per cent within the next six months.

  - Objective 1: Beginning on 1 January, John will increase staff training so that within six months all staff are fully trained.

  - Objective 2: Beginning on 1 January, Helen will organize monthly staff meetings that within two months make suggestions to assist in the reduction of staff turnover.

Active learning point

Using the unit goals that you have developed above, now write objectives for the unit. For each goal set out the objectives as shown in Table 9.2. The table shows how you might plan objective associated with the goals set.

Unit goal	
Objective 1	
Objective 2	
Objective 3	
Objective 4	
Objective 5	
Objective 6	

Table 9.2 Developing unit objectives

Action plans

Action plans take the objectives down to a series of steps that have to be achieved to make the objective happen (Figure 9.3). Depending on the complexity of the objective there may be many or few actions needed to achieve the objective. Again the skills, knowledge and expertise of the person delegated to achieve the objective will be a factor to consider. A more experienced and skilled person will need less guidance and support from you than a person who has yet to develop. The following elements need to be included in the development of the action plan for each objective:

1 *What*: list the tasks needed to be done to achieve the objective.

2 *When*: the time and order that each task is to be completed. Objectives frequently fail because planning starts well but fails in the later stages. Using a time planner can be helpful for complex tasks.

3 *How well*: the standard to be achieved may be an issue, though in most cases it is likely to be a 'done–not done' issue. Training issues may well require the how well evaluation.

4 *Resources*: list the people, material, information, time and money needed to complete the task. It is worth considering all the resources available both within and outside the organization. For example, other units, specialist departments, local government officers, etc. are resources you can use to help you achieve the objective.

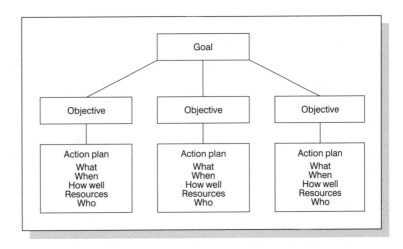

Figure 9.3
Goals, objectives and action plans

5 *Who*: the people who will complete the task. The objective is assigned to an individual who will work with other people who may be delegated to complete various tasks. The process of delegation further develops people in the unit and frees up your time to support people in their work.

A time scheduling sheet can be used to help you to plan more complex and multistaged tasks. In particular it is useful in showing tasks that can be actioned independent of each other and those that are dependent on other tasks being completed.

Table 9.3 is a model to enable you to work out the actions and arrive at a plan of tasks showing the five elements listed above.

Objective:

What	Who	Resources	Begin	Finish	Date finished

How will the task be measured?

Table 9.3 Suggested action plan worksheet

Delegation

Chapter 2 of this book showed how different styles of management can be used to manage the unit as a whole and that varying degrees of delegation are needed for different styles of service to the unit's customers. This section shows that even in command and control type situations operating to 'one best way' of working, you can develop people in your team to take on more of the tasks traditionally seen to be a 'management' task. *Furthermore, delegation to individual team members is a positive requirement for managing your own time effectively.*

Delegation to other people can be defined as:

- The skill of getting work done by people who would not normally undertake these tasks.

- Getting things done by other people.

- Giving people the authority to make decisions on your behalf.

- Developing the skills and talents of others to build their own sense of accomplishment.

- Requiring that the individual be delegated authority to make significant decisions which the person him or herself feels are important and relevant.

- Above all, therefore, effective delegation requires 'buy-in' by the person who is to be delegated.

In this sense delegation is related to developing individuals and you should recognize that effective delegation represents a process that has to be managed. The model in Chapter 2 can be used to develop an understanding of the levels of initiative that are involved in managing different individuals and in showing how people management will require and involve a range of different approaches even with one dominant style. Thus, even in situations where the style is chiefly directive, consultative or participative, you will spend some of your time in different communication relationships with employees and in relationships where the employee displays different levels of initiative. The following section explores five different levels of initiative. Each involves the employee in different ways and requires different levels of instruction, training and support for the team member.

Level 1: Waits to be told • • •

Typically the team member has never performed the task before. They wait too be told and shown how to complete the task. Your involvement is in demonstrating, explaining, training and giving feedback to the employee. You will be present throughout the time the task is being done. Your involvement is shown in the shaded area.

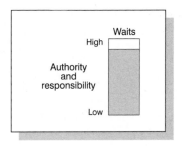

Level 2: Asks what to do • • •

The team member is aware that a task needs doing or that there is a way of getting round a problem, but does not know how to do it. They ask what needs to be done and are shown the task. You would be involved in demonstrating, explaining, training and giving feedback, though this would be reduced compared with Level 1 because the employee has at least a basic grasp of the issue to be undertaken.

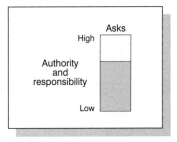

Level 3: Recommends what to do • • •

The team member is familiar with the job or task and is confident enough to make recommendations for correction or improvement. They are still not skilled, experienced or knowledgeable enough to take action themselves. Your involvement should be receiving and deciding on the suggestion, getting the team member working on the task and giving feedback on their efforts. You will need to spend less time on direct supervision of their work

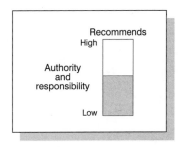

Level 4: Takes action, reports immediately • • •

The team member is confident and familiar with the task, but will not have completed it without supervision in the past. They now need to do the task but check that they have done it correctly. Your involvement is in confirming the correct action or preventing an action that might cause damage to the unit or a loss of confidence in the team member. Minimal supervision of the person undertaking the task

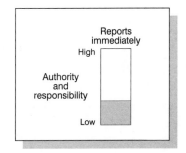

Level 5: *Takes action, reports routinely* • • •

The team member is skilled, knowledgeable and confident enough to carry out the task and do whatever is required. They will not need to inform you of their actions immediately, but will routinely report to you. You will need to provide feedback on a regular basis so that the team member is informed about their progress and their motivation levels are maintained. There is virtually no direct supervision of the team member, though you will be indirectly monitoring progress.

Before moving to act on these five levels, it is important to remember that delegation frequently fails for a number of predictable reasons:

1 Managers pay lip service to employee involvement but do not organize employee development properly.

2 Team members are not given the correct level of training and support.

3 Managers are unclear about what needs to be done and by when.

4 There is a failure to share understanding of what actions are needed.

5 Team members vary in their skills, experience and motivation to take on additional tasks.

As unit manager you need to concentrate solely on doing those tasks that are truly essential and require the expertise and judgement that you alone possess. If you find yourself doing routine tasks that other members of your team could be doing – ordering stock, staff schedules, entering monthly and weekly reports – you are probably not spending sufficient time training, developing and motivating team members or moving the unit forward.

Active learning point

Check your understanding of some of the issues raised in the above section by answering the following questions:

1 What is the likely reaction of a person who has a good grasp of a particular task, yet you manage the person as though they were at a low level of initiative? Are there other likely consequences?

2 What are the likely consequences of delegating tasks to individuals who have not yet developed the skills needed to complete the task correctly?

3 Why do you need to consider the needs and motives of individual team members before delegating tasks to them?

4 What is the likely reaction of a person to whom you have delegated a task, when you constantly check on their progress and closely supervise their actions?

5 Give five reasons why delegation initiatives sometimes fail?

6 Think of occasions when you had tasks delegated to you. What were your feelings and experiences?

Scheduling

The planning of the management team's duties and the appropriate quality scheduling are an important part of your job. In most hospitality retail units you have to ensure that the management team is scheduled to be on duty through the major opening hours, yet have time off duty and their full holiday entitlement. Their involvement in the running of the unit is essential for the delivery of the goals, objectives and actions that have been devised. Scheduling therefore needs to take account of the actions needed by key individuals and the time required to deliver the targets set.

Some of the issues associated with the timetabling of staff are dealt with in more detail in Chapter 11, however, the following section suggests some issues for consideration and the steps that you might take in scheduling the management team's duties.

Principals

The work schedule for the management team needs to recognize and balance the needs of the business and the individuals involved. People do need a life outside of the unit and it is important that this is planned and delivered.

1 You need to establish some basic markers about working a spread of shifts including weekends. Should all managers expect at least on weekend off work each month?

2 Do you need to establish that all managers will work some of the key important shifts, such as the business close shifts or business opening shifts? Different businesses may have different priorities.

3 Work scheduling may need to allow for time to work on the projects that have been delegated to different individuals.

4 The management schedule needs to be completed well in advance of the month end so that people have reasonable notice of when they will be required for duty. You need to fix a time target that will ensure that the plan is available at least ten days before the month end.

5 The priorities arising from the objectives and actions set need to be considered in the planning process.

6 You may also need to consider the relationships between key staff members, so that strong team bonds can be developed. It is difficult for people to get to know each other if they are rarely on duty together.

Planning the schedule ● ● ●

Here are some steps that you might take in scheduling your team:

1 At the agreed date (say fifteen days before implementation) schedule the management team for the following month.

2 Consider the jobholders who are to be included – departmental heads, working supervisors, training personnel, maintenance personnel, clerical staff, key skilled employees.

3 Take into account requests for special time allocations from within the team.

4 Check that all the key posts needed for operational activities are covered and take special account of the action plans, objectives and projects that individuals are working on.

5 Allocate time on the schedule for people to complete the tasks.

6 Plan in the amount of training and counselling needed by individuals doing the tasks, and allow time for yourself to be involved with them when they are at various stages in the delegation process. In some cases, you need to directly train and closely supervise the person.

7 Consult with the individuals once you have made the first draft of the schedule. Act on suggestions and requests where appropriate.

8 Once the schedule is complete, with 'buy-in' from all the relevant parties, ensure that it is made available on the understanding that it will be changed only under exceptional circumstances.

9 Throughout the month monitor its effectiveness. Make sure that you note any difficulties and successes for future reference.

Follow-up

Having devised the unit's goals, objectives and action plans, together with scheduling the time needed for individuals to work on the tasks that have been delegated to them, they should now be capable of making the plans happen. Clearly, this will require focused training and support. Chapter 7 covers the processes for identifying and then delivering individuals training and development needs. It is important to remember that these will be focused on the specific needs of the plan and you will be supporting the individuals completing the tasks delegated to them.

1 Follow-up is an important element in the execution of the task, because it completes the training loop by giving feedback about their actions.

2 Feedback helps individuals develop their understanding of appropriate performance and standards.

3 Follow-up helps motivate people because they are aware of their own development and growing skills.

4 Feedback to individuals helps them understand if there is a problem and understand what needs to be done to correct the problems.

The follow-up element can happen in two ways: *checking progress* and *checking results*.

Checking progress • • •

The process of checking how the individual is progressing through the task can happen at several stages in the completion of the task. Clearly, for more complex tasks, or where the individual has limited experience, you may have to provide more regular checking than where the task is simple or the individual more experienced.

When you check progress you will need to inform the individual of how they are doing. This needs to be done sensitively, particularly where some form of corrective action is needed. In some cases it may be that the individual needs additional training and support. In others you will be confirming that they are on the right lines and reinforcing their actions. Checking progress also keeps you abreast with progress and the likely outcome of the task set.

Checking results

This must always take place on the completion of the task. This stage of the process helps the individual reflect back on what worked or did not work and the total experience. You are able to praise and provide recognition for good work, or encourage the individual to take corrective action where it is needed.

If the checking progress stage has been successful, the number of difficulties and problems will have been minimized. The outcome should be reasonably well known, because you will have a good knowledge of the individual and the progress they are making with the task.

The progress and results stages need to be included in all projects, because they are essential in managing the conduct of delegated tasks, and in ensuring that results genuinely contribute to the improvement of the business and provide learning opportunities for the individual concerned.

Planning follow-up

The following suggests an approach to working the follow-up process into the way you plan and organize the unit:

1 Make a list of the objectives and actions that have been developed in the planning stage.

2 Add the names of the people responsible for the objectives and actions needed.

3 Using your experience and knowledge of the person, evaluate their level of initiative and consider the training and follow-up that will be needed. This may come from you or from the person responsible for the objective.

4 Check that time has been allocated for the training and support activities in the schedule for the coming period. Make any adjustments necessary, or reconsider the allocation of delegated tasks to include more people who have the necessary skills to complete the task.

5 Build in time for training and checking progress with the individual and to assist in developing the individual's motivation and learning from the experience.

6 Ensure that checking results is scheduled and takes place.

Giving feedback on all performance is vital, so make sure that you allocate time for it and make it happen.

Performance review

Most hospitality retail organizations use some form of performance review for both managers and employees. Successful performance reviews need to be established as an ongoing process through an ongoing review system. Accurate documents and records maintained through the review period, together with the feedback and progress-checking processes discussed earlier, are likely to result in a review process that is fair and genuinely beneficial to the individual's development.

A person is most likely to regard the review as unfair if they experience one of the following:

1 There is a lack of facts and accurate information.

2 The review brings up new criticisms that have not been mentioned before.

3 The review is based solely, on the most recent performance and does not explore their performance over the full review period.

4 A failure to acknowledge the person's achievements, and only considers areas for improvement.

5 There is disagreement about issues raised at the checking progress stage.

6 There is a lack of preparation by the reviewer.

7 The review is late and hurried.

Performance reviews need not be damaging, provided they are handled in a positive manner and driven by a genuine concern to register the individual's development thus far as well as build future development. Most people will accept criticism if it is treated as an opportunity to improve.

Your performance review system needs to include three stages:

- performance update
- work review
- performance review.

Hospitality, Leisure & Tourism Series

Performance update

These are unscheduled incidents relating to the individual's performance that are worthy of note. They may be either positive or negative. Typically, they may relate to disciplinary incidents, or successes, say, in dealing with a customer or special project. The key point is that these should be discussed with the individual at the time and recorded on file.

A change of unit or of unit manager should also prompt a performance update, recording the individual's performance up to the date change.

Work review

This is the formal scheduled time to check progress with the individual. You build in a time to your schedule that allows you to discuss progress regarding objectives and responsibilities that have been delegated to the person. There should be a written record of the issues raised and actions agreed. It is essential that the individual is treated as an equal party to the discussion and actions to be planned because they must buy into the process if it is to be genuinely developing. One approach can be that the individual writes up a summary of the review to go on the record, though clearly this will be agreed and signed by you as manager.

Performance review

The final stage is to formally review the performance over the period and identify priorities for the next period. If you have handled the earlier elements in the process correctly, there should be few surprises and it should be a relatively short and straightforward step. The review will be used to formally note the individual's development and needs for future development. In most cases these reviews will be used for promotions and interunit transfers, because they form part of the individual's records of achievement and plans. In other cases, they are used as the basis for bonus payments and salary increases.

Managing performance review • • •

The following list of steps is suggested as a checklist of actions that will help you to plan effective performance reviews for your team:

1 Develop goals, objectives and action plans that will develop the unit.

2 Ensure that these are delegated to individuals.

3 Time should be planned into the work schedules so individuals are able to undertake their allocated tasks.

4 Establish a record-keeping system to keep track of individual's progress including results, responsibilities and performance.

5 Allocate time to check progress and give feedback on performance.

6 During the scheduled sessions ensure two-way communication. Give praise and identify training needs where required. Above all attempt to encourage and be positive. Document all decisions made.

7 Continue the process of recording progress and giving feedback.

8 Plan time to review the results in line with the planned completion dates of each action task or objective.

At the time of the annual performance review you should have a complete documentary record of all these activities on which to base the individual's review.

Conclusion

Effective unit management requires you to plan the direction and priorities of the unit so as to contribute to the overall goals of the organization. You need to manage your own time effectively. As a unit manager, there are many opportunities to keep active and working hard on tasks that are not what you should be doing. Conducting a personal audit helps you identify those tasks that other members could, and should, be doing. Your key role is developing the team to deliver improved unit performance.

Although most goals are set by regional or national management, you will need to understand these and consider the goals that have to be operational priorities for your unit. In some cases, you may want to devise additional unit goals that are specific to your unit. In all cases, you have to devise objectives and action plans that move the business towards the goals identified.

The goals, objectives and action plans identified will form part of the unit business plan – discussed further in Chapter 13. However, this chapter has taken these objectives and action plans and described the processes whereby you manage their implementation and achievement. The detailed allocation of tasks and objectives to named individuals requires planned and carefully managed delegation. The foundation of effective delegation requires a close inspection of the needs of each individual, and training support.

Delegated tasks to trained individuals with the appropriate supervision and support then need to be managed through appropriate time scheduling and follow-up. Checking progress, adjusting and supporting performance, confirming that progress is on the right track and generally keeping some contact with the individual's progress, also has to be managed and planned. The amount of contact you have with different individuals working on different action plans or objectives will vary, but the key point is that some contact will be required in all cases. A well-documented record of these contacts and progress form the basis for effective and motivating performance reviews.

Reflective practice

Answer these questions to check your understanding of this chapter:

1 Critically discuss the need to manage your time more effectively. Conduct an audit of your time showing those actions and tasks that are essential and those that could be delegated to others.
2 For a hospitality retail unit known to you, identify the key goals for the company that might apply to the overall business. Are there other goals you could devise? If so, what are they?
3 In the same business devise the objectives that will help to achieve the goals? For each objective prepare action plans to achieve the objectives.
4 Allocate the tasks and objectives to delegated individuals.
5 What time is required for each individual to complete they delegated task. What additional training and support do they need?
6 Critically discuss the need for effective follow up and performance review. Suggest reasons why this is not so well done at times.

Further reading

Rees, W. D. (1990). *The Skills of Management*. Routledge.

Control and operating profit management

After working through this chapter you should be able to:

- identify cost and sales concepts

- analyse sales and costs for profits generation

- apply a control system

- calculate a range of cost-volume-profit ratios.

It is all about keeping sales and costs under control

The hospitality retail sector, almost by definition, involves the production of hospitality goods and services for commercial reasons. As we have shown in earlier chapters, high volume retail brands are primarily aimed at meeting the needs of customers in a way that satisfies their needs, but also generates a profit for the commercial organization. Services are supplied to customers only when they can produce sales, or revenue, that covers costs and generates surplus.

This chapter introduces some general concepts about the control of costs and sales. It will help you establish a framework for understanding costs and the relationships between different types of costs, as well as understanding how sales can be analysed in a way that might generate extra sales at a lower level of costs. Developing the right kind of control system is essential for effective unit management. The best control systems control the essentials but do not always waste time on those aspects of cost control where the benefit to be gained from the controls is outweighed by the cost of the controls themselves. This point is not as simple as it sounds because there are situations where organizations control incidental expenses – for example, sanctioned equipment repairs – outside of the unit. The attempt to control these 'incidentals' results in a situation where the unit manager cannot call in a service engineer even when a machine is no longer working. Costs are being controlled through a more senior decision-maker, but the cost of lost customers because of increased waiting times, or the cost of staff turnover because of reduced employee satisfaction, are rarely taken into account.

Year XXXX	Nottingham	Leeds
	£	£
Sales:		
Food	800 000	765 000
Beverages	150 000	135 000
	950 000	900 000
Cost of sales:		
Food	320 000	268 000
Beverages	45 000	34 000
Total	365 000	302 000
Trading profit	585 000	598 000
Staff wages (hourly paid)	218 500	216 000
Gross profit	366 500	382 000

Table 10.1
Income statements for Family Restaurants, Nottingham and Leeds

Table 10.1 provides an example of the trading accounts of two units in the same hospitality retail brand. The Nottingham unit is run by a manager who has worked hard to build sales. The Leeds restaurant is the same size as the Nottingham unit and is located in a similar position. In Leeds the restaurant manager had generated fewer sales but has been much more effective in controlling operating costs. Thus with a lower sales level the Leeds restaurant is generating a larger gross profit. However, the extent of the variations is distorted by the fact that sales levels are different. The way to overcome this is to convert the information base in the form of a percentage of sales. The figures given in Table 10.2 show more dramatic differences between the costs in the two units.

Before going on to discuss these figures, the information in Table 10.1 needs further discussion. In the example given, sales revenue is from the sale of two types of items – food and beverage. Both have a different cost base and they are accounted for separately. In other units, say bars or hotels, there may be other income streams from gaming machines and from the sale of accommodation. In addition, some businesses, say, fast-food units, may also generate additional costs associated with sales for paper and packaging.

The key point here is that the cost of sales relates to all those items of expenditure that come about as a direct result of making sales.

Sales and the cost of sales are then compared to produce a *trading profit*, some organizations call this 'gross profit', though strictly speaking the cost of the labour directly involved in producing and serving the food and drink should be included.

Year XXXX	Nottingham		Leeds	
	£	%	£	%
Sales:				
Food	800 000	84.0	765 000	85.0
Beverages	150 000	16.0	135 000	15.0
	950 000	100.0	900 000	100.0
Cost of sales:				
Food	320 000	40.0	268 000	35.0
Beverages	45 000	30.0	34 000	25.0
Total	365 000	38.5	302 000	33.6
Trading profit	585 000	61.5	598 000	66.4
Staff wages (hourly paid)	218 500	23.0	216 000	24.0
Gross profit	366 500	38.5	382 000	42.4

Note: Figures have been rounded.

Table 10.2
Income statements for Family Restaurants, Nottingham and Leeds (proportions of costs)

Hospitality, Leisure & Tourism Series

Thus the costs immediately associated with producing the sales are calculated to produce a gross profit.

In Table 10.2 the income statements for both restaurants use percentages to compare the performance in the two restaurants more effectively. The following are a few pointers for guidance in drawing up the analysis:

1 Sales ratios for food and beverages are both calculated against the total sales, e.g.

$$\frac{800\,000}{950\,000} \times 100 = \text{Food sales as \% of total sales, i.e. } 84.2\% \qquad (10.1)$$

2 Costs of sales are calculated as a percentage of the sales revenue for that item, e.g.

$$\frac{320\,000}{800\,000} \times 100 = \text{Food costs as \% of sales of food. i.e. } 40\% \qquad (10.2)$$

3 Total costs, trading profit and staff wages are all calculated as a percentage against the total sales, e.g.

$$\frac{218\,500}{950\,000} \times 100 = \text{Staff wages as \% of total sales, i.e. } 23\% \qquad (10.3)$$

In Table 10.2 the Nottingham restaurant has generated higher sales whilst making a lower gross profit – 38.5 per cent compared with 42.4 per cent. The reason for this is that both food and beverage costs of sales are higher in Nottingham than in the Leeds. Labour costs, however, are lower.

Active learning point

The examples given above show that the Nottingham restaurant has higher costs in the food, beverage and labour elements and is making a lower gross profit on the sales made. List the reasons that might explain why spending on food, beverages and labour is above those in the Leeds restaurant.

At root the problem is one of cost control and budget management. The Nottingham restaurant manager has been successful in generating extra sales, but it could be that the sales have been generated at a highly discounted rate. The various costs of food and beverages and labour costs might all stem from increased sales that produced lower revenue. There are a number of possible causes of higher costs involving both cost and sales concepts:

- Poor operating standards – portion sizes are being exceeded.

- Wastage – food and drink is being prepared that is subsequently not sold.

- Give-aways – too many products is being given away to customers or staff.

- Theft – food and drink are being stolen.

- Sales generated at a discounted rate – say, a two for one offer – or large price reductions are given to encourage purchases.

- Staff productivity is lower – more staff hours needed to serve a given level of customers.

- Staff are not trained – increasing wastage and lower productivity.

- High staff turnover adds to labour costs because the remaining staff are paid overtime or agency staff are employed.

- Sales per transaction are lower – staff have to serve more customers for any given level of sales.

Clearly, these are not the only costs involved in running a restaurant. You have to pay a number of expenses that cannot be directly linked to production levels. They are either costs that are *fixed* – that is, not changed in the short term, say, property rental or lease – or they are expenses that have to be made and cannot be seen as a direct expense of sales – say, advertising and promotion costs. They are expenses incurred by the restaurant and have to be taken into account before calculating the operating profit.

The figures in Table 10.3 show some of the other costs that restaurants incur – property costs through lease and local charges, management costs, promotional expenses, building and equipment maintenance plus other consumables such as staff uniform costs and depreciation charges for equipment are some examples. There may be others, but these are examples of costs that are typical for hospitality retail operations.

The figures also show how the Nottingham restaurant's performance is well below that of the Leeds restaurant when these other costs are taken into account:

1 Despite having slightly larger sales revenue the Nottingham restaurant is barely covering its costs. The profit, expressed as a percentage of sales, is down to just over 5.5 per cent.

2 Interestingly, the additional sales reduce the proportional charges for fixed costs such as rents and management and administrations charges. This is an important principle – as *sales levels increase the fixed costs are unchanged in the short term, and therefore fall as a proportion of sales.*

Year XXXX	Nottingham		Leeds	
	£	%	£	%
Sales:				
Food	800 000	84.0	765 000	85.0
Beverages	150 000	16.0	135 000	15.0
	950 000	100.0	900 000	100.0
Cost of sales:				
Food	320 000	40.0	268 000	35.0
Beverages	45 000	30.0	34 000	25.0
Total	365 000	38.5	302 000	33.6
Trading profit	585 000	61.5	598 000	66.4
Staff wages (hourly paid)	218 500	23.0	216 000	24.0
Gross profit	366 500	38.5	382 000	42.4
Lease and local tax	90 000	9.5	90 000	10.0
Electricity and gas	20 000	2.1	18 000	2.0
Management and admin.	54 000	5.7	54 000	6.0
Promotional activity	48 000	5.0	45 000	5.0
Maintenance	36 000	4.0	18 000	2.0
Other consumables	36 000	4.0	9 000	1.0
Depreciation	30 000	3.2	30 000	3.3
Restaurant profit	52 500	5.5	118 000	13.1

Table 10.3
Restaurant profits in the Nottingham and Leeds restaurants

3 Whilst most costs are roughly equal in the two restaurants, the Nottingham restaurant spends much more on the maintenance and repair of equipment, and on the consumables such as staff uniforms.

In this case there are a number of possible explanations for the extra expenditure. It could be that equipment in the Nottingham restaurant is older and requires more maintenance and repair. On the other hand, the cause might be poor staff training resulting in accidental damage to the equipment. The additional spending on consumables might be due to high levels of staff turnover and a failure to return uniforms when staff leave the unit.

Active learning point

If you were the manager of the Nottingham restaurant, what would you do to increase the restaurant profit?

Your answer will probably have included a number of strategies to control costs and to have a better understanding of sales. These points are discussed in more detail later in the chapter.

Active learning point

For a restaurant or unit known to you, calculate the percentages for each of the cost and revenue items for at least two trading periods. What are the trends? Can you explain the trends?

Your answer will probably show that many costs have a permanent relationship with volume. Other costs remain the same, but vary as a proportion of costs as sales revenue rises and falls. In other cases, both the actual money costs and the proportion of overall revenue that these represent varies. Your explanation will need to focus on these issues. In particular, are there managerial decisions that have impacted on say labour costs that have added to these costs? Chapter 5 shows that staff turnover can add considerably to labour costs.

Cost–volume–profit relationships

The examples and comments given above show that relationships exist between sales, variable costs, the cost of labour, overheads and profits. These can be expressed as the formula:

$$\text{Sales} = \text{Cost of sales} + \text{Cost of labour}$$
$$+ \text{Cost of overhead} + \text{Profit} \qquad (10.4)$$

In fact this is further simplified to:

$$\text{Sales} = \text{Variable cost} + \text{Fixed costs} + \text{Profit} \qquad (10.5)$$
$$S = VC + FC + P$$

The examples given in Table 10.3 suggest that there is likely to be:

- a relationship between variable costs and sales that will be relatively constant, and this can be expressed as a percentage or as a decimal point

- fixed costs remain constant and do not changes as sales change. However, when these are expressed as percentages or decimals the rates change as sales volumes change.

Hospitality, Leisure & Tourism Series

Using the Leeds restaurant example the following figures establish the total variable costs:

Food cost	£268 000
Beverages	£ 34 000
Staff wages	£216 000
Total variable costs	£518 000

The variable rate is calculated by comparing the variable costs with sales:

$$\frac{\text{Variable costs}}{\text{Sales}} = \text{Variable rate} \tag{10.6}$$

In the case of the Leeds restaurant the variable rate is

$$\frac{518\,000}{900\,000} = 0.575 \tag{10.7}$$

or expressed as a percentage, 57.5 per cent, or as 57.5p for every £1.00 of sales.

The fixed costs are the total of all the other overhead costs:

Lease and local tax	£ 90 000
Electricity and gas	£ 18 000
Management and admin.	£ 54 000
Promotional activity	£ 45 000
Maintenance	£ 18 000
Other consumables	£ 9 000
Depreciation	£ 30 000
Total fixed cost	£264 000

In the Leeds restaurant example, therefore, the figures can be expressed as Sales (£900 000) = Variable cost (£518 000) + Fixed costs (£264 000) + Profit (£118 000)

Contribution rate

If 57.5 pence in every £1.00 of sales is accounted for in the variable cost, then the remaining 42.5 pence is available to:

- meet fixed costs

- provide profit.

Increasing sales result in increasing amounts of money being available to meet the fixed costs. Up to the *breakeven point* the contribution made by sales is not sufficient to meet the fixed costs. Only after the fixed costs have been met does the level of sales generate sufficient contribution to produce a profit. The breakeven point is, therefore, the point at which sales are generating sufficient contributions to meet all costs, but are not yet producing profits. This can be calculated using the *contribution rate* – the rate of contribution after variable costs. In the above example,

Contribution rate $= 1 -$ Variable rate

Contribution rate $= 1 - 0.575$ (10.8)

Contribution rate $= 0.425$.

Breakeven point

To determine the breakeven point for the Leeds restaurant the following formula is applied:

$$\text{Sales} = \frac{\text{Fixed costs}}{\text{Contribution rate}}$$

$$\text{Sales} = \frac{264\,000}{0.425}$$ (10.9)

$$\text{Sales} = £621\,176$$

The Leeds restaurant needs to generate sales of £621 176 before costs are covered and profits can be made. After that point is reached, no additional fixed costs occur and each additional £1.00 generated in sales contributes 42.5 pence profit.

As unit manager it is important that you understand these relationships because:

- if sales are generated at prices below the variable costs, the unit will be making an immediate loss

- sales beyond breakeven point generate profits

- additional profits can be made by all sales that exceed variable costs once the breakeven point is reached.

This latter point is useful because extra sales volumes, even at discounted rates, can make a contribution to profits growth. The relationship between sales, variable costs, fixed cost and profits is usually shown using a graph as in Figure 10.1. Here the fixed costs are a constant, as sales grow the total costs increase through the effect of the increased cost of sales. Sales income eventually reaches breakeven point and profits grow with sales growth after that point.

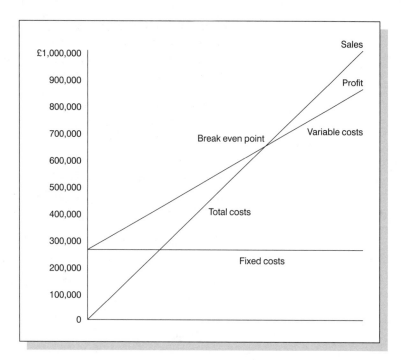

Figure 10.1
Breakeven point, sales and costs for the Leeds restaurant

In the case of the Leeds restaurant, the financial performance given in Table 10.3 shows that sales of £900 000 produced a restaurant profit of £118 000 representing just over 13.1 per cent of sales. If the unit could increase sales to £950,000, the extra sales make an extra contribution of £21 250 (50 000 × 0.425). All this is profit because fixed costs are already covered. Profits rise to £139 250, which is 14.6 per cent of the new sales total of £950 000.

Costs and sales control

The examples given above show that profit is dependent on sales income exceeding costs. Though this seems obvious, the examples show that managers can easily arrive at the wrong decisions driven by what appear to be the right reasons. In the example, the Nottingham manager has prioritized sales growth at the expense of suitable sales and costs controls. The following sections explain some of the ideas the will help you understand the concepts associated with costs, sales and controls.

Cost concepts

In hospitality retail operations costs of food and beverage are the *expenses incurred when goods are consumed*. Food and drink items might legitimately be consumed when served to customers. However, they are also consumed when they are wasted, spoiled or stolen. Labour costs are incurred when staff are on duty and have to be paid for their time. Again, these terms may sound obvious but they raise some important issues about cost management:

1 Effective food and beverage cost control involves ensuring that the minimum costs are incurred for food and drinks that are wasted, spoilt or stolen.

2 Effective use of labour costs requires the careful calculation of the number of staff needed to meet particular levels of demand, and issues to do with labour productivity have to be taken into account.

The costs of food and beverage items can be expressed in a number of ways: units, volume or total value. Food costs can be expressed in costs per weight (kilos), or costs per portion, and drink costs can be expressed as per bottle, per measure or per litre. Labour costs can be can be expressed as hourly, weekly or monthly rates.

Fixed and variable costs · · ·

The examples used above have introduced you to some of the key concepts associated with costs that do not change with levels of production. These *fixed costs* are said to be:

- unchanging in the short term

- not directly associated with the production of individual items.

Both these points need some further explanation. *Fixed costs* in the hospitality retail context refer to costs, such as rent and other property costs as well as depreciation and loan interest. They are fixed in the short-term because all cost can vary over the long term – rents rise, the unit expands capacity with a new extension that increases the rent.

Other costs, such as fuel costs may in reality vary over time, but they are only indirectly related to levels of output. Clearly, higher levels of production might result in more fuel being used, but in most hospitality retail businesses it is not possible to directly link fuel usage with portions produced. It is usual to regard them as fixed costs.

Finally, as fixed costs do not vary dramatically over the short term, increases in sales can be generated without increasing fixed costs, so overall profitability can be improved at a greater rate once fixed costs are covered.

Variable costs are costs related to business volume. Food and beverage costs are the best examples of variable costs in hospitality retail operations. Each sale of a meal or a drink involves the unit incurring the cost of materials involved in the production of the meal and the drink. Food and drink are generally referred to as *direct costs* – they are directly related to sales levels. As sales increase, so these costs increase, and when sales fall these costs also fall.

Payroll costs represent a more complex picture and there is disagreement as to how they should be treated. This text refers to two types of payroll costs, the first relates to the costs of hourly paid employees who are directly involved in producing the goods and services sold to customers. In principle they are variable costs. However, because the link with output is less direct than with food and drink, it is possible to vary the levels of individual sales and the levels of revenue taken with the same number of employees. Hence some people regard labour costs as a *semi-variable cost*. In other words, each employee represents a potential cost base capable of generating a given level of sales. As each employee is added to or taken off the shift roster, he or she represents both an additional cost level and potential sales level. Other payroll costs relate to management and administration staff who represent *fixed costs* in the short term. The examples shown in Table 10.3 treat these two types of payroll costs differently. Payroll costs of those directly involved in producing and serving customers are included in calculations of the cost of producing sales, whilst management and administration payroll charges are treated as a fixed cost.

Controllable and uncontrollable costs • • •

Controllable costs can be changed in the short term. Clearly, variable costs can be controlled and changed. For food and drinks, portion sizes, yields, wastage and theft levels can be controlled to some extent. Redefining the quality standards or ingredients can also change the base of these variable costs. Whilst these are all possibilities, most hospitality retail operations managers have tended to control wastage, yields and theft, and they have tended not to manipulate brand standards because of the potential response from customers confronted with varying portions and quality. At operational level, however, labour has been a key controllable cost. Varying the staffing levels, minimizing the amount of part-time labour and maximizing the workload of full-time staff are examples that were practised in the Wise Owl Hotel example in Chapter 5.

In some cases, nominally defined fixed costs are controllable. The example given in Table 10.3 showed how maintenance charges and consumables could be different in different units and are potentially controllable. For example, improved training could limit damage to equipment and reduces repair charges.

Many hospitality retail operations spend a great deal of time and energy controlling the variable costs, but rarely have a strategy for controlling these fixed costs.

Uncontrollable costs are those costs beyond control in the immediate situation. Rents, depreciation, and license fees are not usually controllable in the short term by unit managers.

Unit and total costs

An analysis of a hospitality retail operation's cost needs to distinguish between *unit costs* – the cost per portion, meal, drink, bedroom serviced, square metre cleaned, etc. – and *total cost* – the total costs of food, drinks, or labour for a period. In the examples given above, the figures show the total costs of food, drink and labour used in the two restaurants. Average costs, or unit cost, can only be calculated once the number of meals served is brought into the equation.

An important consideration, mentioned earlier, is the impact of changes in volume on the average costs per unit for fixed costs. If, say, a restaurant paid a weekly rent of £2000 per week and it served 2000 customers, the average rental charge per customer served would be £1.00, but 4000 customers are served, the average cost per customer served would drop to 50p per customer. Looking at it another way, every customer over 2000 brings in an extra £1.00 because the rent (fixed cost) is already covered.

Sales concepts

Sales are the revenue gained from an exchange of goods and services. In hospitality retail operations, sales result from the sale of food, drink, accommodation and other services such as gaming machines, parking fees, telephone charges, etc. Sales can be measured in a number of ways using monetary and non-monetary terms. Table 10.4 lists some of the measures widely used for analysing sales using monetary terms.

The main benefit of using monetary measures of sales is that they can be used to set against monetary costs. So it is possible to calculate proportions with money. In addition to the monetary measures sales can be analysed using non-monetary measures. Some of these techniques are shown in Table 10.5. The key benefit of non-monetary measures is that they provide sales data that are not distorted by inflation or variations in pricing strategy over time.

By analysing the sales using both monetary terms and non-monetary terms it is possible to select ways of increasing sales that either yield more sales or more profits. By assessing the products according to their level of demand and comparing this with unit profitability it is possible to detect positions within the

Total sales	The total money value through sales and all sources of revenue over a specified time period – day, week, month, year, etc.
Total sales by category	The total money value through sales from the different sources of revenue – food, beverages, gaming machines, accommodation, etc.
Total sales per server	The total money taken by individual employees; using electronic point of sale systems and other sales systems it is possible to track and monitor the amount of money each person serving customers takes.
Total sales per seat	The total sales divided by the number of seats in the restaurant or bar over a set time period. It also possible to use other measures such as per square metre or per table.
Average sales per transaction	Also known as the average bill or average check; the sales divided by the number of bills or checks. The average check may be for one individual or for groups of customers.
Average sale per customer	Similar to the above but aims to create an average price per individual customer; the total sales divided by the total number of covers in a restaurant situation.
Average sale per server	The average sale per individual server comparing sales and numbers of customers sold. Produces a useful measure showing variations in the average sales per server, per customer or per transaction.

Table 10.4
Expressing sales using
monetary terms

sales mix that represent different requirement handling. Figure 10.2 provides a diagram of the four quadrants that emerge from this type of analysis. Some products are *stars*; they are popular and yield high profits. Generally these should be left alone, though they may offer chances to increase prices and thereby profitability. Other items can be described as *dogs* because they are not very popular and also not very profitable. These are items that need to be removed or reviewed in some way that increases profitability or demand. *Cash cows* are products that have a high demand but low profitability. They should not be actively promoted, and ideally they need to have their profitability explored through cost reduction or price increases. At the

Total number sold	The count of each item on the menu or on the list of drinks sold over a given period. Can help to identify the popularity of items. Records can be used to forecast sales for stocking purposes.
Sales mix	Based on the analysis of sales of individual items it is possible to calculate the relative popularity of each item and their contribution to total sales.
Transactions	Number of bills or checks. This figure can help you to calculate the number of sales occasions. May vary through the day – more individuals at lunchtime and groups in the evenings.
Average transactions	Calculated against some other measure. It could be average number of transactions per labour hour, per opening period or for different days in the week. The measure might compare transactions between employees.
Total number of customers	May reveal important differences between the transactions and the people served. In a restaurant situation the calculation might be concerned with covers, or drinks served in a bar.
Occupancy rate	In restaurants the calculation might be seat turnover. In hotels the rate might be rooms occupied or bed-spaces occupied.

Table 10.5
Expressing sales in non-monetary terms

moment, however, they are a good source of revenue and cash flow. Finally, *puzzles* describe products that are profitable but not *very* popular. Ideally you need to actively promote the sale of these items to move them into being 'stars'.

The analysis of sales by individual items and by profitability helps you to consider changing aspects of the sales mix to create a positive effect on sales revenue and products. Here are some examples of what can be done to different products in these categories.

- *Stars*: it may be possible to increase the price of these items without altering their popularity. For the same level of unit sales you are able to lift income without increasing costs – profits rise.

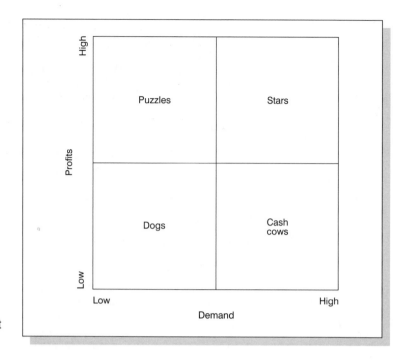

Figure 10.2
Mapping product sales against
demand and profitability

- *Dogs*: can be replaced by items that are more profitable. Even if sales continue to be low you may be able to increase revenue and profitability.

- *Cash cows*: these items are popular and again a price increase may be possible without a negative impact on demand.

- *Puzzles*: may be promoted more effectively through point of sale advertising and staff recommendation to customers. It may even be possible to reclassify these items from puzzles to stars.

The need to achieve financial sales and profit targets is fundamental to your success as a unit manager. This section has been concerned with a basic understanding of the principles involved in making your unit profitable. Ensuring that you control both costs and sales is the way to ensure that you produce a profit. To be able to do this you need a set of control procedures that keep costs down and maximize the surpluses from sales revenues.

The control process

Control is an essential aspect of making sure that the goals and objectives, discussed in Chapter 9, are achieved. Control involves the ongoing process established by the unit manager to ensure that the teamwork within the cost and sales targets is established, worked towards and achieved. Control can be seen in a *negative way* as involving:

- directing
- regulating
- restraining the actions of the team members.

Equally, team involvement and participation in the control process can ensure a more *positive approach* that involves:

- coaching
- counselling
- communicating
- monitoring
- encouraging team members.

Chapter 2 in this book advocated an empowered approach to managing employees in hospitality retail operations. To be effective, empowered employees need to be clear about the objectives that they are attempting to achieve and the actions needed to achieve them. In this situation you need to establish the standards, procedures and training programmes, as well as monitoring and recording processes that will ensure that budgeted targets are achieved through empowered employees.

Although many hospitality retail organizations assume that all employees cannot be trusted and control must be imposed, it is important to recognize that externally imposed control is usually much less effective than internal self-control.

Food, for example, is a perishable product, that can vary in standards and quality:

- It must be purchased to the standard required, stored in appropriate conditions and handled in a safe and hygienic manner.

- Food must also be prepared in a way that meets the demand from customers but does not overproduce so as to generate waste.

- It must also be prepared and served in line with brand standards in terms of portion sizes – too small and customers will be dissatisfied, too large and costs will increase.

- Food has to be served at the appropriate temperature and in a manner and by individuals that meets customer expectations.

- Eating food involves cultural, social and psychological dimensions that mean customers are doing more than just consuming nutrients when they have a meal.

Hospitality, Leisure & Tourism Series

Although different, in some ways the provision of beverages and accommodation services has many requirements in common. At each stage in the organization, purchase, processing and delivery of the products or services, controls need to be established to prevent variations, wastage, oversupply, theft or excessive costs. A series of control techniques are needed, though the precise balance and intensity of these may vary between different types of operations. The following are some of the more common techniques.

Control techniques

Hospitality retail operators have tended to adopt one or more of these techniques as a means of delivering a consistent brand and business format that can be replicated across many units.

Establishing standards

Standard procedures manuals covering product specifications in terms of the quality of ingredients, recipes, presentation, service targets and processes for dealing with customers, employees and communities are at the heart of hospitality retail operations. As unit manager you need to understand the different types of standards that are likely to apply:

1 *Quality standards* are used to define the degree of excellence of raw materials, recipes and final products presented to customers. Obviously, these standards are applied to food and meals, as well as drinks served and accommodation and ancillary aspects to the service, such as crockery, glassware or paper materials. Every aspect of the product offer to customers should be tightly defined as part of the brand definition. Apart from the marketing aspects of defining standards as a way of communicating to customers, quality standards are helpful in shaping costs and cost control. Through setting standards the hospitality retailer is able to be more focused when purchasing, and defining processing steps needed.

2 *Quantity standards* relate to the portion sizes and amounts needed to meet particular sales periods and levels of demand. Quantity standards are important in supporting brand standards so the customers know what to expect in terms of the size of the portion of food or drinks measure. Quantity standards are also important for cost control purposes so that ordering quantities, preparation and service quantities can be managed in a way that makes cost control simpler. Most hospitality retailers now minimize the processing of food and drink and aim to produce standardized quantities through supplier contracts.

3 *Standard costs* are set from the purchase price and quality. In some cases, bought preportioned quantities make this reasonably simple. Hence a negotiated supplier price can be fixed for a given period – each steak has a fixed unit cost. In other cases, items come in a form that has to be measured out, say spirits in a bottle or frozen chips in a bag. These products could involve the service of portions that are more than the standard. Hence standard costs can be used as one of several means of monitoring performance.

4 *Service standards* are set to ensure the nature of the service times and customer contacts are consistent and meet customer expectations. Chapter 8 showed that service quality in hospitality retail operations involves both tangible and intangible aspects of customer service. The tangible measure can be more easily set covering time targets for queuing, order completion, etc. These standards are important, in helping shape and meet customer expectations of their experience. Some of the examples of customer occasions suggested in Chapter 12 follows these points further.

Establishing procedures

Standard procedures establish the correct methods and routines for everyday working. They relate to how individuals undertake their jobs. As we have seen in Chapter 7, people may vary in their previous training and experience and may require a variety of different approaches as they learn to work in the manner required. The standard procedures define how the work should be done in the first instance. That said, some hospitality retail operations require employees to work in a more empowered manner. That is, not all jobs can be predefined and subject to standardized procedures. The work on quality management in Chapter 8 suggested that, in some cases, the performance of employees needs to be flexible and not depend so much on doing the job in 'the one best way'. Here procedures will require a more internalized approach to delivering brand values than the imposed controls.

Training

Team members cannot be expected to work within the standard procedure and to deliver the standards that help deliver the brand and manage costs unless they are:

- informed about what is expected
- provided with the training needed
- told when they are doing the job well
- supported with additional training when needed.

Hospitality, Leisure & Tourism Series

Chapter 7 explored some of the many business benefits of training. Not the least is that trained employees are better able to deliver the brand standards expected by customers and are able to work within the standards and budgets set.

Observing and correcting actions • • •

Training, though essential, is not sufficient in itself to ensure continued effective performance. Your role as unit manager requires that you continue to monitor performance so that employees continue to work in the manner and to the standards set. Many hospitality retail organizations have failed to connect this loop. They train employees and then have no formal process for monitoring and evaluating performance on an ongoing basis.

Example 10.1

McDonald's Restaurants Limited

McDonald's Restaurants' approach to crew training is based on an understanding that crew play an essential role in delivering the brand consistency that customers are buying into. Standardized product specifications and procedures are the basic building blocks of their uniformity dependent offer to customers.

All crew jobs are defined in competence terms in the form of Obsevation Checklists. Each OCL defines the competent behaviour required in the preparation, and execution of the task. They also cover food hygiene, temperature and safe working practice issues, as well as wastage control related to the task. Apart from the descriptions of competent performance of tasks, the OCL requires the trainee to answer questions that test their understanding of the task involved. To be judged competent, and therefore trained, the crew member must achieve a score of 90 per cent or more where job competence is weighted to 70 per cent and the questions are weighted 30 per cent. For a full-time employee, the twenty or so OCLs take aproximately six months to complete. A typical part-time member would complete the training in nine months.

Once trained, the monitoring of performance does not stop there. Each crew member is observed working through the OCLs at least once every six months. The same approach applies and scores are given, this time it is expected that performance will result in scores of 70 per cent or more. Scores averaging above 90 per cent or more earn the crew member an increased hourly rate.

Finally, crew performance and the need to work to the standards set is further underpinned through the employees' performance review procedure and promotion prospects. Competent employees can be promoted through several stages from crew member through to restaurant manager – half of all unit managers started as crew members. This is a considerable motivator to work to the standards set, for those interested in a long-term career with the company.

Requiring records and reports • • •

Monitoring both costs and sales requires the production and recording of reports. Reports on costs such as food and beverages, as well as labour costs for a particular trading period are examples of the sort of information needed to track performance against budgets and standard costs. Similarly, sales information relating to the average bill size, or numbers of customers served and dishes sold, are all examples of some of the information needed for monitoring and managing performance.

Managers increasingly use sophisticated electronic sources of information for monitoring and recording the data needed. In many cases, tills and computers can be set up to provide up-to-date and relevant performance information that enables ongoing monitoring and correction of performance. That said, records and reports are by their very nature historical and are always records of past actions.

Preparing and working to budgets • • •

A budget is a financial plan of the manager's goals and objectives for the trading period expressed in financial terms. There are many different types of budgets in the business as a whole – sales budgets, capital budgets, cash flow budgets, advertising budgets, equipment budgets. At organizational level, these budgets will influence your access to expenditure on new equipment or building maintenance.

The most important budget for a unit manager, however, will be the *operating budget*. Stated in financial terms, the operating budget is the statement of forecasted sales activity and estimated costs associated with that level of sales activity. Clearly, the budget also estimates the level of profit that should be made after the costs have been taken into account. In hospitality retail operations the operating budgets are typically concerned chiefly with food, beverage and labour cost control, though in some businesses other materials such as plastic cups and packaging might also be considered.

In existing units the budgeting process is simpler because, there are past records of performance on which to base future estimates. Here the manager has to consider the impact of changes either on the costs structure or on sales levels. So new legislation, say, increasing the minimum wage, may have an impact on costs or a new competitor may have a negative impact on sales. In a new unit, there are no previous performance figures to work from, but the manager will have company averages and other industry averages to work from.

Preparing an operating budget • • •

An operating budget can be prepared for almost any time period – a day, a week, a month, a quarter or a year. Typically the overall budget would be prepared for the year and then broken down into appropriate periods. It is usual for sales to be spread unevenly through days of the week and months or the year. So the overall budget assumptions have to be matched to the likely time periods. In some cases, it is necessary to budget for hourly periods in the day. Fast-food restaurants, for example, may have sales patterns that move through a number of peaks and troughs through the day. Similarly, pubs will have variations in the levels of sales during lunch times and evenings.

1 Examine past cost performance and identify the fixed and variable costs, and the controllable and uncontrollable costs.

2 Highlight the likely the changes in costs and what can be done to manage the controllable costs.

3 Evaluate the environment to explore possible changes and the impacts these might have on the sales and costs.

4 For each known variable in sales and costs, identify the likely changes.

5 Calculate these into the elements of the budget. Start with the sales mix and estimated total revenue. Follow on through the costs of sales and then go on to the various controllable and uncontrollable costs.

6 Once the budget has been completed for the full year, make the necessary adjustments to the monthly, weekly and daily budgets.

This latter stage is important because it helps you to use the budget on an ongoing basis, tracking performance and making adjustments as you go. This is the key benefit of the budget. It provides a plan of where you want to go and a means of tracking your progress towards the goals set.

Control process

The control techniques used in a single hospitality retail business might well vary according to the key objectives of the operation and the nature of the service being offered to customers. Thus a uniformity dependent unit may require more externally controlled approaches to managing the unit. The need to ensure that customers receive the highly standardized offer, means that controls are likely to focus on defining those standards and ensuring that performance is trained and monitored in a way that delivers the tangibles in products and service.

The more relationship dependent offer is likely to require standards controlling the tangibles, but also will rely on staff interpreting the customer's service needs and working from more internalized self-controls. In these circumstances controls will be associated with developing values, sharing best practice and coaching staff.

Whatever the detail of the control techniques used, the approach and process needs to be the same. Figure 10.3 shows the control cycle that needs to be applied. First, there is a need to establish the standards and standard procedures for the operation. Then train the individuals to the standards and standard procedures. Monitor actual performance against the standards and, where appropriate, take corrective action.

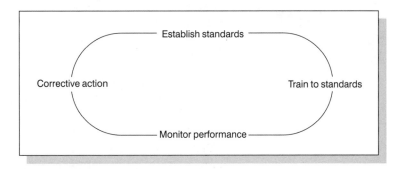

Figure 10.3
The contol cycle

The McDonald's Restaurants example in this chapter showed how important the monitoring of performance is to ensuring that employees continue to work to the standards and standard procedures set.

Conclusions

Hospitality retail management at unit level involves the day to day management of the operation in a way that meets sales and profit targets. A thorough understanding of the different costs and how they can be controlled is at the heart of the activity. Ensuring that food and beverage costs are managed in a way that minimizes overproduction, wastage and theft is essential. Control systems that deliver and monitor the right performance is an approach frequently applied.

That said, the nature of the control systems has to be consistent with the needs of the brand and the business. Many organizations have introduced control systems that produce negative effects on the organization and its performance. For example, in an attempt to manage some of the overhead costs, many organizations require unit management to get head office

Hospitality, Leisure & Tourism Series

permission for even the simplest of repairs. In these circumstances, cost control can have a negative effect on service quality or on employee satisfaction. The marginal benefit of controlling minor expenditure results in a greater loss.

The relationship between variable costs, fixed costs, sales and profits needs to be carefully understood. Thoroughly analysing sales to ensure that the profit contribution of the sales mix is maximized is a good starting point. Similarly, the performance of individual members of staff can be another aspect where focused efforts can increases sales without similarly increasing costs. Indeed, increased profit growth occurs when marginal contribution is being generated from increased sales and fixed costs are already covered.

Reflective practice

Answer these questions to check your understanding of this chapter:

1 Critically discuss the main cost factors that need to be managed so as to generate operational profits.
2 Highlight the steps you would take if a unit's costs were out of line with the budget.
3 Critically review the various measures you would use when analysing sales performance with the unit. Show what steps you would take to maximize sales revenues.
4 Critically evaluate different techniques for controlling performance in hospitality retail operations. Describe the negative and positive effects of control.
5 Describe the control process in a unit known to you. Analyse the strengths and weaknesses of the process. Suggest improvements where appropriate.

Further reading

Coltman, M. (1998). *Hospitality Management Accounting*. Wiley.
Dittmer, P. R. and Griffin, G. G. (1999). *The Principles of Food, Beverage and Labour Costs Controls*. Wiley.

Labour cost management

After working through this chapter you should be able to:

- recognize and manage the elements of labour costs

- calculate effectiveness by measuring productivity

- undertake scheduling and staffing to ensure a number of service goals

- monitor performance against standards and budgets.

There is more to it than cutting wages

Chapter 10 introduced some of the costing and managerial problems associated with labour costs in hospitality retail service operations. Traditionally, labour has been regarded as a fixed cost in hospitality operations – that is, like other fixed costs, an expense that had to be met with little direct linkage to the costs of producing individual sales. More recently labour has come to be regarded as a *semi-variable cost* because the amount of labour can be varied to meet different levels of expected sales. The key problem is that labour is frequently treated as a cost to be minimized, and too many hospitality organizations keep wage levels down and minimize the number of staff on duty.

This tendency to see labour chiefly as a cost results in two problems:

1 It fails to recognize that employees deliver the service, and that insufficient staff on duty or poorly trained staff can result in service breakdowns and customer dissatisfaction.

2 The labour as cost approach also fails to recognize that the wage cost to the employer is also a source of income to the employee. Attempts to cut pay rates, or hours worked, reduce the employee's income and can cause employee dissatisfaction leading to staff turnover and other problems.

Part of the problem lies with the limited information systems used in the past. The trading account and profit and loss account generally only register labour as a cost, and there has been no tradition of costing other labour costs, such as staff turnover, or reduced productivity for inexperienced staff. Similarly there have been few, if any, attempts to see labour as an asset to be developed. Thus an investment in training that improves employee effectiveness and productivity is mostly regarded as cost and there is no attempt to value the benefit of the trained employee.

Elements of labour costs

The 'labour as cost' model is powerful because in most hospitality retail operations labour represents a considerable part of the operating costs. In a simple hospitality operation labour is likely to represent 15 per cent of total sales revenue, and in complex operations represents over 30 per cent of sales income. It is perhaps not surprising that managers have tried to reduce the labour costs as a way of increasing profits.

Under the pressure of commercial objectives it easy to forget that labour costs to the unit represent income and key motive for working for the employees. Before going on to look at the compensation and reward package that make up 'cost' and 'pay', we need to consider the different time relationships involved in employment.

1 *Full-time employees*: employed for a fixed number of hours for a set weekly wage. Typically the hours would be fixed at say forty hours and work beyond this entitles the employee to overtime pay. The employee has protection against a maximum number of hours, and is regarded as permanent until such time as one or both parties decide to end the relationship.

2 *Part-time employees*: work for a variable number of hours per week. The relationship is semi-permanent in that employees still have protection under the law. In other words, there is an expectation that hours will be provided. Most part-time employees expect a reasonably predictable number of hours, as this helps them plan their income and domestic lives.

3 *Casual employees*: work irregular hours; usually they are brought in for a special job, say, a banquet, or to cover a temporary shortage. The relationship is less regular but employees may still need some training to be effective in their role.

4 *Agency staff*: in emergencies, many firms use agency or contract staff to fill gaps. This is particularly true of the skilled jobs in the kitchens or in some of the administration and management jobs. Usually, rates paid are higher than for employees, but the contract can be terminated with no notice.

When managing employees as a cost, the temptation is to treat them differently because each represents a different cost relationship. In the example in Chapter 5, managers at the Wise Owl Hotel:

- made full-time employees work longer shifts than their contracted hours, in sessions where there were not enough staff on duty

- part-time employees were brought in and then sent home if the unit was not as busy as predicted

- casual employees were only employed for special events, or in emergencies

- agency staff were used as a quick fix to a desperate situation – problems about commitment and knowledge of the immediate team and situation are typical.

Employee reward and payment

All employees are paid wages, though the reward package can be made up of several elements. Figure 11.1 provides an overview of the various elements that make up the direct, statutory and

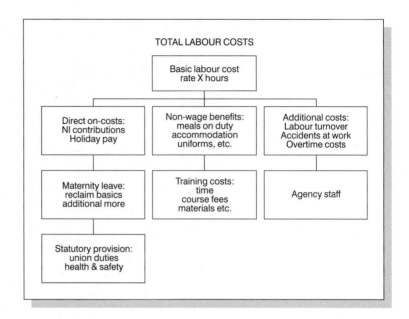

Figure 11.1
The total labour costs

indirect elements of the total costs of labour. As we have seen, traditional approaches to labour costs have been to regard these as a semi-variable and related to the costs of sales in calculating the gross profit. This view causes problems because:

- it often fails to allow for the fact that various legal responsibilities add to the cost of employing people

- it fails to recognize there are additional non-wage benefits given to employees and these are a direct cost of employment

- it fails to show that training is a necessary additional cost that can produce benefits to the employer through improved outputs from staff

- additional costs are caused by high levels of staff turnover.

The *basic labour cost* is the standard pay rate multiplied by the number of hours worked. Full-time employees may be paid a standard wage at a fixed amount per week, and this represents an agreed number of hours – and thereby an agreed rate per hour. Both part-time and casual staff are paid at an hourly rate. In most European countries, this standard rate is regulated by law in that there is a rate below which pay cannot drop. In the UK this is known as the *national minimum wage*.

It is common practice in many hospitality firms for the rate to be fixed at the statutory minimum, though some firms – McDonald's Restaurants, for example – aim to pay above this amount. In addition, local labour market conditions and competitor employers may pay above these rates, thereby forcing hospitality employers to pay more.

In addition to these direct wage costs paid to the employee, employers in the UK have to pay a National Insurance contribution, as well as holiday pay entitlements and, in many cases, towards pension funds. These are *additional costs* of employment.

Female employees are also entitled to Statutory Maternity Pay, though the basic amount can be reclaimed by the employer from the state. In some cases these rights are extended by employers and this represents an additional set of costs associated with employment. Though they are not directly associated with the costs of sales they are a cost to be met and are additional costs to the basic wage cost.

Similarly, employers are required to provide paid time off for employees' representatives involved with health and safety or for trade union representatives to be paid to attend to their duties. Again these represent an indirect cost of employment, but they are a cost to be accounted for nevertheless.

It is usual for the various additional costs of employment to amount to an additional 25 per cent of the basic wage bill.

As well as these payments associated with legal responsibilities and duties that have to be paid, either to the employee, or the state, hospitality retail employers often provide additional benefits to employees that also adds to the cost of labour.

Meals on duty • • •

Meals on duty are usually provided by most firms though the arrangements vary:

1 The staff choose menu items – as do McDonald's crew. The items must be accounted for because they are stock that has been used.

2 Staff eat items that are left over from the service period. Again these should be accounted for because they represent sales stock that has not resulted in sales.

3 Special meals are prepared for the staff as separate menus and costs. Again, costs are controlled but they do not relate to stock that has not been used to generate sales.

Each of these approaches to providing staff meals can result in benefits and difficulties. There are clearly benefits, from a training point of view to letting staff sample the meal they are serving, though controls are important so that you know what has been used for sales. Similarly, using up leftover items for staff meals may help reduce wastage loss, but may cause staff dissatisfaction because they have to eat unpopular items.

Prepared staff meals are easier to isolate and control, but again staff may not like the food prepared because it is of low quality.

Accommodation

Accommodation is another benefit provided to employees in some businesses. Hotels and some pubs have provided accommodation to full-time employees. This has been seen as a benefit because employees are available on the premises when needed. For employees the provision was something of a mixed blessing. It was useful to have accommodation, but being available to the employer – even during days off – was seen as a major disadvantage. Increasingly, hospitality retailers do not provide accommodation – particularly where the units are in tailor-made buildings.

Where accommodation is provided, it is usual for the employee to pay some form of rent, and there are a number of different ways of charging this to employees. Usually, the rental is deducted from the employee's pay, and building costs etc. are covered as an overhead cost deducted after gross profit. Accommodation is an indirect cost of employing employees.

Uniforms

Uniforms are provided in many hospitality retail operations. Staff uniforms are one of the means by which brand identity is established. The provision of uniforms involves two types of costs:

- the purchase of the uniform – sometimes more than one set per employee
- the cleaning and maintenance of the uniform.

The purchase of sets of uniforms for all new employees can cost anything from £30 to £80 per set. It is not unusual for employees who leave the company to take the uniforms with them, thereby adding to the costs of staff turnover. Usually, the costs of these are borne through the overheads and represent an indirect cost of employment.

Uniform cleaning is charged to the unit as part of the general laundry and cleaning function in the overheads. Again, these are regarded as indirect costs of labour.

Staff training provision

Staff training provision varies in its scope and cost to the organization:

1 *Training off the job*: where an employee is paid to do a college course or an in-company programme their wages for the time

away from work are counted as a cost of training. Even if the employee attends the course on their day off, the costs of course fees and other expenses such as books may all involve charges to the business.

2 *Training on the job*: even in lightly structured approaches to training employees there will be associated costs that should be accounted for. The trainee's time during instruction, the time of the instructor, the cost of materials used in demonstrations, the cost of wastage during learning, and the cost of any other printed documents, all involve direct costs associated with training someone. As well as these direct costs, indirect costs occur through lost productivity, customer dissatisfaction and added employee stress as the trainee is learning all add to the true cost of training.

Where training is taking place off the job, it is not unusual for the cost of training to be a substantial amount, once all the fees and time away from work are taken into account. Even in situations where the training occurs at work, direct costs can be high. A recent study at McDonald's (1999) suggested that on average these costs amount to just under £600.

Traditionally many hospitality retail organizations have regarded training as a luxury; with a few exceptions, they have tended to cut training budgets when trading situations were difficult. Yet a recent study at McDonald's showed that the best training units outperformed the worse training units through:

- higher productivity per labour hour

- registered higher service quality grades

- better employee satisfaction scores

- a more flexible workforce because more staff were available to work in all sections of the restaurants

- lower levels of staff turnover and lower costs associated with staff replacement.

Although this and other studies show that training is an essential element of running a hospitality retail brand, when times are hard and costs have to be cut many managers continue to treat training as an expensive luxury to be trimmed. There are several reasons for this:

1 Current accounting methods often only account for labour as a cost to the business.

2 Comparisons are only made with sales revenues in total amounts.

3 There is little consideration of productivity through transactions or sales per labour hour per employee.

4 Training benefits are rarely recognized and accounted for in performance.

5 The costs of not training are never calculated.

This latter point needs some expansion. Some of the potential costs of not training are:

- absolute productivity loss

- productivity loss from reduced learning speed

- increased staff turnover costs

- increased levels of wastage

- reduced service quality

- reduced employee satisfaction

- increased employee accident rate

- limited flexibility

- resistance to change.

People do eventually learn from experience and by trial and error, but this approach is not without cost. *It is just not recognized.* The productivity levels of untrained employees, when measured by output, are lower for untrained employees. They are also more likely to leave their jobs more quickly, produce higher levels of wastage, have fewer satisfied customers, be more dissatisfied at work, have more accidents at work and be less flexible in their working practices and more resistant to change.

Furthermore, training is one of the key techniques for managing a brand in hospitality retail operations. Training helps:

- employees deliver consistent brand standards

- establish portion, quantity and cost controls

- deliver quality goods and services

- meet customer expectations

- increase sales and profitability.

In addition to the costs of labour that are a direct consequence of the employment relations, and the additional costs that are incurred through the package of on-wage benefits and need to train employees, there are some additional and often *hidden costs of employment*. These are costs that come about from the need to recruit and cover employee shortages through the use of overtime payment, or the employment of agency staff in times of shortage. Sometimes these costs are a result of unforeseen high levels of customer demand or staffing difficulties because of illness. More often that not, however, they are the result of *staff turnover*. Chapter 5 deals with the causes and remedies for staff turnover in detail, but the following focuses on some of the key costs involved in replacing staff in hospitality retail operations.

Staff turnover • • •

It is not unusual for individual hospitality retail businesses to have no detailed records of unit by unit levels of staff turnover, and it is almost unheard of for the firm to account for the costs of losing and replacing staff.

Recent research conducted by staff at Leeds Metropolitan University (Eaglen et al., 1999) suggests that the direct costs are between *£580 and £1000 per person*. The direct costs only take account of the immediate expenditure involved in:

- advertising for replacements
- management time spent recruiting, interviewing, selecting, inducting, training
- recruitment agency fees
- travel expenses for interviews
- postage and stationery
- induction and orientation
- training
- overtime cover
- agency staff cover
- processing new recruit's documents
- processing ex-employee's documents
- uniforms.

These various cost headings may not apply to all businesses but many of them are likely to be common to every hospitality retail operation. In addition, there are considerable *indirect costs* that are more difficult to count but nevertheless are costs to the business.

Some of the costs involved when staff leave and have to be replaced are:

- lost investment in training

- lost staff expertise

- reduced service quality

- reduced productivity

- increased wastage and costs

- customer dissatisfaction

- negative impact on remaining staff

- opportunity cost of lost management time.

Usually, the most highly trained employees are the first to leave the unit. When they leave their skills and talents go with them. Whilst it is possible to calculate the cost of training an individual, the additional talents and expertise developed are difficult to calculate. Similarly, it is not easy to calculate the cost of lost customers, but Chapter 8 suggested that this could easily represent thousands of pounds. Finally, the lost opportunities of management time involved should not be underestimated. If managers are spending time recruiting new staff, they are not doing other things that could be developing the business.

Bearing in mind these points, it is not unreasonable to see that the true costs of staff turnover could easily double the direct

Restaurants	Headline rate (%)	Rate after temporary staff (%)	Temporary staff leavers	Leavers after temporary staff	Cost of staff turnover in restaurant (£)
Alpha1	42.07	42.07	0	14	6 300
Alpha2	52.57	46.88	4	33	14 850
Alpha3	74.09	74.09	0	23	10 350
Alpha4	60.06	60.06	0	38	17 100
Alpha5	74.03	67.35	3	33	14 850
Alpha6	78.8	43.01	15	18	8 100
Av Alpha		55.57			11 925
Beta1	128.1	118.6	7	87	39 150
Beta2	158.0	152.4	2	55	24 750
Beta3	175.0	166.1	5	93	41 850
Beta4	128.4	126.0	1	54	24 300
Beta5	176.1	155.5	9	68	30 600
Beta6	169.7	118.2	27	62	27 900
Av Beta		139.46			31 425

Table 11.1 Staff turnover in a sample of McDonald's Restaurants

costs. Certainly the Institute of Personnel and Development figure of £735 per person for 'unskilled routine labour', given in Chapter 5, is not unrealistic.

Example 11.1

McDonald's Restaurants Limited: the costs

McDonald's Restaurants is an example of a hospitality retail organization that has had a poor reputation for staff turnover in the past but that has made attempts to manage it, with successful results. Staff turnover in the past has been similar to that in many other hospitality retail organizations. An average rate of about 150 per cent per year was quite normal for the group, with some large variations across units.

The company has adopted policies designed to bring these rates down, and the average rate in 1998 was below 90 per cent and the company has a national target to reduce the rate to below 70 per cent. Key to this approach has been the recognition that staff turnover is a problem that can be managed and unit mangers make a considerable impact on staff retention. Performance monitors for every unit in the group include a monthly staff turnover rate calculated for the preceding twelve months. Unit managers' performance reviews include staff turnover targets, and performance bonuses are only paid if these targets are met.

As yet the company does not account for the cost of staff turnover in each unit, but staff at Leeds Metropolitan University recently estimated that the direct cost of staff turnover averaged £450 per person. A sample of restaurants showed the extent of these extra costs. Table 12.1 highlights the rates in two clusters of restaurants based on their training activities. The Beta group of restaurants were lower than average trainers and had higher than average staff turnover rates. The main point is that the extra costs of staff turnover added considerably to operating costs. For example, in 1997 the number of staff employed in directly managed restaurants totalled 42 982, based on an average of 90 per cent staff turnover and a direct cost of £450 per head; staff turnover of crew alone cost £17 407 710.

Agency staff • • •

The use of agency staff, particularly for skilled kitchen staff, can fill an immediate gap in staffing. However, agency staff are considerably more expensive. The hourly rates are frequently three or four times the normal wage. In addition to the extra hourly rate, agency staff can also cause added indirect costs:

- Agency staff are unlikely to understand the immediate brand standards and operating procedures.

- They are not part of the permanent team and may cause friction with other staff.

- They are not as committed to the business and its goals in the long term.

This section has shown that staff costs account for more than just the hourly rate and the broad variable cost of traditional management approaches. Some costs like National Insurance and pension costs are directly related to hourly rates and payment for work done. Other costs are more indirectly linked to providing staff with an array of other benefits such as meals on duty and costs of ensuring effective performance through training and employee development. Finally, some costs result from mishandling staffing and labour costs. The added costs due to staff turnover and staff shortages are neither direct costs of producing hospitality goods and services, nor are they indirect cost of employing people. They are extra costs that arise from not managing labour stability and ensuring that the right staff are available as and when needed. As we have seen, these costs are rarely recognized and accounted for, but they do add to real operating costs.

Measuring staff costs

At its most simple and crude the measurement of staff costs involves solely the consideration of the amount of hours bought and the rate paid. Thus using this approach, attempts to control labour costs involve strategies that:

- keep the rate paid per hour low
- reduce the number of hours paid for
- make employees work without pay for additional hours
- increase the work rate of those who are employed.

Managers at the 'Wise Owl Hotel' in the example in Chapter 5 followed all these strategies. They paid the lowest rate possible, they minimized the hours for part-time staff – even sending staff home after just one hour, they made full-time staff work longer hours than the agreed forty-hour week and with lower staffing levels. As we saw, they also generated high labour turnover and the extra costs associated with replacing staff. Like many other hospitality operators, *because they did not ask any questions about these costs, they had no idea of the real cost of their actions.*

Labour performance indicators

As in many other aspects of management information, a failure to ask the right questions means that you have an unsound basis on which to make decisions – you do not even know what decisions have to be made.

Given the team nature of much of hospitality industry work, it is not always possible to measure the precise output of every individual. In particular, kitchen work cannot always be related to individual efforts and the work of ancillary workers such as cleaners, storekeepers and administrators is also part of the operational need but not directly linked to specific levels of output or sales. In these circumstances, it is possible to aggregate employee performance and apply some general ratios:

1 *Sales per labour hour*: the sales take is divided by the number of labour hours purchased in the period. For example, the Leeds restaurant takes £900 000 in the year and employs 24 137 labour hours in the year. This averages £37.28 per labour hour. This average is £32.60 per labour hour in the Nottingham restaurant.

2 *Transactions per labour hour*: the total number of transactions for the period is divided by the total number of labour hours. For example, in the Leeds restaurant there were 56 250 transactions delivered through the total of 24 137 labour hours. This averages 2.33 transactions per labour hour, compared with 2.1 transactions per labour hour in Nottingham.

3 *Transactions per customer*: the total number of individual customers or covers, divided by the labour hours. In the Leeds restaurant average 6.52 customers per labour hour, compared with 5.88 in Nottingham.

4 *Sales per transaction*: the average sales revenue from each transaction. The total sales figure divided by the number of transactions. In the two examples the average transaction sale was £16.00 in the Leeds restaurant and £15.50 in the Nottingham restaurant.

5 *Training activity*: there are a number of ways of measuring the training activity in different units. McDonald's Restaurants have specific performance indicators and monthly audits of training. In other cases, the activity may be measured through a simple calculation of the cost expressed as a percentage of direct wage costs.

6 *Labour turnover rate*: there are a number of indexes of staff turnover and retention, but the simplest measure is to express the number of leavers over the year divided by the normal establishment – as Chapter 5 demonstrates. These can also be expressed for different job categories, levels and departments.

7 *Labour turnover cost*: the number of job leavers in the period priced out at a rate per head. This may vary between different types of employees and managers. For example, skilled kitchen staff will be more expensive to replace than unskilled routine restaurant and bar workers.

Using these global labour ratios it is possible to focus on different approaches to managing the labour budget. Table 11.2 lists some of these measures for the Leeds and Nottingham restaurants and this shows that, although the labour budget appears higher in the Leeds restaurant, labour productivity is higher and the staff generate higher sales, lower operating costs and, ultimately, greater profitability. The Leeds manager allocates £20 000 per annum for staff training and this represents an additional 10 per cent on the labour budget. The Leeds restaurant, however, generates more sales per labour hour, more transactions per hour and more sales per average transaction. That unit, although similar in most essentials, is able to operate a lower cost of sales ratio and has lower levels of staff turnover and all the costs associated with staff replacement. The pay rate averaged over all staff categories is higher in the Nottingham restaurant, yet profitability is greater.

The Nottingham restaurant, on the surface, is more successful because the manager has generated more sales and operates with lower labour costs. Yet despite operating with lower wage levels and cutting out training, the managers needs to employ more labour hours because the labour productivity is lower.

- With the same transactions per hour as the Leeds, the Nottingham restaurant could have served the same number of customers with 26 647 labour hours – a saving of 2486 hours, or £18 645.

	Leeds restaurant	Nottingham restaurant
Sales for year	£900 000	£950 000
Labour cost	£216 000	£218 500
Training	£20 000	Nil
Net cost	£196 000	£218 500
Pay rate averaged + 25%	£8.12	£7.50
Labour hours	24 137	29 133
Transactions	56 215	61 290
Average transaction	£16.00	£15.50
Transactions per hour	2.33	2.10
Average sales per hour	£37.28	£32.60
Normal establishment	25 (full/part time)	30 (full/part time)
Leavers in past year	10	54
Staff turnover rate	40%	180%
Cost of staff turnover		
Direct (£500)	£5 000	£27 000
Indirect (£800)	£8 000	£43 200

Table 11.2 Labour performance indicators for the Leeds and Nottingham restaurants

- Similarly, if the average sales per transaction matched those in the Leeds restaurant, the business would have generated another £30 645.

- The staff turnover costs could be brought down to £6000 if the rate matched the Leeds restaurant, making a further saving of £21 000.

All these savings do not take account of the differences in the costs of sales in the two restaurants where staff training and staff commitment are important factors in attempting to control these costs.

Active learning point

Using figures from a restaurant, bar or other unit known to you, establish the real staff costs by exploring the wider range of measures as given above. Is there potential to provide better wages and training as a result of saving on staff turnover costs and other gains in performance?

In addition to the broad performance indicators that you can use to compare your employee's general performance with those in other restaurants or in the group as a whole, electronic point of sale (EPOS) systems allow comparison of individual employees in selling roles. Thus a comparison of frontline staff in bars and restaurants is much simpler using EPOS.

Table 11.3 gives an example of different levels of staff performance depending on whether the employee was experienced in bar work or not. The data were collected from a range of different pubs in different settings over one shift period. The

Locations	Inexperienced staff		Experienced staff		Difference	
	Served	(£)	Served	(£)	Served	(£)
Community pub, Lancs	1) 173	590	198	665	24	75
	2) 175	560	177	603	2	43
City Centre Bar, Manch.	147	448	234	712	87	264
Country pub, North	71	254	88	313	17	59
Country pub, North	75	304	111	458	36	154
City Centre Bar, Liv.	1) 154	495	218	689	64	194
	2) 178	584	287	859	109	275
City Centre Bar, Manch,	164	450	221	621	57	171

Table 11.3 Comparison of experienced staff and inexperienced staff

figures show considerable differences and highlight a need to ensure that inexperienced staff move quickly up the learning curve. Training and coaching is an essential technique in ensuring that the learning stage is short.

As well as the statistics given in customers served and sales made, it is also possible to explore differences in sales mix and the achievement of targets to feature certain products.

This section has attempted to show that the traditional approach to managing labour costs tends to focus on the cost of labour, but this approach is limited because it fails to consider wider aspects of cost associated with employing staff. *It is a matter not so much of what labour costs, but what labour does*:

- the skills that staff bring to their work
- their ability to work within cost targets
- the numbers of customers that can be served
- and the revenue gained from each transaction
- the additional costs generated by staff replacements.

All the above items are important considerations.

Adding to staff income

In addition to the basic wage paid to staff, there are a number of other means by which their income can be increased. Tips from customers and a set service charge are both additional payments made by customers. Commission is paid by the employer and is directly linked to some additional incentive – sales typically, though several organizations make additional payments based on other aspects of performance. All of these arrangements can be seen to have strengths and weaknesses.

The assumptions that they all share are that money is a prime motivator and that employee effort will be directed to earning the maximum income. There are several problem with this view:

1 Money is only a motivator if the individual is generally dissatisfied with the level of pay, or needs to maximize income for some other reason. In Herzberg's terms it is a 'hygiene' factor but not a 'motivator'. In other words, money can be the cause of dissatisfaction and can lead employees to leave the firm, but in the long run money is not a primary motivator.

2 Whilst it is possible to identify individual contributions in some cases, mostly hospitality operations are based on team-working and several individuals contribute to producing the goods and service supplied to customers.

3 Where money rewards are low, individuals may say that they are not worth the extra effort.

4 Money rewards can be the source of envy and conflict, which adds further to employee stress.

5 When ranking issues important to their subordinates, managers frequently overestimate the value of material (extrinsic) rewards (see Chapter 3).

6 For any approach – tips, service charge or commission – the incentives vary considerably and there needs to be a clear understanding of the aims of the incentive scheme.

Tips from customers

Although a widespread practice in hospitality services, tips from customers present both employees and customers with many anxieties. In the UK in particular, the rules about tipping – when to tip, how much to tip, the reasons for tipping a norm or for excellence – are not culturally shared and there are different expectations between staff and customers, and between staff and staff and customers. Apart from these confusions, arrangements for dealing with tips vary and can represent different benefits to the individuals and teams involved.

1 *Individualized tips*: service staff in the restaurant or bar receive tips from customers and these are the property of the person receiving them. Probably the most widely practised form of additional income in hospitality retail operations. In some units staff can double or treble their wages through tips. Although it benefits the individual and in theory makes them more concerned about service quality, the practice can be divisive amongst employees. Competition for the 'best' tables and customers, and jealousies between kitchen and restaurant can be counterproductive.

2 *Shared tips*: tips received by staff are shared out amongst the entire staff. This prevents some of the jealousy, but it is difficult to police and a lack of trust might lead to tensions amongst staff. This method may also challenge the supposed incentive to good service. There are a number of variations to this approach. A points system, for example, may weight the benefits to different groups.

Service charges

The management levy a set charge on all bills for the service given. This removes some of the uncertainties about what to give and when to give the tip, but it can cause customers stress, particularly where the service has not been satisfactory. The arrangements for paying the charge levied are also somewhat vague. Is the charge paid in addition to basic pay, or does it in part meet the cost of basic pay? Many firms use the charge to help meet labour costs, and so it is not an extra payment. Differences in arrangements make the service charge of variable benefit to employees. If staff will be paid it in any case, it is unlikely to motivate staff to give priority to service quality. Nor will it be an incentive if the charge is being used to meet basic pay.

Commission on sales made • • •

Some organizations pay staff a basic pay and then add a bonus related to the customers served and sales made. It is assumed that staff will work to maximize their income by 'up-selling' to customers.

Example 11.2

TGI Friday Restaurants

TGI Fridays use this approach. Service staff are paid 3 per cent of all sales made in the evening and kitchen staff receive 6 per cent. The restaurant and bar staff are paid the commission on the sales they individually make, whereas kitchen staff are paid a commission for the session shared equally amongst those on duty. On a regular basis managers select the top ten service workers and they are allowed to select the shift periods they work and the restaurant areas they work.

Again, there is a fine line between individual incentives and setting up reward systems in which some people will always lose out. When there are winners there are also losers, and in this situation employees not earning the best commissions may become demotivated.

Extra payments for performance • • •

Several hospitality retail organizations use some form of additional payment related to performance or the achievement of a desired goal. One approach involves monitoring employee performance over a period and then paying an extra amount to staff who achieve a particular performance level.

Example 11.3

McDonald's Restaurants Limited

McDonald's Restaurants evaluate staff performance through the observation checklist. Crew who achieve scores over 90 per cent in all the OCLs in a six-month period are paid 15p per hour extra during the next period. This scheme reinforces 'one best way' of operation, because it rewards a consistent adherence to the company's standards.

Other organizations link the extra payment to achieving a training standard or award. Usually the extra payment is made as an added hourly rate, paid once a person has achieved the required training level.

Example 11.4

Harvester Restaurants

Harvester Restaurants linked an extra 20p per hour bonus to the achievement of 'Silver Badge'. This is paid on the achievement of at least eight of the team's key skills related to the team's accountability.

Whilst the extra amounts that can be earned by staff are relatively small, they do at least reward the achievement of a desired company objective and send a message to staff about the priorities. Extra money rewards can benefit the employee and create an incentive pay structure that encourages employees to aim at the priorities set by management. However, there can be problems where the additional pay is marginal and does not compensate for the added effort involved. In some cases, these schemes can be divisive and lead to harmful competition between employees.

Scheduling employees

The preceding sections have shown that the calculation and management of labour costs is more complex than the mere calculation of cost of labour to the organization. It is equally necessary to consider the outputs from labour. That is, it is as important to ask *'what does labour do?'* as it is to ask *'what does labour cost?'* Giving consideration to productivity, skills, service quality and customer satisfaction is crucial. Having the correct number of staff on duty to meet customer demand is clearly a matter related to these issues. Too few staff and customer service targets and service quality may be threatened. Too many staff increases costs and reduces profitability.

Staff scheduling has to take into account the staff needed on each day, at various times during the day, and at the same time ensure that part-time employees, in particular, have sufficient hours to ensure a reasonable pay level for their period on duty.

The Wise Owl Hotel example in Chapter 5 and comments earlier in this chapter, show that there is a temptation to treat full-time and part-time employees differently. Part-time staff are

Hospitality, Leisure & Tourism Series

frequently treated like a water tap to be turned on and off as customer demand dictates. A lack of sensitivity to their income needs can have motivational and staff turnover consequences that are counterproductive and, ultimately, more expensive.

A thorough analysis of past sales, together with a consideration of influencing factors, such as

- the influences of weather conditions
- competitor activity
- special promotional activity
- general sales trends
- macroeconomic activity,

enables a reasonably well-informed estimate of likely sales levels over the next months, weeks, days and hours of the day to be developed.

This task is made simpler through the use of information technology. Electronic point of sales information can produce sophisticated data about sales that then help to build an estimate of the employees needed on duty. Figure 11.2 provides an example of a typical sales pattern over a full week. The number of customers' mean individual portions, is probably the more accurate measure than transactions, though the transaction count needs to be studied as well because there may be implications for the numbers of service staff required.

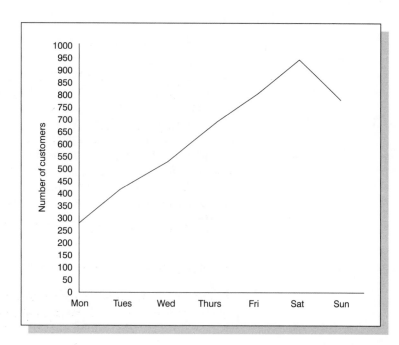

Figure 11.2
Number of customers served per day

Similarly, an analysis of sales by hours through the day can help to identify when staff cover needs to be adjusted to satisfy the different levels of sales at different times during opening hours. Table 11.4 lists the number of customers served in a themed restaurant for just one day. As stated earlier, the records set up must keep some account of the weather conditions, competitor activity, as well as own promotional activities such as 'early bird' promotions or other activities that influence sales at a particular time of day so these can be factored into the calculations.

Table 11.4
Hourly business volumes in the restaurant, Friday

Hourly period Weather: fine and dry	Customers served External factors: low competitor activity
11.00 a.m.–Noon	33
Noon–1.00 p.m.	90
1.00 p.m.–2.00 p.m.	89
2.00 p.m.–3.00 p.m.	51
3.00 p.m.–4.00 p.m.	6
4.00 p.m.–5.00 p.m.	7
5.00 p.m.–6.00 p.m.	45
6.00 p.m.–7.00 p.m.	78
7.00 p.m.–8.00 p.m.	95
8.00 p.m.–9.00 p.m.	95
9.00 p.m.–10.00 p.m.	73
10.00 p.m.–11.00 p.m.	48

The figures in Table 11.4 show sales on one day and within given internal and external conditions. There will be fluctuations in these sales per hour and the model built up needs to allow for a number of variables:

- the range of fluctuations per hour within the same conditions

- the impact of weather on sales in each hour

- the effects of specific competitor promotions or other activities

- the impact of own promotions and activities.

In each case, the judgement has to fix the likely levels of sales given the variables, and the normal fluctuations between peaks and troughs of sales on the same day and in the same month.

Active learning point

Using figures from a restaurant, bar or other unit known to you, estimate the sales levels for a week. Taking the figures for one day, estimate the sales through each part of the day that the unit is open. Where possible, show how many staff are needed.

Once you have arrived at an estimated sales volume you need to calculate the number of staff needed for each period through the day. The process involves the following key stages:

1 Identify the key job roles needed to service any level of sales. For example, simple tasks of 'food preparation' and service may be undertaken by just one person during quiet periods. In the more complex settings it is likely that several posts are needed to prepare, cook and serve the food.

2 Match the job with the normal output level and the estimated sales for each period during the day. Table 11.5 gives an example for the restaurant service staff needed for the sales levels indicated for the day in Table 11.4.

3 The staffing requirement is then compared with the skill profile of each member of staff. Typically, these might be available solely for specific jobs, though increasingly staff are being trained to be multiskilled and thereby able to work in several areas. Staff at McDonald's Restaurants, for example are trained to do the full range of production and service jobs.

Hours of operation	Estimated sales levels	Staff required
10.00 a.m.–11.00 a.m.	0	2
11.00 a.m.–Noon	33	2
Noon–1.00 p.m.	90	5
1.00 p.m.–2.00 p.m.	89	5
2.00 p.m.–3.00 p.m.	51	3
3.00 p.m.–4.00 p.m.	6	1
4.00 p.m.–5.00 p.m.	7	1
5.00 p.m.–6.00 p.m.	45	3
6.00 p.m.–7.00 p.m.	78	5
7.00 p.m.–8.00 p.m.	95	5
8.00 p.m.–9.00 p.m.	95	5
9.00 p.m.–10.00 p.m.	73	4
10.00 p.m.–11.00 p.m.	48	3
11.00 p.m.–Midnight	0	2

Table 11.5
Staffing needs in the restaurant, Friday

The schedule of hourly staffing needs (Figure 11.3) based on Table 11.5, allows for two staff to be on duty to set up before service commences and then for two staff to be on duty after service. Also, to increase flexibility, the schedule uses four full-time and three part-time staff. Three of the full-time staff are scheduled for split shifts. The part-time staff need to have sufficient hours to ensure an agreed income level. In this case, it could be possible to have employee B do the work roster of employee G if needed. Some employers prefer to employ mostly part-time staff because it enhances flexibility and potential to minimize costs. On the other hand, some employers see the value of employee commitment and employee skills, and prefer to maximize the use of full-time staff.

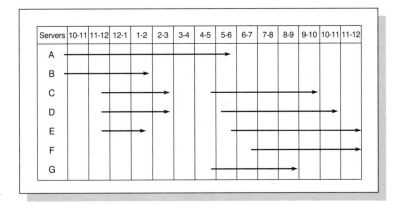

Figure 11.3
Sample hourly schedule for restaurant staff

In modern hospitality retail organizations the calculations of potential sales and staff needs can be done with a computer programme. For example, McDonald's Restaurants' Human Resources and Training programme allows each manager to record the training undertaken by each individual employee. This is then fed into the computer programme, which then calculates the predicted weekly sales and staffing rosters for the restaurant. Whilst most unit managers prefer to use their own knowledge and judgements about how best to staff the restaurant and use the skill profiles of individual employees, this type of programme provides valuable support to human judgements.

Conclusion

This chapter has shown that managing labour costs in hospitality retail operations involves more than wage rates, hours worked and keeping the labour account within budget. These direct costs of staffing are only part of the story. Labour costs also include some indirect fees – for example, to meet tax, pensions and

National Insurance responsibilities. In addition there are costs associated with other employer responsibilities, such as providing time off for union or health and safety duties.

Additional costs are incurred when providing non-wage benefits such as meals on duty and uniforms. These are rarely taken into account as part of the direct costs of employment. Similarly, the cost of training is not shown as part of the direct costs of employment, if it is shown at all. More often than not training is treated as a luxury that can be cut in bad times. Yet training is a fundamental feature of brand management. Without adequate training it is impossible to meet the brand standards and customer expectations. No firm in the sector calculates the costs of not training. Lost productivity, reduced customer satisfaction and added wastage all increase costs for the firms who do not train. Another and related aspect of these hidden costs in hospitality retail operations is labour turnover. The cost of losing and replacing staff is high, particularly when the excessive rates of staff turnover are considered.

When these additional costs of staffing are taken into account, the old certainties of hospitality business management are brought into question. An organization that cuts wage costs, shaves employee hours and eliminates the training budget, only to find that staff productivity is lower, customer satisfaction reduced, wastage increased and staff turnover cost raised, is often saving money with one hand and throwing it away with the other.

As a hospitality retail operator you need to adopt more searching approaches to labour cost management. The approach must take into account these wider issues. The added costs produced by short-sighted management practices have to be calculated. Paying higher wages, giving people a decent wage, ensuring that training and career progression are built into normal management practices, and that labour turnover is calculated, costed and recognized as a real cost to the business need to become the norm in hospitality retail businesses.

Reflective practice

Answer these questions to check your understanding of this chapter:

1 In a hospitality business known to you, critically discuss current management information systems being used to monitor and control labour costs.
2 In the same operation suggest how the information system could be improved to have a broader understanding of the true costs of employment in the unit.
3 Using the figures gained from the unit, calculate the added costs of employment – using the model outlined in Figure 11.1.

4 Critically evaluate the forms of added payment that employees receive in the unit. If staff are not given added income through tips etc., suggest some schemes and discuss the strengths and weaknesses of each approach.

5 Using the same unit, describe different ways of considering labour productivity. What is the range of productivity rates for staff doing the same type of work, say, in the bar, restaurant, accommodation and reception. What would be the effect of all staff working at the rate of the best? How might that happen? Discuss ways of increasing employee productivity.

6 Within the unit calculate the likely sales level and work out the staff roster for one day. Explain your answer.

References

Eaglen, A., Lashley, C. and Thomas, R. (1999). *Benefits and Costs Analysis: the impact of training on business performance.* Leeds Metropolitan University.

Lashley, C. and Rowan, W. (2000). *Wasted Millions: the costs of staff turnover in licensed retailing.* CHME Hospitality Research Conference Proceedings. University of Huddersfield.

Further reading

Coltman, M. (1998). *Hospitality Management Accounting.* Wiley.

Dittmer, P. R. and Griffin, G. G. (1999). *The Principles of Food, Beverage and Labour Costs Controls.* Wiley.

Sales generation and marketing

After working through this chapter you should be able to:

- critically discuss models of hospitality service business segments and marketing mix
- define and deliver the key customer occasions within given business contexts
- promote and enhance sales within the unit
- produce and evaluate marketing plans within a branded hospitality retail operation.

Meeting and exceeding customer expectations

As a unit manager in a branded hospitality retail organization your control over the wider marketing strategy will be limited when compared with an independent business owner. The brand values within which you work are a given. However, you have a key role in delivering those brand values to customers. One of the reasons why branded hospitality services are experiencing success, compared to the independent sector, is their consistency and reliability. Customers are given clear messages about what to expect and the operating system is designed to deliver these expectations. It is your job to ensure that the consistency and reliability are provided in the form of customer experiences.

To be able to do this effectively, you need first to understand the nature of the service's marketing and the different aspects of service segmentation of customers. Chapter 1 showed that services are different to products because services are:

- intangible – they cannot be touched
- heterogeneous – they are unique to every customer
- perishable – they can't be stored
- personal – the customer has to be present.

It is for these reasons that branded hospitality services have emerged. Given the potential uncertainty of the quality of the bar, restaurant or hotel, the brand helps customers understand what to expect. Marketing hospitality retail therefore is concerned with sending clear messages to customers and ensuring that when they enter the establishment they both know what to expect and their expectations are met.

Each brand should focus on the reasons why customers use the establishment and the delivery of experiences that are consistent with their reasons for entering the unit. At local level you have to ensure the business communicates with its customers effectively and ensures that all local potential markets are targeted and sales opportunities are maximized.

Marketing services

There have been many debates about the marketing of services and the extent of the differences with marketing products. Marketing has been largely concerned with ensuring *the marketing mix* is appropriate. That is, ensuring the product, place, price and promotion (the 4Ps) are consistent with each other and focused at an identified *market segment* of customers. The 4Ps have been added to in the case of services because of the elements of services listed earlier. Table 12.1 lists the marketing mix for services, these now include people, processes and premises.

Product	In hospitality retailing this would include all food and drink items as well as the accommodation and range of ancillary services, say, games machines in pubs.
Price	This will include the overall pricing strategy – this communicates something about the product – high price good quality, low prices value for money.
Place	In this case, the overall location strategy for outlets – city centre, suburban, motorway, ring road, rural.
Promotion	The messages and media for telling customers about the brand and developing their understanding of what to expect.
People	The type of employees and the service expectations that they need to deliver have implications for recruitment, training and development and rewards.
Processes	How customers are served and the range of support services available to them. Here service speeds and potential critical success factors are important.
Premises	The overall décor, arrangements for seats, tables, games machines together with cleanliness and ambience-creating factors like music need to be consistent with the brand.

Table 12.1
The services marketing mix

The services marketing mix provides hospitality retail organizations with a framework for focusing on the related aspects of the brand, so that all the elements of the brand are consistent with each other. In this way the products sold and prices charged, together with people delivering products and services and the processes they use, reinforce the key features of the brand. This all takes place in premises that are located close to their markets and that also help to build the brand image.

Example 12.1

TGI Friday Restaurants

TGI Fridays is an American bar and diner concept which is operated in the UK by Whitbread's Restaurant and Leisure Division under license from the parent company in the USA. In the past, site location has required a minimum population of 250 000, though there have now been some variations in the design of the basic units, and plans are under way to expand the chain with smaller units over the next few years. There are now restaurants located in most major cities in the UK. Apart from two large units in central London, most of the brand's restaurants are located on major roads away from the city centre and include ample car parking.

Since the first unit was opened in New York in 1965, the décor and physical attributes have remained essentially unchanged. A uniform feature of the unit design is that the bar occupies a central position, with dining facilities surrounding the bar. Décor is similar throughout all units and is similar to that in the American television series, *Cheers*. Red and white striped awnings, wooden floors, Tiffany lampshades, cane chairs, and striped tablecloths create an aura of the American bar/diner. Each restaurant offers a range of approximately one hundred American/Mexican food menu items and approximately the same number of cocktails. Menus and the product range are designed and priced centrally at head office. Recipes' production together with service instructions are also designed centrally and then *trained out* to the units. Staff uniforms add to décor and logo factors to convey the brand across units located in different regions.

In the UK, food accounts for 60 per cent of turnover and drinks 40 per cent. Executives describe the brand as being located in a casual themed dining market and in the UK is reckoned to be the market leader. One executive described the brand as 'offering a premium price at the top of a very small market segment'. The pricing strategy and layout of the bar/restaurant are seen by business managers as important aspects of the customer offer. For their customers, largely drawn from professional and white-collar occupations, seeing and being seen to participate in this premium brand is key. Again this was described as 'you are buying almost a look, it's why you buy Yves Saint Laurent as against Marks and Spencer, it's a label'.

In addition to these premium label elements to the customer, the brand offers a fun atmosphere, which reflects controlled spontaneity – a party atmosphere where people can go without knowing but hoping to meet the other guests. In many ways it performs the community meeting point in cities where many people live an individualized existence. TGI Fridays provides a service which 'creates a sense of social connection to others'. Many customers need to feel important as individuals, but also want the security of knowing what to expect from a mass-produced standardized service. Service target times require that starters are served within seven minutes of receipt of the order. Main course items must be served within twelve minutes. A computer programme helps managers to monitor the achievement of these service times. Here the security of a highly standardized layout, décor, menu and process is balanced by an extensive menu that allows the customer to select what they consume within the range. In many ways the offer is similar to mass customization in manufactured products. The customer knows what to expect, but they can personalize the experience through the extensive menu.

The company's own research shows that 25 per cent of customers return to the restaurant at least once a month. During weekdays the typical customer is female in her thirties and is in a professional, managerial or white-collar occupation. However, the typical customer profile changes through the day: business lunches, families in the afternoon and early evening, couples and young adults in the later evening. At the weekend customers typically include large numbers of families. There are also some significant differences between customer profiles in London and the provinces.

A second feature of marketing services is that they are targeted at specific customer groups. Again an understanding of who your customers are can be developed by looking at a number of variables that describe them as people. Table 12.2 lists some of these variables, from which you can build a profile of key customer groups. Often hospitality retail organizations attract different customers at different times of day, or times of the week.

Socio-economic group	Income and status groups:
	A Professional, doctors, senior managers
	B Intermediates, middle managers, teachers
	C1 White-collar, clerical, administrative
	C2 Skilled manual, crafts, engineers
	D Unskilled, routine jobs, services/product
	E Low income, unemployed, pensioners
Life cycle position	People in different stages of life
	Bachelor stage
	Newly marrieds, no children
	Full nest I (child under 6)
	Full nest II (child over 6)
	Full nest III (dependent older children)
	Empty nest I (no children family head in work)
	Empty nest II (family head retired)
	Solitary survivor (in work)
	Solitary survivor (retired)
Gender	Male
	Female
	Gay men
	Gay women
Geographical	A classification of residential networks (ACORN):
	Divides people according to the area in which they live. Seventeen groups and fifty-four neighbourhood types.
Lifestyle	Based round educational, income, occupations, social contacts and individual preferences, e.g.:
	Environmentally aware
	Health conscious
	Materialistic
Personality	Extrovert, introvert
	Stable, unstable
	Tough minded, tender minded

Table 12.2 Market segment characteristics

Having defined the customers and customer groups, you are in a much better position to focus on their service needs and the key channels of communication with them. In reality no single method of segmentation is totally satisfactory and most hospitality retailers will use *multivariable segmentation* to better define the market position and target the marketing mix.

Active learning point

In a brand known to you describe the marketing mix that makes up the offer to customers and define the customer market segment or segments that make up the most significant customer group(s). Do different types of customers use the business at different times of the day, or week?

Customer occasions

Increasingly, hospitality retailers are defining and developing their brands round the occasions that customers use their type of business. To some extent, this breaks out of the somewhat constrained way of segmenting customers by the characteristics outlined in Table 12.2. In recent years it has been recognized that the same hospitality retail customers may visit different types of premises for different reasons and at different times of the week. As the unit manager, you need to be focused on why customers visit the premises and what customers using the unit for different occasions require.

The following sections are examples of different customer occasions that apply to a range of hospitality retail operations: restaurants, bars and branded hotels. In each case there is a suggestion of critical success factors together with some factors that might put customers off, because they cut across the customer's primary needs on this occasion, for example, customers out for a 'special occasion' being mixed in with people who are 'out on the town'. In each case, some suggested selling points are also included.

Refuel

Lunch and early evening particularly in city centres or on main routes into and out of cities. Associated with major office or work environments in general, or shopping developments. The emphasis is on having a break – lunch time, coffee time, tea time. Customers may be business people, shoppers, shop workers, office workers, tourists or visitors to the area. The visit is usually restricted by time pressures and the need to return to the primary activity – work or shopping, etc. Timing and speed of service are essential. In some cases, a takeaway, drive-through, or preordering service might be offered so that customers – particularly those who are at work – can telephone their orders in advance and speed collection.

Critical success factors

- Quick service of food and drink.
- In some units express tills and drive-through opportunities.
- Good customer–staff service; friendly but quick.
- Smoke free areas.
- Strong communication of sales offers – good signage, chalkboards, tent cards, etc.
- Female friendly – good vision into the unit, high levels of cleanliness.

Brand examples include:

- McDonald's Restaurants
- Burger King Restaurants
- Pret A Manger
- Rat and Parrot
- All Bar One.

In addition to these core elements of critical success you, as unit manager, need to focus on the different customer types and their specific needs. Here are some additional factors that are important:

- High standards of visibility – customers want to be able to see inside and feel secure.
- Limited queuing – customers need visual evidence that they will be served quickly, or will find a seat, etc.
- Good levels of cleanliness throughout – toilets and car parks.
- Clear offer visible – product and service style must be clearly communicated and consistent with the customer need.
- Attractive external décor – flowers, plants, outside seating, ample parking.
- Mix of large and small tables consistent with variety of customer group sizes for your unit.
- Trained service staff with good product knowledge and customer care skills.
- Up-selling techniques for additional sales.

Sales promotion suggestions • • •

- Links with other businesses – shops, offices, transport companies, car parks, promotional materials or linked offers price reductions etc. – to customers of both businesses or some other encouragement for their captive audience to use your unit.

- Special offers and occasional new items to attract new customers and entertain existing customers. Chosen well, these can yield an additional margin through pricing based on unusualness.

- Up-selling by staff – providing staff with additional targets to promote additional sales or side orders, extra products etc.

Cannot be bothered to cook

Covers all times of day and potential meal occasions from breakfast onwards. Customers need no-effort feeding that is value for money, though the way this is defined will depend on customer income levels. The decision to use the restaurant, pub or bar is usually taken on the spur of the moment. So, dress is often informal and all family members may be present. The decision to go out for a meal may be taken as the result of a 'hard' day or working late, traffic problems, etc. As unit manager, you need to understand who makes the decision to go out for a meal, and why. The nature of the offer and the type of meal occasions need to be carefully considered and focused. You may need, for example, a child's menu and/or a menu that is capable of delivering both snack and main meal options. These units are most likely to be located near key residential areas or on city ring roads, and require adequate parking.

Critical success factors • • •

- Communicate that food is available all day, using typical meal occasions – breakfast, morning coffee, lunch, afternoon tea, dinner.

- Nature of menus and pricing clearly stated to customers – menus displayed outside and on tables.

- Food delivered quickly within time targets, e.g. within fifteen minutes of placing the order.

- Good menu knowledge.

- Good customer care skills – able to relate to different types of customers.

- Mixed range of table sizes to accommodate different customer groups.

- No-smoking areas.

- Credit card payment facility.

Brand examples include:

- Pizza Hut Restaurants
- Homespreads
- Rat and Parrot
- J D Wetherspoons
- Chef and Brewer.

As unit manager you need to build up a profile of customer types and the occasions they visit the unit. Are there differences between customer visits on different times of day and days of the week? It may be that customers on weekday evenings are largely made up of young, two income, childless couples, whilst at the weekend parties are made up of families. The following are some additional points that need to be available for customers for this occasion:

- Drinks to include wines, soft drinks and coffees.
- Children's menu available if families are a significant customer base.
- Outdoor seating can be an additional attraction in summer.
- Lighting so customers can see what they are eating.
- High standards of cleanliness throughout – toilets and car parks.
- Offer cash back facilities.

Sales promotion suggestions

- Make special offers to expand customer usage at different time periods – 'early birds', for example, give customers a price incentive to use the restaurant prior to 7.00 p.m. Usually, this would involve some form of free offer – free starter and sweet with every main course.
- Special offers to retired people, aimed particularly at non-busy periods. Again this may take the form of linked offers – 'free starters' or even two for the price of one on set items.
- A set low-price menu that is offered at lunch time or dinner. If customers know they can get a meal at a 'value price' they are more likely to decide to come in the first place. A more ambitious 'a la carte' menu can be used to up-sell.
- Good publication relations through local newspapers and 'free sheets' can be used to promote the unit.

- Links to clubs for the elderly, major local employers, sports and social clubs can all help to promote the business.

- Up-selling and selling additional items such as side orders extra coffee, wine and other drinks.

Family outing

Families with children under ten years old usually visit in the early evenings, at the weekends or during school holidays. In some cases, for example, where a single parent is looking after preschool children, visits might occur during the daytime on weekdays. In these circumstances budget lunch menus or coffee or tea events may attract the parent whilst the children play with the children's facilities. These play facilities are an essential part of the provision for family outings, and groups may stay for several hours if the children are entertained in a safe environment. Customers may travel considerable distances if the facilities are attractive enough. Hence good parking and access from a reasonable road network is essential.

Critical success factors • • •

- Children's facilities internal and external.

- Reliable food offer and drink offer that cater for children; children's menu essential.

- Children's pack including puzzles, games and colouring packs; free crayons.

- Female friendly – safe, clean and smoke free areas.

- Healthy menu options.

- Staff and management child friendly.

- Value for money food and drink.

Brand examples include:

- Miller's Kitchen

- Brewer's Fayre

- Homespreads

- Happy Eater

- Tom Cobleigh.

Again, as unit manager, you will be expected to analyse customer visits and build a picture of the people who come to the unit at different times of the day, week and year. In particular, you need to consider the potential for building entertainment events and reasons to visit that trigger customer attention. Thus it is possible to see that small children who accompany their mothers may require types of entertainment different from those for older, perhaps teenage, children who accompany two parents. The following are some suggestions that customers who visit units for the occasions might need:

- Signs and promotional material must communicate that families are welcome.
- Highchairs, booster seats, and pushchair access must be available.
- Easy and ample parking required.
- Promote games and play equipment.
- External presentation needs to be welcoming and friendly – flowers, lighting, signs.
- Nappy-changing areas, bottle-warming services with additional supplies of appropriate materials and foods for small children.
- Confectionery and sweets available.
- Children's vending machines and games.
- Zoning customers according to family types – children's age, etc.
- High standards of cleanliness throughout the unit including toilet and car park areas.

Sales promotion suggestions • • •

- Maximize the promotional opportunities from calendar events through the year – Halloween, Mothering Sunday, Father's Day, Bonfire Night, and school holidays in general. At Christmas a Santa's grotto or other attraction for children.
- Organize fun days with a bouncy castle or other attractions such as clowns or fete-type events.
- Links with play groups and local nurseries with the sponsorship of prizes or events.
- Promotion of birthday events via mailing lists and the development of a database of existing customers who have used the unit on earlier birthday occasions – for example, sending birthday cards and offering incentives for repeat business.
- Coverage of special events in local papers and free sheets.
- Links with other business, toyshops, petrol stations and other businesses that might be prepared to make linked promotional offers.

Special meal out

This appeals to couples and groups. All ages are catered for, though the children would typically be older and specialist play equipment would not be provided. Food and drink offers are aimed at the traditional meal, though menus need to reflect the specific themes of the brand – 'British', 'French', 'Southern European', etc. Visits are usually not time pressured and customers want to linger over their meal. That said, there are some requirements in service speeds – to be acknowledged quickly, to gain access to a menu and be offered drink service within a short time of entering the restaurant. Customers have high expectations of both the quality of service and the quality of food and drink served. They expect to make reservations to book a table. Customers' visits will occur on special occasions which are peculiar to them – anniversaries, birthdays, Valentine's Day, Mother's Day, business lunches, etc.

Critical success factors • • •

- High quality environment – décor, toilets, cleanliness, smoke free areas.

- Multicourse menus with a wide choice of items; vegetarian options.

- Service levels relevant to the occasion – table ordering, credit card payment, appropriate staffing to ensure attentive service.

- Drinks offer to match the menu – wines, cocktails, liqueurs, coffees, etc.

- Well-trained staff with good customer service skills and menu knowledge.

Brand examples include:

- Cafe Rouge

- The Dome

- Chef and Brewer

- Beefeater Restaurants

- Cafe Uno

- Est, Est, Est.

Customers who use the hospitality retail outlets on these occasions are looking for a consistent quality experience from both the menu items and the staff. They want the occasion to be special, particularly, when the occasion is triggered by some significant personal event such as a birthday or anniversary. Staff interactions are particularly important because the way they handle customer orders and requests will have an added significance on these occasions. Customers are usually prepared to pay a premium for these special meal occasions, so there are considerable opportunities for 'up-selling' or for selling special items such as fine wines and champagnes. Here are some additional suggestions for success:

- Table reservation service, particularly at busy times of the week or round busy times of the year, say, Christmas or Easter. Accept bookings via fax and e-mail.

- Provide a full table service with all service interactions at the table.

- Tables prelaid with interesting table décor, napkins, glasses, flowers etc.

- Interesting menu, with 'specials' board to maintain interest for regular clients.

- Good wine list and additional drinks such as cocktails, interesting coffees, etc.

- Smoke-free areas, and good quality air conditioning help maintain clean air.

- Staff uniforms and personal hygiene, together with customer care skills, are vital. Staff must be able to make decisions about unusual customer requests and deal at once with customer complaints. High levels of staff training and empowerment are recommended.

- Staff encouraged to pick up on the reasons for special occasions and provide little extras, such as additional flowers, or candles on desserts, etc. to help customers feel special.

- Food production skills through trained chefs are an essential ingredient of this business.

- Excellent external features, décor, signage, visual appearance welcoming and inviting.

- Open fires in winter.

Sales promotion suggestions

- Ensure inclusion in good food guides and local directories that register pubs and restaurants offering meals. Try to generate special features in the local press. Associated with this develop strong links with local journalist, particularly those specializing on dining and leisure features.

- Directed mailshots to existing customers, say, from business cards. Help to promote special offers or special occasions. At less busy times these might be linked to price reductions or two for one, or fixed price menu offers.

- Links with local business organizations – offices or other workplaces – where executives might be encouraged to prioritize the use of the restaurant for business entertaining. Special discounts or party occasions that give a 'thank you' are some ways of developing these links.

- In some cases links with local theatres or cinemas can encourage use, again special offer links can stimulate joint visits to both businesses.

- The availability of menus and cards for customers to take away with them enable customers to have a record of the restaurant and numbers to contact for reservation.

- Increasingly businesses are making web sites and Internet orders and reservations.

Out on the town

This usually occurs in town or city centres and involves younger customers eighteen to forty years of age, normally in groups or couples often based round students or work colleagues. The occasion is typified as 'letting you hair down' and depends on a lively and friendly atmosphere. Customers are out for 'a few drinks' rather than just for 'a drink'. Customers are casually dressed and may go on after the occasion to a curry house, Chinese restaurant or pizza place. The occasion is based round pubs and bars, where having a good time is communicated through the general atmosphere of the place, fellow customers and staff.

Critical success factors

- 'Something happening' atmosphere – good music and entertainment.

- Staff who enjoy the 'party' atmosphere and can communicate with customers in their own terms – recruitment and selection are particularly significant.

- Up-front promotion of the party atmosphere externally and internally.

- Rapid service – lots of service points and minimal waiting by customers.

- Latest fashions drinks and full range of drinks available, prominent displays, staff trained to promote 'star' lines.

Hospitality, Leisure & Tourism Series

Brand examples include:

- It's A Scream
- Firkin
- Bar Oz
- O'Neils
- Comedy clubs.

The key to this type of occasion is in the production of a party atmosphere. Lots of fun, entertainment and music is supported by staff who are 'up for it' are essential elements of the customers' expectations. The music might be provided by a disc jockey, or managed music or a carefully profiled jukebox would provide the necessary sounds for the party atmosphere. A public entertainment licence is required for the unit and late drinking licences might also be required, particularly on the busy weekend nights or when there are key holiday events. Here are some additional factors to ensure success:

- Operational arrangements need to be well planned before the major service event – fridges stocked, buckets with beer bottles on ice, cellar arrangements allowing for quick changeover at peak service times, sufficient glass-clearing and washing capacity.

- Ensure that all service points flow well – review service periods and adjust points where service was held up or slowed down.

- Staff training builds service speeds and up-selling – performance review and monitoring are also helpful in developing service staff.

- Floor space – maximize usage of space for groups standing and seating.

- Themed nights involve employees dressing up and creating the necessary party atmosphere with appropriate performance and fun.

- Stage area might be used for entertainment events.

- Games and entertainment, karaoke can be part of the party atmosphere.

Sales promotion suggestions

- Headline nights allow for customers and staff to feature a particular dress code or musical style, period or band on which to build a 'special' event.

- Staff prepromote forthcoming events to customers.

- Promotion round special dates – St Patrick's night, 4 July US Independence Day, etc.

- Links with students' groups – Students Union or specialist student clubs and societies. Employ students to serve students.

- Links with clubs and recreation facilities as well as workplaces that might be a source of potential customers. In some cases, preferential discounts on the first drink or cash-back offers are useful ways of introducing new customers.

- The use of strong external signage as well as advertising in prominent parts of town – on buses or billboards.

Staying away

Guest are looking for a convenient and safe place to stay overnight – price and location are often most important determinants of usage. Guests are frequently business travellers staying for a short period (one or two nights) during the week. Weekend visitors are often couples or families visiting friends and relatives or attending special functions and conferences. Family weddings and parties are occasions when people in this latter group might visit the hotel. In both cases, the guest spends a limited amount of time on the premises. The main reason for the visit for business and leisure travellers is somewhere in the area, and their time is largely outside the hotel. Usually these properties are best located on a major road or intersection that maximizes the possibility of spontaneous custom and allows speedy access to the unit. The key motive for the visit is efficiency and price sensitivity, whilst at the same time providing reasonable 'no frills' quality facilities, cleanliness and security.

Critical success factors ● ● ●

- Speedy and efficient reception of guests – quick exit service, prepayment assists.

- Business services through fax, in and out, photocopying, message services.

- Comfortable, warm clean rooms with en suite facilities.

- Safe and friendly environment.

- Consistency in offer and services.

- Well-trained service staff capable of delivering the efficiency customers require.

- Quality food and drink available throughout the day.

Brand examples include:

- Travel Inn
- Travel Lodge
- Holiday Inn Express
- Lodge Inns
- Toby Hotels.

Customers are essentially concerned with a basic accommodation provision that meets consistent standards of service, which allow customers privacy and somewhere to 'rest their head'. As the time spent in the accommodation is minimal, additional service such as minibars and even trouser presses are not essential elements. Prepayment of room and breakfast, and pay as you call telephone facilities mean that customers pay for their accommodation on check in and there are no retrospective billing requirements. Hence guests can leave the hotel without further interaction with staff. Evening meal facilities are advertised in rooms and paid for in the restaurant. These hospitality retail services have cut the accommodation service to the minimum required by customers, focusing on speed and price together with cleanliness and consistency. Here are some additional factors that may make the stay a success.

- Reservations staff know the nature of customer needs and can give directions to the unit by telephone or fax.
- Staff knowledgeable about local tourist attractions and business companies and facilities. Local maps available to explain to guests how to get popular locations.
- Friendly, efficient reception staff, capable of welcoming guests and provide efficient check-in and payment.
- Emergency supplies of toiletries available for those who have forgotten razors, toothbrushes, deodorants, etc.
- Car parking facilities need to be adequate and well maintained.
- Room cleaning and maintenance must be checked and up to brand standards.
- Mixture of smoking and non-smoking rooms needed.
- Female guests given 'first floor' rooms because they are perceived to be safer.
- Television and tea- and coffee-making facilities are valued.

Sales promotion suggestions • • •

- Rooms in this hospitality retail market are not usually price discounted but there can be opportunities for you to develop relationships with local organizations who frequently bring employees, suppliers or clients to the area: local universities and colleges, training organizations that have a training facility in the area, local firms with large sales forces that visit the area.

- In some cases, you might be able to develop mutual offers with organizations who jointly promote your accommodation and other leisure services – theatres, cinemas, sports venues such as football clubs.

- Frequent stayers may be offered extra incentives particularly associated with food or free courses or discounted 'two for one' rates.

The above section suggested a number of customer occasions that customers would choose to visit hospitality retail venues. This list is not exhaustive, but it is sufficient to show:

1 Customers visit restaurants, bars and hotels for a discernible reasons and with expectations of the service they will encounter.

2 Different customers visit theses premises for different reasons.

3 Some of these different occasions are compatible with others, but it is a mistake to mix people with different needs who are visiting the premises for very different reasons.

Example 12.2

Chef and Brewer

Chef and Brewer attracts customers who are:

- out for a special meal
- cannot be bothered to cook
- are refuelling

but would lose customers if a unit manager tried to attract customers who are:

- out on the town
- on family outings.

Active learning point

In a brand known to you, describe the customer occasions and motives for using the hospitality retail unit. Describe the different main occasions, as well as the potential occasions that would not conflict with the main occasions, and identify the contradictory occasions that conflict with the main occasion.

Brand _____

Main occasions	
Potential occasions	
Contradictory occasions	

Know your customers

Table 12.3 is a checklist of questions that will help you to focus on your customers so that you better understand who they are and their motives for coming to the unit. You may need to adapt it for your business or produce more than one for different time periods – for example, for lunch-time customers and for evening customers.

Key customer occasion(s)	
Where do customers live in relation to the unit?	
Where have your customers been *before* visiting the unit?	
Where are your customers going directly *after* visiting the unit?	
How long do customers take to make the decision to visit the unit?	
What mode of transport do they use?	
How often do they visit the unit?	
How often do your customers visit the area?	
What competition do your customers also use?	
What is the main age range of customers?	
What is the male: female ratio?	
What is the average party size?	
How many customers bring children with them?	

Table 12.3 Suggested customer profile

Local community

Although some hospitality retail businesses serve customers who come from a wide area, most units serve a local community, and it is a good idea to add to your knowledge of customers by considering some factors about the communities from whence they come (Table 12.4). It is important to build up a picture of your trading area so that potential opportunities can be identified. You will find this information useful when you come to develop a strengths, weakness, opportunities and threats (SWOT) analysis.

	Name(s)	Level of involvement (current/potential)
Local MP/MEP		
Councillors/chief officers/mayor		
Key local charities		
Schools, colleges and universities in the area		
Services: police, fire brigade, etc.		
Local sponsorship		
Business community: chambers of commerce, education business partnerships		
Local press, radio, television media		
Key local employer organizations		
Major sports or other venue		

Table 12.4 Suggested local community audit

Sales analysis

In addition to a detailed knowledge of customer types and reason for using your hospitality retail outlet, you need a thorough understanding of the pattern of current sales. From these you are able to see:

- what is being sold and at which times

- when sales levels are high and low

- why sales patterns are shaped as they are

- where there is potential to increase sales by focusing on light periods

- how sales growth might be prioritized.

	Breakfast	Lunch	Dinner
January	10	25	65
February	11	27	62
March	10	28	62
April	9	30	61
May	9	30	61
June	8	35	57
July	7	40	53
August	7	35	58
September	8	30	62
October	9	25	66
November	9	25	66
December	10	25	65

Table 12.5
Example of sales analysis by meal occasions over twelve months (percentage of monthly sales)

The example given in Table 12.5 can be adapted and changed to meet any business situation. It is merely a device for showing general trends in sales over the year and the shifting importance of different sales occasions – the table could just as easily compare:

- food and drink sales

- snacks and meal sales

- special meal items – leader lines

- overall sales patterns compared with national averages within the brand.

Whilst Table 12.5 provides an overall picture that might show potential areas to build sales in different parts of the year, the information is not detailed enough to show daily or weekly

Hospitality, Leisure & Tourism Series

patterns on which to base actions. Tables 12.6 and 12.7 give examples of the sorts of tables that can be used to establish daily sales patterns and weekly sales patterns respectively.

Using the sales analysis you may see that opportunities present themselves to build sales with target users and user occasions. For example, in a fast-food restaurant it may be possible to build sales through encouraging more breakfast sales aimed at nearby office workers on their way to work, or by attracting more shoppers to visit the unit for morning coffee and a pastry.

Time bands	Percentage of daily sales
11 p.m.–7 a.m.	
7 a.m.–11 a.m.	
11 a.m.–2 p.m.	
2 p.m.–5 p.m.	
5 p.m.–8 p.m.	
8 p.m.–11 p.m.	

Table 12.6
Example of sales analysis of daily sales by time bands

Days of the week	Percentage of weekly sales
Monday	
Tuesday	
Wednesday	
Thursday	
Friday	
Saturday	
Sunday	

Table 12.7
Example of sales analysis of weekly sales by days

Finally, this picture can be further developed by exploring the average sale per sale. Modern till equipment can provide very valuable information about sales rates over time periods, as indicated, but it can also show the average cash value of each transaction together with sales analysis product by product and the amounts of money taken by individual staff members. As shown in Chapter 7 this information can also highlight training needs. Table 12.8 provides a model for analysing sales in a restaurant chain.

Having identified current sales patterns you are able to identify specific targets for sales growth. These should always be expressed in *measurable objectives*, that is, words that define a target that can be measured, so you know when you have achieved it. For example, the objective is to increase the average transaction value by 50p per transaction.

	Average restaurant cheque	National average cheque	Difference +/−	Comments
January				
February				
March				
April				
May				
June				
July				
August				
September				
October				
November				
December				

Table 12.8 Example of comparison of average sales unit/brand over twelve months

Name of competitor _____

Element	General comments	Score
Visibility and location – how effective is it?		
Access – how easy is it to use the unit? Car parking?		
Menu and range?		
Service style?		

Additional offers:
   Specials
   Drinks		

Facilities – standards:
   Baby changing areas
   High chairs
   Disabled toilets
   Disabled access		

Seating:
   Numbers
   Tables and variety		

Pricing and special offers		

General cleanliness:
   External
   Internal
   Toilets		

Promotional activities:
   External signage
   Internal notices
   Special discounts		

Table 12.9 Suggested competitor analysis

Competitor activity

The hospitality retail business environment is highly competitive. There are two issues about competition that you need to consider:

1 There are immediate competitors, that is, units within the same catchment area of customers that offer similar goods and service and meet similar customer occasions as your unit. Examples given earlier list potential brand competitors to McDonald's – Burger King; Harvester Restaurants – Beefeater.

2 There are competitors who might meet customer needs in a different way. Here the customer might take some other service on an occasion that might have been satisfied by a visit to a hospitality retail outlet. For example, the 'cannot be bothered to cook' occasion could be met by a takeaway meal delivered to their home or by a meal bought in a supermarket and reheated at home.

In both cases, it is important that you are aware of prices, the range being offered, service levels, access and other issues that might influence customer choice. You need to be aware also of the general quality issues that customers experience. Competitor analysis needs to consider both the general aspects of the competitor activity and the quality of the service provided (using the example in Table 12.9 and a scoring system, 10 = excellent, 5 = average, 1 = poor).

It is useful to conduct a regular competitor audit comparing your major immediate competitors with your own unit assessment. It is important to be as honest as possible and think carefully where your unit has strengths over competitors and where competitors have strengths. Table 12.10 provides an example of what can be learnt from competitor analysis.

Obviously the above examples of customer analysis and sales analysis in general are given to provide examples of the sort of documents you might use. They should be adapted to the needs of your individual business. However, they cover many issues that are common to many hospitality retail organizations.

Local environment

In addition to information about competitors, a sound marketing plan for the unit needs a clear understanding of developments in the local environment. Economic trends, say, in the form of new organizations locating in the area or the closure of existing operations, create a situation that will offer either opportunities or threats for your units. Similarly, changes in the local housing mix that results in changes in the profile of local residents may also create changes to the customer base that you need to be aware of and plan for (Table 12.11).

Service	Possible	Actual
Manager's and employees appearance	10	
Speed of service	10	
Order correct	10	
Correct staff levels	10	
Polite and friendly service	10	
Temperature comfortable	10	
Music level and quality	10	
Product range visible and clear	10	
Manager visible	10	
Cutlery, napkins, etc. available	10	
Service sub-total	100	
Quality		
Temperature of food	20	
Temperature of drinks	15	
Appearance of food	20	
Appearance of drinks	10	
Taste of food	20	
Taste of drinks	15	
Quality subtotal	100	
Cleanliness		
External litter and cleanliness	10	
Main signage clean	10	
Litter bins clean	10	
Tables and chairs clean	20	
Floors clean and tidy	10	
Toilets, clean, stocked and fresh smelling	20	
Doors and windows clean	10	
Landscaping and plants	10	
Cleanliness subtotal	100	
Total	300	

Table 12.10 Suggested internal competitor audit

Issues to evaluate	Yes	No	Comments
Are there any factories, shops or offices in the area that are likely to close down and negatively impact on your sales?			
Are there any planned factories, shops or offices in your area that are likely to increase your sales?			
Are there are any planned new facilities that might bring more customers to the area, and thereby increase sales?			
Are there any planning restrictions that might impact on your business?			
Are there any minor traffic changes that might impact on your business, e.g. double yellow lines?			
Are there any major traffic plans that will result in new roads that might impact on the business?			
Are there any local council policies that might impact on your business – opening hours, noise control, etc.?			

Table 12.11 Suggested local environment audit

Again, the list in Table 12.11 is not exhaustive. Each type of hospitality retail business will have its own peculiar features that need to be taken into account when considering the local environment. Licensed retail operations, for example, may have to consider the general attitudes of the local council and the licensing magistrates to the spread of licensed premises. Some areas have covenants to and local restrictions on the number of pubs and bars in an area.

The SWOT analysis

A thorough and honest analysis of the strengths, weaknesses, opportunities and threats to your hospitality retail unit is essential to your production of a marketing strategy and plan for the business. The analysis brings together much of the information already gathered – sales analysis, customer profiles, local

Table 12.12 Suggested SWOT analysis and action priorities

In each case enter the facts from your earlier analysis.

Service quality audit – customer contacts and mystery diner reports plus internal audit (e.g. service times are too slow)	Is this a strength or weakness?	Priorities: high, medium or low?
Sales or costs targets – may relate to increasing sales or priority products or reducing costs (e.g. increase breakfast sales or increase average sales)	Is this a strength or weakness?	Priorities: high, medium or low?
Merchandising – exploring all external and internal promotional activity (e.g. improve the effectiveness of promotional material)	Is this a strength or weakness?	Priorities: high, medium or low?
Visibility – the awareness of the location of the unit and issues related to poor visibility (e.g. improve the visibility from the north)	Is this a strength or weakness?	Priorities: high, medium or low?

Access – ability of all potential customers to gain access to the unit (e.g. no wheelchair ramp)	Is this a strength or weakness?	Priorities: high, medium or low?
Facilities – full range of spaces available and facilities or needs to be competitive (e.g. children's play area, insufficient seating)	Is this a strength or weakness?	Priorities: high, medium or low?
Customers – the current customer profile and usage occasions (e.g. high number of shoppers, need to look at other customer groups, office workers)	Is this a strength or weakness?	Priorities: high, medium or low?
Local trading area business generators – surrounding facilities that can bring customers into the area (e.g. local swimming pool nearby)	Is this a strength or weakness?	Priorities: high, medium or low?

Local community links – police, fire brigade and other community groups who support the unit (e.g. excellent links with local police)	Is this a strength or weakness?	Priorities: high, medium or low?
Competition – current provision and quality issues, exploiting common promotions or weaknesses in service (e.g. competitor restaurant is running major promotion)	Is this a strength or weakness?	Priorities: high, medium or low?
Environment – issues likely to effect the local trading conditions, fewer or more potential customers (e.g. new housing development ion near completion)	Is this a strength or weakness?	Priorities: high, medium or low?

community, competitors and local environmental issues. The example given in Table 12.12 is just one possible way of undertaking the exercise; others invite you draw up a four-quadrant table with strengths, weaknesses, opportunities and threats each occupying one of the four quadrants. The benefit of this model is that it does lead you to a consideration of the priorities for action.

SWOT high priority actions

Having considered the full range of strengths and weakness together with the opportunities and threats open to the unit, you now need to decide on the key priorities. It is unlikely that you will be able to do everything so:

- consider the long-term goal (sales growth, quality improvement)
- decide which can be achieved with least effort
- which will yield the quickest returns
- what you need to put in place for long-term gain.

From this, you should be able to list and prioritize the immediate priority actions (Table 12.13). This in turn will help you set your goals and define the actions needed to make your marketing plan happen.

Setting goals

The SWOT summary has provided you with a list of priorities that have to be actioned. Your goals need to address each of the priorities and clearly state what it is you want to achieve, by how much and by when. Setting price targets is important because you must be able to determine whether you have achieved what you set out to do, and if not why not? Table 12.14 provides a simple format for listing these goals and showing what you intend to achieve.

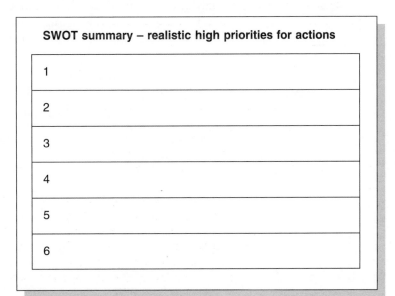

SWOT summary – realistic high priorities for actions

| 1 |
| 2 |
| 3 |
| 4 |
| 5 |
| 6 |

Table 12.13
Suggested SWOT summary sheet

Hospitality, Leisure & Tourism Series

What is to be achieved?	By how much?	By when?
E.g. increase average sale value	50p	3 months

Table 12.14
Setting goals in hospitality retailing

Marketing plan

Successful actions are based on clearly thought through goals that are then converted into a plan of action that essentially answers the question, 'How will I achieve the goals set?' (Table 12.15). You may need to target particular customer groups or promote customer occasions that are complementary to the core occasions that make up your main business. For example, a restaurant that relies heavily on customers who are *refuelling* may promote the *cannot be bothered to cook* occasions. To achieve other goals you may need to make changes to the way the unit and employees operate. For example, increasing sales may require employees to make suggestions and jointly decide on actions.

Goal, e.g. increase average spend by 50 pence within three months	By a) training staff in up-selling, b) setting up action teams of staff
1	
2	
3	

Table 12.15
Marketing action plan

Conclusion

This chapter has attempted to give you some appreciation of, and tools to be able to understand customers and their motives for visiting hospitality retail outlets, and show how your unit can be marketed effectively. In most cases, hospitality retail brands have clearly defined qualities that are communicated to customers. In part it is your job to ensure that customer expectations are at least met, if not exceeded, when they visit your outlet. In these circumstances, understanding the nature of the service offer made by the brand and the critical factors needed for success are essential, because this gives your work focus and objectives.

Furthermore, the chapter has shown that you as unit manager have considerable scope to build on the brand and identify those aspects of the brand that might be offered to customers who have complementary needs to those of your core business. Sales growth can therefore be delivered by ensuring that core customer needs are satisfied and that additional customers are encouraged to use the business in different, though supportable, ways. Clearly, this is not about merely adding numbers because potentially the wrong type of customers who have needs different to the core customer base might alienate your core business.

Whatever the broad approach you take, your business needs to .be carefully analysed and a detailed plan devised that shows how the unit matches with competitors and others in the local marketplace. A well-informed analysis of the local community and the environment as well as the customer base helps build the priorities, goals and marketing plan of actions through which you will be able to build sales and thereby profits.

Reflective practice

Answer these questions to check your understanding of this chapter:

1 For a hospitality retail unit known to you, describe the customers who make up the main customer base for the business. Do different groups use the business at different times? How are their needs different?
2 In the same business, consider the main customer occasions which are served by the unit. Describe the benefits of the customer occasions model of thinking about your customers?
3 Identify customer occasions you might be able to attract that might provide a new source of customers. What occasions would contradict current core customer uses.
4 Highlight the steps required to draw up a unit marketing plan. What information is needed about the local community and environment?

5 Critically discuss the need for a unit marketing plan. Pick out the key problems and tensions in matching this to the overall brand marketing plan.

Further reading

Buttle, F. (1986). *Hotel and Food Service Marketing: A Managerial Approach*. Cassell.

Honer, S. and Swarbrooke, J. (1996). *Marketing Tourism Hospitality and Leisure in Europe*. International Thompson Business Press.

Lewis, R. C. (1997). *Cases in Hospitality Marketing Management*. Wiley.

Preparing a unit business plan

After working through this chapter you should be able to:

- understand the need to produce and work to a unit business plan

- gather the information and background details needed for the plan

- write up and present an effective business plan

- work to the plan and make any necessary adjustments.

Business plans, like any map, improve the chance of reaching the destination

Although you may be working for a large branded hospitality retailer, and managing a unit that is already covered by the plan for the overall business, it is useful to prepare a business plan for your unit. For independent business in freehold, tenanted, leased or franchised businesses a business plan is essential. As the above statement indicates, business plans assist managers to plan the direction of the business, compare performance with the plan and take corrective action.

Preparing a business plan allows you to:

• think about the mission, goals and objectives of the business, and the actions needed to achieve the objectives

• identify the information needed to understand the customers and competition

• develop a competitive business strategy for the unit

• plan all the activities needed to make the strategy work

• forecast the results of the unit and plan to overcome difficulties

• keep track of the business and take corrective action where needed.

Preparing a business plan helps you understand the business and the planning process. It is this process that is important to your role as unit manager, because the hospitality retail sector is fast-moving and dynamic and a plan gives you a sense of direction and purpose. It gives you a basis from which to make changes and amendments as circumstances unfold. As part of a group, the business plan shows how your unit will contribute to the goals and objectives of the company.

Describing the business

The business planning process starts with a clear description of the business, the management and team and the core business activities.

Mission statement, goals, objectives and actions

The mission statement, goals and objectives (Figure 13.1) are important because they help to give everyone in the unit focus and a sense of purpose. Also they help everyone to consider problems and difficulties to be overcome.

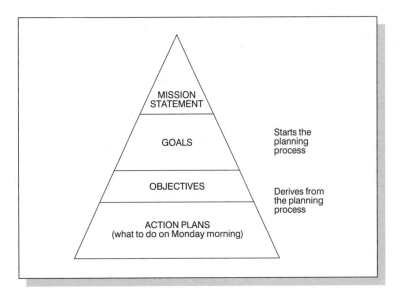

Figure 13.1
The pyramid of goals

Mission statement ● ● ●

In large organizations the mission statement will be provided by the organization, but as unit manager you will need to understand the statement and encourage team members to understand their contribution to achieving the mission. A good mission statement provides an organization with focus, and helps to concentrate managerial and other employees on the key activities. In particular the mission statement should cover the following points:

● what business you are in and your purpose

● what you want to achieve over the next one to three years

● how you will achieve this – your values and standards.

A mission statement should not be too bland, nor should it be so general that is difficult to know what business you are in.

Goals ● ● ●

These are the specific goals to be achieved over the next three years. They have to be written in specific and measurable terms. For example:

1 Increase sales by 20 per cent over three years.

2 Reduce employee turnover by 10 per cent each year.

3 Increase customer satisfaction scores by 5 per cent within one year.

By defining the key goals you are providing a set of targets so that you are more likely to achieve the overall purpose of the business. They provide you with a measurable set of pointers that guide actions over the forthcoming period.

Objectives ● ● ●

Objectives are the specific activities that you need to undertake to achieve the goals set. They are the 'how' statements that will make the objectives happen. For example:

1 Identify complementary customer occasions, so as to attract new customers to the business.

2 Target businesses that might undertake joint products with my products and services.

3 Direct promotional material and special offers to customers who use the unit in quiet periods.

Actions ● ● ●

In this case you are showing what needs to be done and when – what you will do on Monday morning – thinking ahead to the various actions needed, and when. For example:

1 Survey existing customers and potential customers.

2 Visit all competitor units in the area.

3 In August start recruitment and training of staff needed for the Christmas season.

In your case, as a unit manager, the identification of goals, strategies and actions are most important because they are useful in helping you achieve the overall mission as set by the organization. It is your job to run the unit in such a way that it makes its contribution to the overall success of the brand. Regional and senior managers will be monitoring your performance, and the business plan helps you and them overview progress.

Description of the products and services

Even in situations where you are managing a unit of a branded hospitality retail organization, it is worthwhile focusing on the key products and services that you are supplying to customers. Hospitality retail operations often involve the sale of a mixture of food and beverage items. These need to be analysed:

● by meal types – say between set meals and snacks, or

● between types of drinks – alcoholic and soft drinks

● through other income streams – say from machines.

Where accommodation is also offered for sale, the analysis should include room sales and types.

Increasingly, as we have seen in Chapter 12, the analysis should also consider the primary customer occasions the business is servicing, and identify potential complementary occasions that might be tapped as a source of sales growth. A suggested format for this analysis is shown in Table 13.1.

Product/service	Description	% of sales
1		
2		
3		
4		
5		

Table 13.1
Product and service analysis

This statement of the key product and service together with a statement relating to product and service quality and some targets for its management is a crucial planning tool. Chapter 8 provides an overview of different approaches to quality management, but this statement with its clear objectives is an important aspect of the way you plan to manage the business. Also flowing from your analysis of the customer occasions at the core of your business, it is possible also to list the key critical success factors so that you focus on those aspects of the product and service offer most important to meeting customer expectations.

You and your team

A careful consideration of the experience, training and development and skills available within both the management team and among the employees is a valuable starting point to considering the skill needs of the unit. Clearly the plan can help you to:

- identify potential strengths in the team

- highlight key skills and experiences that can be used for projects and special initiatives

- focus on skill shortages and development needs for the future

- progression plan employees' and managers' career development.

Increasingly, hospitality retail units are concerned with availability of key staff at all levels. The right management team skills and experiences capable of running and developing a multi-million pound business are vital. In addition, the inability to attract, recruit and train employees is further compounded in many hospitality retail organizations by high levels of staff turnover that often represent a key weakness and substantial additional cost to the business. A clear commitment to building a strong team and increasing staff retention need to be a key part of your overall policies and objectives, and your analysis of the team.

1 Explain the thinking behind the company's mission statement and show how you will work to achieving the mission in your unit.

2 List your goals for the unit: (a) for the long term, (b) for the short term.

3 List the objectives you need to do and actions you need to take to achieve the goals.

4 Describe your products and service as if to a new employee.

5 How do your goods and services differ from competitors?

6 Are there possible complementary occasions through which you could attract new customers?

7 What relevant skills and talents are available to you?

8 What are the shortages of skills and talents? How do you plan to fill the gaps?

'9 What are current levels of staff retention and staff turnover?

10 What are the current levels of financial performance – cost levels, sales growth, profit levels, etc. – and the targets for the future?

Market research

Many branded hospitality retail operators commission research on the brand, customers, competitors and markets, and you will usually have access to this national information. However, you need to understand these issues as they relate to your particular unit and the community in which it is located. Chapter 12 has dealt with many of these issues. The following list provides a checklist of issues to be included in the business plan. An important element of your job as unit manager, therefore, is:

- you thinking about the core customer needs the unit is servicing
- the types of customer who are attracted to the business
- the activities of competitors
- the general conduct of the market in which you operate.

An ongoing analysis of these issues helps you keep the plan in focus and to react to any changes that come up. Thus the unforeseen opening of a competitor unit or the closure of a major local employer may have adverse impacts to which you need to react.

Customers

The focus of this text suggests that each brand represents a series of tangible and intangible benefits in products and services to customers. These can be best understood through an analysis of the 'occasions' that customers visit the establishment.

The key starting point of your plan is to consider the various customer needs you are servicing through the business and the factors that are critical for success. Furthermore this needs to be further developed by an analysis of the customers themselves.

1 *Socioeconomic group*: how do customers comprise the key socioeconomic groups? Issues to do with income, status and employment can have important consequences, particularly if you build up a picture of key employers for whom your customers work.

2 *Life cycle position*: a description of the life cycle position(s) of key customer also helps you to analyse the number of potential customers in your locality and their needs and concerns from businesses like yours.

3 *Gender*: the mixture of male and female customers has a number of consequences for the product and services you offer. Healthy eating options on the menu, the provision of non-smoking areas and security are issues that may be important issues where a substantial number of customers are women.

4 *Geographical*: what kind of area do customers mostly live in? What housing types and locations? Are there other similar areas that might yield customers? What developments are there in these areas that might impact on your business?

5 *Lifestyle*: are there issues about environmental awareness, health consciousness or appeals that can be made to those concerned with material rewards? In some units, a series of healthy options might attract customers to use the unit more frequently.

6 *Personality*: what personality types mostly dominate the customer base? Are there additional opportunities to attract similar customers or a different sort of customer at different times?

These matters need your careful consideration because, over recent decades, hospitality retail brands have emerged around changes in the population and their spending power. Here are just a few examples:

- More women are working, taking careers breaks to have children and then returning to work.

- There are more two income households than previously.

- There are more single households than previously.

- More elderly people are living longer and have higher incomes.

- There is a general increase in the number of people eating out.

- There has been an increase in people preferring healthy eating.

These changes have resulted in some additional opportunities; for example, retired customers can be attracted to use restaurants and pubs during the late afternoon and early evening through price offers or special offers. More women with independent income mean that more women are looking to be able to eat and drink on their own. More health consciousness and growth in vegetarianism mean that most menu offers have to include vegetarian and healthy eating options, and increasing non-smoking customers are demanding smoke-free atmospheres or no smoking areas in restaurants and bars.

Key customer occasions and critical success factors ● ● ●

Chapter 12 outlined these in detail but the following acts as a reminder of the key customer occasions most appropriate to hospitality retail operations in general. The list provided is not exhaustive and your business may well be meeting other customer needs that result in them visiting the restaurant, bar or hotel and are not included here. Your business plan needs to list the core customer occasions and the potential complementary occasions that might yield more customers:

- refuel

- cannot be bothered to cook

- family outing

- special meal out

- out on the town

- staying away from home.

In addition, your business plan needs to list the critical success factors that are at the heart of customer expectations of a successful visit to the unit.

Competitors

Research on local competitors is an important source of information on which to plan your own activities. Many retail hospitality markets are dominated by 'me too' brands, that is, brands that are aiming at similar market segments and offering to satisfy similar customer needs on similar customer occasions. You need to know their current strengths and weaknesses so that you can:

- learn from their strengths

- attack their weaknesses.

Remember the points made in Chapter 12, there are both immediate and second order competitors for your customers' spend. Initially concentrate on the immediate, first order competitors, but you need also to think about the other competitors who are also meeting similar customer needs to the same customer base as you. Your business may well have its own features in relation to customers that will add to the list of key concerns in Table 13.2. The important point is that the issue you investigate needs to be relevant to your business and to the customer needs it is aiming to satisfy.

When drawing up your business plan you need to have an honest and accurate picture of the strengths and weaknesses of competitors, and this should then inform your plan. Where can you build genuine competitive advantage? What actions and targets are required to gain the competitive edge needed?

Flowing from the initial research, you should be constantly tracking competitors. You need to explore issues beyond the immediate customers, goods and services offered. Usually you are competing in the same labour markets and in the same local environment so you may also need to explore wage rates and incomes, and their links with local employers, schools, local government, planning offices, etc.

Factor	Competitor	Own unit
Visibility and access		
Menu and range		
Service style		
Additional offers		
Facilities		
Seating		
Opening hours		
Pricing and special offers		
General cleanliness		
Promotional activities		
Estimated sales revenue		
Average check size or transaction value		
Internal competitor audit		

Table 13.2 Competitor analysis

The local environment

Your business plan now must take into account the local environment because it provides opportunities and threats that will impact on the business. Contacts with relevant government authorities can help you identify some useful data about the economic, political, social and legal environment. These items flow from your marketing analysis, but here are some issues you might like to consider:

- local population demographic profile – trends and changes

- general level of economic activity – employment, incomes, changes and future trends

- local offices or factories – major employers that may impact on your business, either closing or expanding

- any planned traffic changes or other planning decisions that might impact

- the general approach of the planning authorities to your type of business.

The key is scanning the future for potential impacts on the business you are in. Do they potentially generate more customers or fewer? As Wellington once said, 'The value of recognizance is knowing what is over the hill'. In fast-moving hospitality retail businesses you have to be aware of changes before they occur. In this way you will be in the best situation to benefit from increased customer or best suited to deal with problems.

1 What is the geographical area from which customers are likely to be drawn? Consider numbers, locations, housing stock, etc.

2 What are the customer needs expressed in customer occasions that will be your core customer base? Identify potential customer occasions.

3 Consider the critical success factors for each of these customer groups, and differences between groups.

4 Are the markets you aim to draw from increasing or declining?

5 Might potential changes in customer tastes, or habits, either increase or reduce sales?

6 List the competitors with whom you will directly compete.

7 List competitor opportunities to satisfy the same customer needs.

8 Highlight the strengths and weaknesses of their approach to serving these customers.

9 Match these with strengths and weaknesses you have compared with them for the same customers.

10 Describe the local economic and social context in which your business is located.

11 Identify local firms with whom you might be able to form alliances.

12 Identify the key threats and opportunities posed by the local environment.

Competitive business strategy

You should now be in a position to formulate a competitive business strategy that will help you plan your tactics and actions over the short, medium and long term. As a unit manager you need to regard the short term as actions within the next year, medium term as over one but under two years and long term as three years or more.

Working within a branded environment, the business strategy in terms of the overall direction of the business will be decided and shaped at head office. Your role as unit manager is to understand the strategy and interpret it within the local context. Broadly, there are three types of strategy that organizations follow:

1 *Overall cost leadership* is usually used by large firms who can take advantage of reduced costs through economies of scale. The size of the business allows the firm to work on reduced costs due to lower production and distribution costs, greater purchasing power with suppliers and reduced advertising and selling costs. In addition to providing a uniformity dependent service, McDonald's Restaurants also follows a policy that has much in common with cost leadership.

2 *Differentiation* through quality, good design and image, that creates brand loyalty and a willingness to pay a price premium. In some cases, the 'label' is the key benefit to the customer. TGI Friday Restaurants are in part attempting to gain competitive advantage in this way.

3 *Focus* is where a company focuses on a particular market segment, or a narrow market segment that is too specialized to attract competitors. By specializing in this way the firm makes the market its own. In some cases, being the only supplier of a particular hospitality service to a particular local market can have elements of this, though in many cases the entry barriers for hospitality firms are too low to make it a realistic national strategy.

The overall business strategy brings together the various elements of the mission and objectives, market research, and marketing strategies, the market place and the marketing mix leading to an overall plan. The service marketing mix needs to be stated in your business plan, and you need to give it the local flavour that will help you action the overall brand strategy.

Pricing

As shown in the previous chapter, pricing is one of the elements of the marketing mix. In branded situations you have to manage to work with national brand selling price strategies. Here are a few key pointers to pricing:

- The selling price shapes customer perceptions – higher prices can communicate a perception of higher quality.

- Price is associated with concept of value, but customers use the perceptions of the benefits to assess whether the price paid represents good value.

- Many competitive markets are price sensitive, and small changes in price can result in large changes in customer demand.

- It is possible to adopt approaches where prices are held constant but bonus offers and the promotional mix increases sales. McDonald's Restaurants' 1999 campaign giving away 'Beanie Babies' is an example.

Your business plan needs a clear statement about the pricing strategy of the brand and how you will use this in local campaigns.

Advertising and promotion

You need to communicate with your local market, both customers and would-be customers. Advertising is paid-for messages in the form of, say, local press advertising, whilst promotion is those activities that will help generate sales, like the McDonald's campaign mentioned above.

Your marketing plan needs to take account of how you will promote sales through an array of different activities. Here are some examples that you might consider:

- Local newspapers and 'free sheets' are often effective in that they reach target markets and are increasingly able to tailor their messages to specific localities. These are most effective when tied to an editorial piece, say, a story about your unit that is of local interest.

- Leaflets dropped through doors or sent by post to targeted postcode areas are also useful in that you can direct your messages to the people most likely to use your establishment.

- Links with complementary firms – cinemas, theatres and other leisure venues – can provide joint offers such as pre-theatre dinners, or price-off vouchers to attract them to your business.

Your business plan needs to show how you will promote the business over the period:

- What are the goals and objectives?

- How much is it worth?

- Which methods will you use?

- What benefits do you expect to receive?

- How will you check the results?

Place

Your business plan needs to consider the nature of the premises as these provide sources of tangible and intangible benefits to customers. As we saw, issues such as the approach and appearance externally, the signage form various approaches, the cleanliness, visibility to the inside, external décor and car parking facilities may all be issues that are benefits or limitations.

Internally, the atmosphere, cleanliness, décor, music, toilet provision, no smoking areas, availability of children's play areas etc. are also issues that need to be considered, because they may require capital expenditure to meet changed customer expectations.

Often it is said that location is the key to success in hospitality businesses, but difficulties in this area can be overcome with the right attention to service, customer expectations and promotional activity.

Your business plan should include an analysis of the facilities so that you can analyse and act upon the strengths and weaknesses they pose for meeting and exceeding customer expectations:

1 What are the key cost elements that your business has to incur to make an operating profit?

2 What is the overall price strategy?

3 How do your prices compare with those of your competitors?

4 Are there differences amongst customers in their price sensitivity?

5 What are your key objectives for advertising and promotional activities?

6 What methods will you use to achieve the objectives, and why?

7 How will the results be monitored and evaluated?

8 Are premises adequate for future needs?

9 What development work is needed and why?

Operations

'Operations' is the name given to the activities required in order to fulfil the strategy. In hospitality retail operations these activities cover the production and service of food and drink and, in some cases, accommodation. Your business plan needs to show in detail how products and service will be supplied to customers.

1 It is useful to start with an indication in broad terms of what it is you are selling, though an appendix could include the full product range.

2 From this you indicate the opening hours of the unit and the sales mix at different times of each day.

3 Provide an organizational plan that shows the organization of the unit and indicates the key job roles required to produce the goods and services. This will indicate the management posts involved and broad areas of responsibilities. Again, the appendix can be used in which to provide job descriptions (showing duties and responsibilities) and person specifications (showing skills and qualities) needed for each job title.

4 You also indicate how the individuals will be managed, rewarded and motivated, issues to do with group work and teamwork in the management of particular customer groups and customer occasions. In other words, how will you manage the critical success factors?

5 Following from this you should indicate your approach to customer complaint handling and the responsibilities for achieving customer satisfaction.

6 Your business plan needs to consider the management of materials and cash involved in the operation.

7 In most hospitality retail operations there are strict legal responsibilities associated with food hygiene, health and safety, licensing, and other responsibilities to customers and staff. Your plan should show how these matters are handled and managed.

The operational plan lays down a blueprint of the key issues that are priorities for the delivery of a successful unit likely to satisfy customers and employees.

Forecasting results

The business plan was described earlier in the chapter as a map, and the ultimate aim of a unit offering hospitality retail products is to deliver a profitable operation that will make a positive contribution to the company's financial performance.

Sales forecasts

The sales forecast is, arguably, the most important set of figures to arise from the planning process. The sales forecast helps to establish the targets that you will use throughout the year and establishes a set of unit profit and loss accounts that will indicate the success or otherwise of the unit.

Your estimate of sales from various income streams – meals, non-alcoholic and alcoholic beverages, machines and accommodation, etc. – will need above all else to be based on sound reasoning. As part of a branded multiunit operational you will have previous trading experience on which to build, even in a new unit. In many cases, however, you will be managing a unit that has been trading for some time. The following points provide a checklist of issues to bear in mind when calculating and justifying the sales forecasts:

- How big is the market, bearing in mind the customer profile you will be wanting to attract and the local population within the unit's catchment area. Is the overall market growing or shrinking, and at what rate? Avoid unsubstantiated statements – you need to be convinced that the targets are achievable.

- How many customers are there who are likely to buy from you and how much do they spend on average per visit? Are there seasonal variations or variations between customer types? Hospitality retailers can obtain some information about the area, customer types, traffic flows, footfalls, etc. from the local authority and from research organizations.

- The desired income approach is appropriate for these operations and your aim is to achieve the forecast. By a thorough analysis of potential sales you are able to make adjustments if sales slip for some reason.

- Are there any product life cycle issues to consider? Some hospitality retail operations, pubs for example, are working in markets where customer visits are in decline, though there are growing opportunities in the restaurant sector.

How long a period should your sales forecasts cover? In fast-moving retail markets it would be unusual to plan more than three years ahead and most will operate a twelve-month cycle.

Operating profit statement

The operating profit statement sets out to match income with expenditure over the appropriate time period of your business plan. It is the way profit and loss can be calculated for the period.

Sales income • • •

This shows the total budget sales income for each month over the year. The figure will include the total income from all the unit's revenue earning activities – sales of meals, snacks, alcoholic and non-alcoholic drinks, machines, accommodation, etc.– for each month as they are likely to occur. You must consider potential variations month by month. Traditionally, hospitality retail operations experience low sales in January after peaks in December.

Cost of sales

To calculate a trading profit deduct the costs of the materials purchased to produce the goods sold – all the food, drinks and other materials directly used – from the sales revenue. Usually these costs could represent an average and be calculated as a percentage, though there may be major differences between the profitability of different income streams and products.

Labour costs

Again these relate to the costs of producing the products and services associated with the sales revenue generated. Thus the total direct labour costs of kitchen, bar, restaurant and accommodation are calculated as a means of arriving at a gross profit, that is, the surplus after the costs directly associated with generating the sales revenue have been taken into account. Again the costs of labour can be calculated as a percentage, though there are differences between departments and sections depending on the labour intensity and the use of supplies that require different amounts of handling by staff.

Table 13.3 shows an example of an extract from accounts for a hospitality retail operation. The gross profit shows you how much income will be generated after the immediate costs of producing the products and services sold. However, these are not

Year XXXX	Chelmsford
	£
Sales	
Food	900,000
Beverages	50,000
	950,000
Cost of sales	
Food	225,000
Beverages	20,000
Total	245,000
Trading profit	705,000
Staff wages (hourly paid)	175,000
GROSS PROFIT	530,000

Table 13.3
Extract 1 from gross profit budget for Mr Bean Restaurant, Chelmsford

Year XXXX	Nottingham
	£
Sales	
Food	900,000
Beverages	50,000
	950,000
Cost of sales	
Food	225,000
Beverages	20,000
Total	245,000
Trading profit	705,000
Staff wages (hourly paid)	175,000
GROSS PROFIT	530,000
Lease and local tax	90,000
Electricity and gas	20,000
Management and admin	54,000
Promotional activity	48,000
Maintenance	36,000
Other consumable	36,000
Depreciation	30,000
RESTAURANT PROFIT CONTRIBUTION	216,000

Table 13.4
Extract 2 from gross profit budget for Mr Bean Restaurant, Chelmsford

the only unit-based expenses. Managers' salaries and other administration costs, as well as rents, rates, lighting and electricity, unit-based advertising, staff uniforms and other expenses will need to be taken into account to show the profit contribution that your unit makes to the business.

Table 13.4 is an example from the same organization, but shows how the operation profit can be calculated.

Clearly, a branded hospitality retail unit is different from an independent business because it unusual for the latter organization to produce unit-specific balance sheets. However, each business will be considered as a business investment and the return on capital employed might be an issue that the company accounts might include.

Writing up, presenting and working with your business plan

The business plan is a document both to be presented to colleagues – showing how you plan to manage the unit – and that you will use throughout the year to work from and to assess your progress. The business plan, therefore, needs to be presented in a professional manner, and be easily accessible.

Presentation of the written document

The business plan needs to conform to professional standards in the way it is written and presented:

- A simple business folder with a spiral binding will be sufficient.
- It must be word-processed (typed).
- The layout should be much closer to that of a report than a memo or essay.
- The page layout should use wide margins and be pleasing on the eye, and it should be printed on single sides of A4 paper.
- It should paginated.
- Tables, figures and graphs should aid understanding and are a quick way of communicating information, though these should also be explained and discussed in the text.

Remember, the appendix should be used to provide useful background information; all information that is essential to the plan must be included in the text.

Layout and content

There is no formally accepted business plan format, and a business plan for a unit that is part of an multiunit organization has to be different to a plan for an independent business. The balance sheet section and the justifications that an independent business is required to include are not needed in a document for these purposes.

The front cover of the document should clearly state the name of the business and the date of the business plan. It is important that it is clear that this is the latest version of the plan. The second sheet behind the front cover should include:

- the current trading position of the restaurant, past successes and the general appraisal of performance over recent years
- the products and services currently being sold and the units ranking compared with competitors
- the customers and the potential customer base in the area, and the reasons why they use the unit
- the unit's aims and objectives in the short term, and the strategies to be employed in achieving them
- a summary of forecasts, sales and profits.

The table of contents • • •

The table of contents is valuable because it helps readers to find their way round the document and focus on the issues of immediate concern. Remember that you will be using this document so you need to be able to turn quickly to the sections that are of particular interest at a specific time.

There are a number of ways of numbering pages and sections. It is most appropriate to use a system that gives every section a new number, and subsections are differentiated by using decimal points.

Though there are likely to be variations between different businesses, the following is an example to work from and might be useful as basis for designing your own document.

Example 13.1

Sample table of contents

Section

Executive Summary

1 The Unit and Management
 1.1 History and overview of progress to date
 1.2 Current mission
 1.3 Objectives and actions needed
 1.4 The team

2 The Products and Services
 2.1 Products and services
 2.2 Current sales mix

3 Market and Competition
 3.1 Description of customers
 3.2 Customer occasions, needs and benefits
 3.3 Market segments
 3.4 Market size in the area
 3.5 Location of customers and flows
 3.6 Market projects over the period
 3.7 Competition

4 Competitive Business Strategy
 4.1 Pricing policy
 4.2 Promotional plans
 4.3 Premises
 4.4 Competitor responses

5 Operations
 5.1 Critical success factors
 5.2 Quality management and control
 5.3 Organization structure
 5.4 Employee management and motivation

6 Forecasts and Results
 6.1 Sales forecasts
 6.2 Operational budget

Appendix

The writing of the plan may have to go through several stages: at least a first draft that you will show to and discuss with colleagues, and a second draft that will be the final document. It is important that the final draft is clear and well written, and free from spelling and grammatical errors. The document has to be detailed enough to show that you have thought through the issues and to record your thinking, but it must not be overly long. So part of the editing process is to ensure that the information that is needed is in the document and that you have not overdone parts.

Working with the business plan

The business plan should be used throughout the year to monitor progress. The assumptions and calculations built into the plan made sense to you and your colleagues at the time, so you need to think critically about the how you will use the plan to guide your trading performance.

1 *Sales analysis*: hourly, daily, weekly and monthly sales audits can keep track of issues such as the sales mix, sales of most profitable lines, average transaction values, numbers of transactions, party sizes, irregular flows in the times customer use the business, etc.

2 *Promotional plans and activities*: impacts of particular offers, bonuses, national and local initiatives that were more or less successful.

3 *Customers*: regular users and customer retention, location and reasons for coming to the unit, demographic profiles, complaints and comments of satisfaction, customer focus groups, mystery customer reports.

4 *Employees*: staff retention and labour turnover, staff satisfaction surveys, costs of training, benefits from training and developments, sales analysis and up-selling opportunities, labour costs and investment in human capital.

5 *Competitor activities*: making records of their initiatives that impact negatively on your sales, and how they respond to your initiatives.

6 *Cost control and profitability*: ensuring that you keep to the costs of the materials and labour needed for the production of goods and services is essential in developing the basis for profitable performance.

Hospitality, Leisure & Tourism Series

Conclusion

There are some differences from a traditional business plan. Our business plans are rarely used in support of a request for finance, as would be the case with an independent business, though there are times when a business plan might be used to justify an increased investment in the unit. In the main, however, business plans in multiunit branded hospitality retail operations do not involve calculations that consider the investment benefits of the business. So it is unusual for this type of business plan to consider the balance sheet and the various ratios associated with return on capital employed, etc.

The business plan provides you with a detailed map of how the unit will develop and undertake its activities. It is essentially a tactical account of the unit and the issues that need to be managed for it to meet the brand's commitment to customer satisfaction, sales and profitability growth, and continued success in the community in which it is located.

Though there are no hard and fast rules about how this type of business plan should be presented, it is important that you undertake the research necessary and undertake the activities suggested in this chapter in as thorough a manner as possible. The more you invest in making rational decisions based on a sound understanding of the most relevant information the more likely that your plan will form a reliable basis for arriving at your desired objectives.

Further reading

Barrow, C., Barrow, P. and Brown, B. (1998). *The Business Plan Workbook*. Kogan Page.

Quick Serve Restaurants Limited: case study

After working through this chapter you should be able to:

- analyse the key features of hospitality retail service

- identify problems and their causes in hospitality service operations

- show how problems in hospitality service operations are interrelated

- suggest improvements to hospitality service operations.

The case study outlined in this section is designed to help you practise an analysis of hospitality retail unit management in a context based on a real-life situation. Although the incident and characters have been embellished to provide levels of analysis, the basic details and figures provided are taken from a hospitality retail operator. The preceding chapters give you a range of tools and ideas that can be applied to overcome the difficulties experienced in this case study.

Background: Quick Serve Restaurants Limited

Quick Serve Restaurants is one of the world's fastest growing restaurant chains. The UK operation is currently run under licence from the American parent company by a major British licensed retail company. The first UK restaurant opened in 1993. At the time of the incident there are twelve restaurants operating in two areas in the UK. A further twelve restaurants are either under construction or at various stages of planning to commence operations within the next twelve months. The US parent company expects the UK company to double the number of operating restaurants each year for at least the next five years.

Brand attributes suggest value for money, consistent quality and speedy service. The menu on offer is adequate in size but limited to fewer than ten main menu items, though this is supplemented by a children's menu and an ongoing programme of special offer products. These latter products help to overcome the 'menu fatigue' that is inherently a problem in this type of business.

Key customer occasions involve 'cannot be bothered to cook', refuelling, and family outings. Some of the larger units have a 'kids area' and specialize in children's parties. On average, regular customers visit the restaurants 3.5 times per month. Sixty per cent of customers are regular users, and a further 20 per cent visit the restaurants more than once per quarter. The average spend per transaction is in the region of £3.41, and each transaction accounts for 1.4 customers, though these amounts increase when there is a special promotion.

The two areas are loosely 'north' and 'south' with little difference in the mix of restaurants in the two areas. All restaurants are located in major cities along the motorway corridors between London and Leeds and Manchester. Though there are some variations, most units in both areas are in city-centre sites. The company is a fast-moving hospitality retailer and considers that restaurants with sales below £400 000 per annum are too small.

A minority of the kitchen and restaurant staff (crew) are employed on thirty-five hour full-time contracts; most of the crew are employed part-time on an hourly basis. Typically, the latter would involve sixteen to twenty hours per week. At the time of the incident rates are £3.70 per hour. Where staff shortages occur, 'agency' staff are employed from a contract agency and these are charged at £10.00 per hour.

Quick Serve Restaurants Limited operate quick service restaurants in a manner which has been described as a 'production line' or 'service factory' approach to service delivery – that is, the production and delivery of the company's services are informed by Weberian 'formal rationality' and have much in common with Taylor's approach to factory production. The extreme division of labour, production and service tasks are routinized, requiring minimal discretion by operational crew (as

Unit	Av. wk sales (£)	Av. wk trans.	Av. trans (£)
North 1	15 953	4347	3.67
North 2	33 434	8235	4.06
North 3	17 699	5601	3.16
North 4	26 767	7044	3.80
North 5	26 321	6051	4.35
North 6	20 962	5027	4.17
South 1	30 013	8446	3.55
South 2	14 535	4895	2.96
South 3	30 457	8515	3.57
South 4	18 162	5513	3.29
South 5	27 919	7386	3.77
South 6	27 150	7536	3.60

Table 14.1
The twelve restaurants at
the time of the incident

production and service staff are called). Operating manuals and procedures do not just specify product standards but also give a detailed breakdown of service times and targets.

In these circumstances, the US parent company states that training crew to perform tasks in 'the one best way' is an essential feature of delivering the company's highly standardized and uniformity dependent offer to customers. Production and service operations are tightly defined and the subject of detailed training programmes. Crew are supposed to be trained to these standards and a management development programme supports manager training for each stage of the management hierarchy up to unit management.

The key elements of the Quick Serve approach to training are:

- All crew are trained including full-time and part-time employees.

- Training is competence based.

- Ultimately training aims to develop a flexible workforce capable of undertaking all crew jobs.

- Much of the crew training involves learning to do the job in 'the one best way'.

- Competencies are defined for each task on *observation checklists.*

- Completed training is rewarded through the '*five-star badge*' and pay increases.

- Training is delivered through a '*training squad*' (crew members trained to train).

- Observation checklists are also used to monitor ongoing employee performance.

- Unit managers are accountable for training and are monitored through the '*training log*' and training audits to ensure that crew training is being administered correctly and OCLs are being completed to plan. The Human Resource and Training (HRAT) computer system enables both unit managers and regional executives to monitor training in each restaurant.

Crew training . . .

All crew should be trained according to the company's standard procedures. Though there are some exceptions, particularly in jobs such as 'hostess' or 'maintenance', the standard approach to training involves functional flexibility. In other words, crew are generally trained to do the full range of production and service tasks in the restaurant. Although, some employees have personal preferences and skills which mean they do specialized jobs either in the 'kitchen' or on the 'counter', most employees seem to like the variety which this approach to training allows.

Observation checklists . . .

Observation checklists play an important role in both defining and monitoring crew member performance. As we have seen they are used to check competence after initial training. An OCL exists for each job undertaken by crew. It contains two elements. The first is a detailed outline of the skills and behaviours that comprise competent behaviour in the task. The second element checks the knowledge that underpins competent performance. Total scores are weighted 80 per cent for the first element and 20 per cent for knowledge. After initial training the trainee is expected to achieve a total score of over 90 per cent on a checklist. Observation checklists are also used to monitor employee performance in each restaurant. Every crew member should be observed against each task in each six-month period. The key issue is that the management of the OCL monitoring process is seen as an important indicator of line management performance.

Monitoring and development . . .

Observation checklists play an important role in defining the standard performance for each of the restaurant's key tasks and in providing a standard against which ongoing performance can be monitored. Each restaurant has its own computer that is used to record the individual training record and, subsequently, the OCL record for each member of staff. Information from these records is also used by the computer-generated staffing schedule that assists managers planning the duty roster for the forthcoming week. The system identifies the skills needed for each shift period, matches these against the skill levels of each individual and makes a recommendation for the manager's action. Clearly, the training approach allows flexibility in staffing options. The HRAT programme identifies training and staffing priorities.

Regional monitoring of each restaurant's training log shows how many employees have been fully trained and identifies the priorities for training. This regional record also shows the state of OCL tracking in each restaurant. Consequently each restaurant can be evaluated against the management of crew training and performance monitoring. Information on the training activity of each restaurant is used to provide a 'training grade' and it is expected that these will be above 90 per cent.

For the purposes of this study, the training grades were used to identify restaurants that appeared to be meeting and exceeding the company's training standards, and those that were operating below the expected standards.

In summary, Quick Serve Restaurants Limited is in many ways a benchmark organization for the provision of training amongst UK hospitality organizations. Their systematic and detailed approach, together with the universality of training for all employees and line management accountability for training, is an example that could be adopted by others.

The current situation

You have been recently appointed to the post of Area Manager for the South area, responsible for the six restaurants in the area. The post has been vacant for nine months and has been directly managed by the Operations Director, Graham Fastbuck. You have just completed a three-week induction programme.

Graham Fastbuck was appointed from one of the major UK restaurant chains – a competitor of Quick Serve Restaurants in preparation for the rapid expansion of the chain. The board of directors was keen to appoint a Britsh executive who had a proven record in 'the UK market place'. Since being appointed, Fastbuck has indeed tightened up on controls within the company. He viewed the more autonomous management style that was in place before he joined as 'anarchy'. He has fixed stringent budgets for each unit. He monitors budgets with the managers and supervisors concerned at monthly meetings. He uses these meetings to 'jolly up' individuals whose actual costs vary from budgeted performance.

Fastbuck approves items on the menu. He likes to ensure that dishes are developed that meet his expectations. Where appropriate he will make alterations to planned recipes. He does not like food with strong flavours. Fastbuck approves all selling prices to be paid by customer in all restaurants. He makes all other marketing decisions about both unit promotional material and general brand marketing strategy.

Fastbuck has attempted to delegate the selection and recruitment of staff at operative level to the Recruitment and Training Officer, Val Pole. She has recruited all staff in the South area. Unit managers inform her of their staff needs and she appoints accordingly. Fastbook recruits all unit managers personally – he likes to ensure that those entering the management team are 'the sort of people who will fit in'. He particularly values people who are prepared 'to get things done and make things happen', people like himself, 'with a bit of get up and go'.

Fastbuck recognizes the importance of good communications. He holds weekly meetings with senior managers in the business when he tells them his decisions and gives them their instructions for the week. He makes sure that he personally visits each of the units once per month and is thereby available to hear staff grievances during his tour of inspection.

Despite all Fastbuck's efforts, operational accounts show a stubborn resistance to cost reduction and are currently showing a considerable budget variance. In addition there are some worryingly performance indicators in the South area, and despite his direct intervention over the past nine months the situation appears to be getting worse.

Other members of the management team • • •

Val Pole, the Recruitment and Training Officer; has been in this post for almost two years. She was one of the first appointments Fastbuck made on becoming Operations Director. Val had been the Personnel Officer at AVCO Engineering prior to her appointment. Fastbuck said that her expertise was 'just what Quick Serve Restaurants needed'.

Since joining the business she has certainly made an impact on the selection and recruitment of staff in the South region. The amount of work has grown over the past couple of years. Recently she has attempted to persuade management that she needs an Assistant Recruitment Officer to help with this work in the North region, though Ann Jackson has been resistant to Val and Graham's attempt to the centralize recruitment in her area. The post would attract a salary of £13 000 per annum.

Val takes her job seriously and values a systematic and organized approach to recruitment. She designs all advertisements, short-lists and selects all operative staff herself. Given the growth in selection and recruitment activities, Val has not been able to spend much time on training activities over the last twelve months, but this is as well because the training budget had to be cut to save money.

Three clerical assistants also work in Val's section. They help with record-keeping, wages calculations and the administration needed for staff recruitment/separations etc.

Val feels that she certainly earns her £17 000 salary each year. She prides herself on being able to carry through her ideas and 'make them stick'. She had to overcome a lot of resistance from the unit managers when she first arrived and centralized the recruitment of staff, but she did not mind stepping on a few toes and eventually got her own way. Val has a reputation for being fair with staff in the business, but can be sarcastic with people she considers to be less committed to the job than she is.

Terry Ball, the Property Development Manager; has worked for Quick Serve since it opened and has over thirty years' experience in hospitality management. He has been the Operations Manager with one or other of the major brands since 1979. In fact, he was asked to set up the current Quick Serve Restaurants division when the company took on the franchise from the US company, and was Chief Executive until Fastbuck was appointed and the business was reorganized in preparation for the coming wave of expansion.

Although he is close to retirement, Terry has been an innovator and force for change, particularly in the early years. He organized much of the provision, bringing in an empowered management style that delegated much of the decision-making to the unit managers. As an 'old hand' Terry has always valued the part that a high-quality provision can contribute to business performance. Throughout his time working in the UK branded restaurant business he has always said, 'Consistent quality is the key to customer loyalty'.

Over the last couple of years, Terry has been increasingly fond of telling people that he is looking forward to retirement. He does not like all the recent changes that have taken place; Quick Serve Restaurants just is not the same place to work, 'too many bloody accountants in charge'. At one time he argued against the changes which he felt were not in the interests of staff and customers, but nowadays he does not let things get to him – life is too short. He tends to go along with Fastbuck's decisions, does not take sides and likes to remain neutral when some of the unit managers come to him with complaints or disagreements. He is happy that his job involves site visits to progress the new restaurant openings, so he spends a lot of time out of the office and tries to avoid being in Fastbuck's company.

John Marsh, the Distribution Manager; has worked for Quick Serve for five years. He is responsible for the team of drivers who take product ingredients and packaging to the restaurants. Food is distributed in vans. Recent legislation has laid down strict requirements for food temperatures during transportation, and John places high value on maintaining good relations with his staff. He often feels as though he is torn between loyalties to his management colleagues and to the staff in his section. He likes to avoid conflict and tries to soothe feelings when conflicts occur within his team. Often he uses humour to maintain friendly relationships.

Ann Jackson, Operations Manager, North Region, has responsibility for the six restaurants in the North. Over the next year, another nine restaurants will be opened in her region. Work is organized through the unit managers. She has resisted Fastbuck's attempts to impose more centralized control in her region, and there have been several very heated discussions about the way to run the business. Up to this point Fastbuck has been unwilling to dismiss her, although he hopes that she will buckle under his pressure and resign from her post.

Ann has five years' experience of working in Quick Serve Restaurants She joined after completing an HND in Hotel, Catering and Institutional Management. Ann has been in her current post for just over two years. During that time Ann has shown herself to be concerned to ensure that decisions are taken seeking out the opinions and ideas of other people in her region. When conflicts have arisen, she has attempted to discover the underlying causes and resolve them. She has sometimes upset Fastbuck because she has frequently argued against his policies and has personally been prepared to change her mind when convinced by other people's arguments. Fastbuck has privately described her as 'a bit of a wimp' and a mistake in his normally accurate selection process. That said, Ann's subordinates generally like working for her and value her sense of humour even under pressure. And there has certainly been plenty of that. There have been difficulties caused by Fastbuck's insistence on financial performance measures as the only indicator of business success. She has argued that customer and employee satisfaction should also be taken into account. In line with this she has recently calculated that staff turnover incurs a direct cost of £450 per head.

She has recently further angered Fastbuck by telling him she will be taking maternity leave in three months, though she does plan to return. Fastbuck told Terry Ball that this was one of the problems of recruiting women to senior management positions.

You, the Operations Manager – South Region, have recently been appointed to this post having worked as an area supervisor in one of Quick Serve's other restaurant chains. You have been in post for three weeks. Your predecessor had been in post for approximately eighteen months and has now taken up a similar job in a competitor organization in Derby. The post has been vacant for nine months because Fastbuck wanted to run these restaurants himself, and the opportunity to save the salary enabled him to save on the administration and management budget.

The incident

On the Monday morning of your fourth week you are summoned to the Quick Serve's Chief Executive's office. She tells you that Graham Fastbuck has been suspended prior to a disciplinary hearing relating to a matter of gross misconduct. He is not expected to return to work. She also gives you the impression that Fastbuck's removal has been at the insistence of the Quick Serve parent company in the US. They have been particularly concerned that the South region's performance has suffered since Fastbuck took over.

She asks you to temporarily take over as Operations Director, she expects that it will be two or three months before the company will be able to begin to find a replacement. Whilst mindful of the need to observe equal opportunities policies, she gives you the clear impression that you might be offered the post on a permanent basis, providing you make a good job of running the business.

She wants your assessment of the chain's problems in two weeks time. She says she wants you to prepare for a meeting in which you will be expected to identify the causes of the problems and highlight the actions needed to improve business performance. You will need to start by making an analysis of the management reports in Tables 14.2 to 14.6.

MANAGEMENT REPORTS

Unit	Av. wk sales (£)	Av. wk trans.	Av. trans. (£)	No. crew	Over 35 hrs	Over 35 hrs (%)	Av. hrs wrkd
North 1	15 953	4347	3.67	35	9	25.7	23.68
North 2	33 434	8235	4.06	71	17	24.3	23.68
North 3	17 699	5601	3.16	33	9	27.2	23.93
North 4	26 767	7044	3.80	54	8	11.3	20.16
North 5	26 321	6051	4.35	46	7	15.2	22.17
North 6	20 962	5027	4.17	41	7	17.1	23.83
South 1	30 013	8446	3.55	72	12	16.6	19.43
South 2	14 535	4895	2.96	34	11	32.3	27.30
South 3	30 457	8515	3.57	70	3	4.3	17.04
South 4	18 162	5513	3.29	47	9	19.1	21.30
South 5	27 919	7386	3.77	44	11	25.0	22.20
South 6	27 150	7536	3.60	49	7	14.3	21.57

Table 14.2 Restaurant sales information

Units	Overall training grade	Av. crew numbers	Fully rotatable crew	Fully trained crew	(%)	Training squad	Outstanding OCLs	Employee satisfaction training (%)
North 1	92.00	35	21	15	71	6	8	64
North 2	91.00	71	46	35	76	5	9	56
North 3	93.00	33	15	10	67	3	7	66
North 4	85.00	54	27	13	48	3	15	63
North 5	85.00	46	26	15	58	6	15	80
North 6	93.00	41	33	20	61	3	7	71
South 1	76.00	72	38	19	50	8	26	55
South 2	80.00	34	26	8	31	4	19	36
South 3	74.00	70	39	16	41	4	26	46
South 4	80.00	47	27	13	48	3	23	39
South 5	72.00	44	26	13	50	3	27	38
South 6	54.00	49	35	13	37	5	36	44

Table 14.3 Training in the restaurants

Units	Headline rate (%)	Rate after temporary staff (%)	Temporary staff leavers	Leavers after temporary staff	Cost of staff turnover in restaurant (£)
North 1	42.07	42.07	0	14	
North 2	52.57	46.88	4	33	
North 3	74.09	74.09	0	23	
North 4	60.06	60.06	0	38	
North 5	74.03	67.35	3	33	
North 6	78.8	43.01	15	18	
Av. North		**55.57**			
South 1	128.1	118.6	7	87	
South 2	158.0	152.4	2	55	
South 3	175.0	166.1	5	93	
South 4	128.4	126.0	1	54	
South 5	176.1	155.5	9	68	
South 6	169.7	118.2	27	62	
Av South		**139.46**			

Table 14.4 Staff turnover in the restaurants

Units	Mystery shopper	Quality	Service	Cleanliness
North 1	96.7	100.0	92.0	98.3
North 2	92.9	96.8	92.1	95.6
North 3	89.1	96.4	83.6	88.0
North 4	91.2	93.6	88.9	90.7
North 5	88.5	90.7	82.9	95.1
North 6	94.7	96.8	92.1	95.6
South 1	85.5	96.8	74.4	84.5
South 2	86.7	93.1	80.9	85.4
South 3	86.7	88.4	84.1	86.9
South 4	92.7	96.2	87.4	96.7
South 5	81.9	87.4	72.8	82.7
South 6	83.4	87.4	76.0	82.7

Table 14.5 External customer satisfaction ratings

Units	Overall	Your job	Performance and training	Pay and work	Management and leader	Customers	Communication	The company
Average	57	49	57	57	59	65	53	58
North 1	65	51	64	67	64	79	62	64
North 2	64	52	56	62	75	76	54	65
North 3	65	53	66	64	76	68	56	63
North 4	68	59	63	68	72	80	60	66
North 5	81	74	80	74	84	86	80	84
North 6	66	51	71	64	66	83	58	68
South 1	51	44	55	62	46	64	42	46
South 2	33	23	36	39	37	23	35	31
South 3	43	26	46	46	41	49	41	46
South 4	35	33	39	34	34	42	27	37
South 5	38	25	38	35	46	40	32	40
South 6	49	43	44	53	57	49	46	47

Table 14.6 Employee satisfaction survey results (percentages)

Index